Karl Marx and Friedrich Engels

THE COMMUNIST MANIFESTO

With an Introduction and Notes by
GARETH STEDMAN JONES

P9-CPX-439

PENGUIN BOOKS

To the memory of Raphael Samuel

PENGUIN BOOKS

Published by the Penguin Group
Penguin Books Ltd, 80 Strand, London WC2R 0RL, England
Penguin Putnam Inc., 375 Hudson Street, New York, New York 10014, USA
Penguin Books Australia Ltd, 250 Camberwell Road, Camberwell, Victoria 3124, Australia
Penguin Books Canada Ltd, 10 Alcorn Avenue, Toronto, Ontario, Canada M4V 3B2
Penguin Books India (P) Ltd, 11 Community Centre, Panchsheel Park, New Delhi – 110 017, India
Penguin Books (NZ) Ltd, Cnr Rosedale and Airborne Roads, Albany, Auckland, New Zealand
Penguin Books (South Africa) (Pty) Ltd, 24 Sturdee Avenue, Rosebank 2196, South Africa

Penguin Books Ltd, Registered Offices: 80 Strand, London WC2R 0RL, England

www.penguin.com

This translation, by Samuel Moore, first published 1888
Published in Penguin Books 1967
This edition, with Introduction and Notes, published in Penguin Classics 2002

13

Introduction and Notes copyright © Gareth Stedman Jones, 2002
All rights reserved

The moral right of the editor has been asserted

Set in 10.25/12.5 pt Monotype Baskerville
Typeset by Rowland Phototypesetting Ltd, Bury St Edmunds, Suffolk
Printed in England by Clays Ltd, St Ives plc

PENGUIN ⊕ CLASSICS

THE COMMUNIST MANIFESTO

Born in Trier in the Rhineland in 1818, KARL MARX was the son of a Jewish lawyer, recently converted to Christianity. As a student in Bonn and Berlin, Marx studied law and then philosophy. He joined with the Young Hegelians, the most radical of Hegel's followers, in denying that Hegel's philosophy could be reconciled with Christianity or the existing State. Forced out of university by his radicalism, he became a journalist and, soon after, a socialist. He left Prussia for Paris and then Brussels, where he stayed until 1848. In 1844 he began his collaboration with Friedrich Engels and developed a new theory of communism to be brought into being by a proletarian revolution. This theory was brilliantly outlined in *The Communist Manifesto*. Marx participated in the 1848 revolutions as a newspaper editor in Cologne. Exiled together with his family to London, he tried to make a living writing for the *New York Herald Tribune* and other journals, but remained financially dependent on Engels. His researches in the British Museum were aimed at underpinning his conception of communism with a theory of history that demonstrated that capitalism was a transient economic form destined to break down and be superseded by a society without classes, private property or state authority. This study was never completed, but its first part, which was published as *Capital* in 1867, established him as the principal theorist of revolutionary socialism. He died in London in 1883.

Born in Westphalia in 1820, FRIEDRICH ENGELS was the son of a textile manufacturer. After military training in Berlin and already a convert to communism, Engels went to Manchester in 1842 to represent the family firm. A relationship with a mill-hand, Mary Burns, and friendship with local Owenites and Chartists helped to inspire his famous early work, *The Condition of the Working Class in England in 1844*. Collaboration with Marx began in 1844 and in 1847 he composed the first drafts of the *Manifesto*. After playing an active part in the German revolutions, Engels returned to work in Manchester until 1870, when he moved to London. He not only helped Marx financially, but reinforced their shared position through his own expositions of the new theory. After Marx's death, he prepared the unfinished volumes of *Capital* for publication. He died in London in 1895.

GARETH STEDMAN JONES is Professor of Political Science in the History Faculty of Cambridge University and a Fellow of King's College, Cambridge. He is also a Director of the Centre of History and Economics at Cambridge. His publications include *Outcast London* (1971), *Languages of Class* (1983) and an edition of Charles Fourier, *Theory of the Four Movements* (1995). He is especially interested in the history of political thought after the French Revolution.

Contents

PART II

Karl Marx and Friedrich Engels:

THE COMMUNIST MANIFESTO

Acknowledgements

In preparing this book, I have drawn upon the insight and inspiration of many whom I cannot mention here. But I must record my special thanks to those who knowingly or unknowingly have contributed so much to the interpretation I have developed in the introduction: to Raymond Geuss and Istvan Hont, with whom I have taught Hegel; to Emma Rothschild with whom I have explored the history of economic thought. I would also like to thank those who read my essay in manuscript: Chimen Abramsky, Sally Alexander, Edward Castleton, Tristram Hunt, Daniel Pick, Miri Rubin and Bee Wilson. Their criticisms and suggestions and their scholarly knowledge have been invaluable. In preparing the manuscript for publication, I would particularly like to thank Susanne Lohmann, Inga Huld Markan and others at the Centre of History and Economics, and my copy editor, Caroline Knight. I also owe much to Margaret Hanbury and, at Penguin, to Simon Winder, for making possible the present shape of this volume. Lastly, my greatest debt is to my family whose constant stimulation and encouragement spurred me on to complete this project.

PART I

INTRODUCTION

I. *Preface*

Through most of the twentieth century, the importance of *The Communist Manifesto* was uncontested. It was important not because of its intrinsic merits, but because of the brute facts of world politics. In the twenty or thirty years after 1950, millions in the Soviet Union, China, Cuba and Eastern Europe lived under communist rule. Millions more, whether engaged in civil wars in Southern Africa, Latin America and South East Asia or in political struggles in France, Greece, Italy or Portugal, lived in countries in which communism was a powerful and inescapable presence.

In Western Europe communism was rejected as unacceptably authoritarian. But, strange though it now seems, until the 1960s it continued to be identified with an image of ruthless and energetic modernity. At the time of the Soviet five-year plans in the 1930s it had been thought to possess an answer to mass unemployment. Through to the 1970s it was widely believed to have the most effective solutions to economic backwardness. In many parts of the Third World national liberation and anti-colonial movements concocted their creeds from a mixture of Marxism and nationalism, while even in Northern and Western Europe, a blend of Keynesianism and moderate versions of socialist planning appeared to be in the ascendant. In Britain in 1964, for example, the prime minister, Mr Wilson, as champion of the forces of modernity, believed he had to produce a 'national plan' to regenerate the country. Only in the United States – and even there, only after a sustained period of persecution in the McCarthy era – did the population appear immune to the appeal of socialism. Clearly, therefore, an understanding of the modern world appeared to require a knowledge of Marx; and Marx's message was most memorably set out in *The Communist Manifesto*.

But in the 1980s and 1990s the political landscape of this mid twentieth-century world was transformed beyond recognition. The fall of the Berlin Wall in 1989, the collapse of the Soviet Union in 1992 and the extinction of communist parties everywhere outside China and South East Asia brought to an abrupt end a 'Cold War' that most had come to accept as part of the order of things. No one had anticipated that communism would make such a rapid and undignified exit from history.

Socialist and Social-Democratic parties had also been forced onto the defensive. From the time of the events in Paris in May 1968 libertarian and anti-authoritarian movements had emerged both on the left and on the right. The rise of a new and more aggressive laissez-faire conservatism, spearheaded by Mrs Thatcher in Britain and President Reagan in the United States, brought to an end the post-Second World War consensus built upon exchange stability, full employment and social security. At the same time, the electoral basis of social democracy began to break up as traditional industrial occupations throughout the developed world disappeared in the face of a shift of manufacture to the Third World. In addition, developments in electronics and information technology led to the down-sizing of corporations, the casualization of office employment and yet more shedding of manual labour. In the new era, a growing prosperity of the majority of wage earners in the advanced economies was accompanied by increasing insecurity and the emergence of an underclass lacking any useful function in the post-industrial economy. Traditional socialist and social-democratic aspirations to shape the economy or to redistribute wealth were all but abandoned.

The increase in female employment has made the language of the *Manifesto* appear dated: appeals for the unity of 'working men' have all but ceased. The growth of more individualized political concerns and the proliferation of single-issue campaigns have made the ambition to turn the working class into a party appear incomprehensible. Belief in the possibility or even the desirability of a future communist society has become extinct. In this new era the *Manifesto* can no longer command automatic attention and its importance needs to be thought out afresh. Will it become one of a very small number of political texts – Plato's *Republic*, Machiavelli's *Prince*, Hobbes's *Leviathan*, Rousseau's *Social Contract* may be others – that even centuries after their original composition still retain their power to shock? Or will it, like the communist movement it once inspired, shrink in importance until it is little more than an object of curiosity for specialists in the history of political thought?

To this question, there is one simple answer. The *Manifesto* will remain a classic, if only because of its brief but still quite unsurpassed depiction of modern capitalism. Marx was the first to evoke the seemingly limitless powers of the modern economy and its truly global reach. He was first to chart the staggering transformation produced in less than a century by the emergence of a world market and the unleashing of the unparalleled productive powers of modern industry. He also delineated the endlessly inchoate, incessantly restless and unfinished character of modern capitalism as a phenomenon. He emphasized its inherent tendency to invent new needs and the means to satisfy them, its subversion of all inherited cultural practices and beliefs, its disregard of all boundaries, whether sacred or secular, its destabilization of every hallowed hierarchy, whether of ruler and ruled, man and woman or parent and child, its turning of everything into an object for sale.

In short, the *Manifesto* sketches a vision of reality that, at the start of a new millennium and against a background of endless chatter about globalization and deregulation, looks as powerful and contemporary a picture of our own world as it might have appeared to those reading it in 1848.

In the period before 1870, political economists were slow to recognize the transforming power of industrialization because they remained haunted by fears of overpopulation and the spectre of diminishing returns.[1] It was left to socialists in the 1830s and 1840s, particularly the followers of Robert Owen, as apostles of what was then called 'social science', to identify themselves with the prospect of abundance and the possibility of a society freed from scarcity. But these potentialities were identified with science and cooperation. They were not usually associated with the market, which was denounced as a system of unequal exchange, of the 'war of all against all' or of 'buying cheap and selling dear'. From this position it was easy to slip back into a nostalgia for a 'simpler' society with predictable expectations and fixed needs. What was unusual, if not unique, about the *Manifesto* – and this is by no means true of all Marx's other writings – was its unflinchingly modernist vision, in which the capitalist world market was not simply identified with destabilization and exploitation but also with a liberating power, the power to release people from backwardness and tradition-bound dependence.

The continual process of innovation, the incessant invention of new needs and the creation of new markets have not ceased since the time the *Manifesto* was written. The tendency towards limitless expansion remains, even if it is now hindered by environmental dangers, as it once was by diminishing returns. Communism, as subsequent history was to prove, was not the answer to the contradictory tendencies at work in the world depicted by the *Manifesto*. But, whatever is said about the rest of the *Manifesto*, its great achievement was to have built its theory upon a highly distinctive and strikingly novel vision of the modern world that, for all the immense changes of a century and a half, still remains visibly our own.

The case for the historical importance of the *Manifesto* is also powerful. For a century or more, its now seemingly extraordinary theory of history as a class struggle leading inevitably towards the triumph of world communism constituted a credo embraced by tens of thousands, sometimes hundreds of thousands, of adherents in every

1. On the continuing fear of diminishing returns, see in particular E. A. Wrigley, *Continuity, Chance and Change: the Character of the Industrial Revolution in England*, Cambridge, 1988; on the lateness of a recognition of an 'industrial revolution' among economists, see D. C. Coleman, *Myth, History and the Industrial Revolution*, London, 1992, pp. 1–42.

part of the world. Enunciated not as a statement of principle or an expression of desire, but as a set of predictions, the formulations of the *Manifesto* underpinned the creation of a worldwide labour movement in the last third of the nineteenth century and, in the twentieth century, fuelled many of the political struggles – and not a few of the wars – that tore the world apart from 1917 to 1989.

A more diluted form of the view of history expressed in the *Manifesto* also made an impact far beyond the ranks of socialists and communists. It profoundly affected both the writing of history and the understanding of society among those without any direct acquaintance with the works of Marx. In place of a battle of ideas and creeds, it substituted the clash of social forces judged according to the goal of imminent or eventual social revolution. The 'materialist conception of history' that Marx and Engels applied to the history of communism in the *Manifesto* also gained wide acceptance beyond the ranks of communists, and it was to generate a mode of social and historical understanding which continues even after communism itself has begun to fade into history.

Even now, for example, a spectrum stretching from despairing veterans of the 'old left' to brash new champions of the free-enterprise right have appeared to agree that the development of world capitalism encountered only one major challenge in its history, that of revolutionary socialism representing the industrial working class. Both groups appear to conclude that with the final overcoming of this challenge, the future progress of an unconstrained and fully globalized capitalism will proceed unimpeded.

If this short-term stocktaking after the Cold War reveals the lingering after-effects of the *Manifesto*, so perhaps at a more stylish level does the stance adopted by a certain strand of post-modernist writing. This is the approach of all those French and American theorists who have concluded that because the class struggle over communism is over, history itself must have come to an end. One way to counter such conclusions is to point out that challenges to the global development of laissez-faire capitalism did not begin with industrialization and revolutionary socialism. Nor is it likely that the collapse of communism and the end of the industrial epoch will bring about their disappearance.

Already the end of the old millennium has witnessed the beginnings of other and differently inspired attempts to set the global economic system within a more sustainable and ethically acceptable framework.

But the best answer to this kind of post-modernism is to draw attention to the now forgotten sequence of events which resulted in the construction of the grand historical narrative associated with Marx. An investigation into the construction of the *Manifesto* can explain how this still compelling vision of the world was first stitched together. Such an explanation requires the telling of a rather lengthy and complicated story. But the story is important because it makes clear that much of what was first put forward in the *Manifesto* and later accepted as a commonsense understanding of the making of the modern world belongs more to the realm of mythology than fact.

In particular, such an account will show that what became Marxian socialism in Germany in the beginning had nothing to do with industrialization or the social and political aspirations of industrial workers. On the contrary, it emerged from debates among radical disciples of the German philosopher Hegel, about what should replace Christianity or Hegel's rationalized variant of it, 'absolute spirit'. Furthermore, when seen in a larger European perspective this emergence of German socialism out of a movement of religious reform was not particularly surprising. Socialism had also emerged out of post-Christian movements of religious reform in Britain and France at the beginning of the nineteenth century.[2]

2. In France, the origins of what came to be called socialism went back to the 1790s, the decade of the French Revolution, and the search for a replacement for the Christian religion, which, it was hoped, would disappear like the monarchy. Socialism – the 'harmony' of Fourier or 'the religion of Newton' (later 'the new Christianity' of Saint-Simon) – was to provide 'the spiritual power' once possessed by the Catholic Church. In Britain, 'the new moral world' promised by Robert Owen was presented without irony as a message from the second Messiah. The 'rational religion' of the Owenites was a direct extension of the eighteenth-century tradition of rational dissent. It was put forward as the scientific replacement of traditional Christianity based upon original sin. What distinguished the German path from religious reform to Marxian socialism was not a difference in kind from the process that had produced so-called 'utopian socialism' in France and Britain, but a difference between preceding religious and philosophical traditions. This account of the origins of socialism is elaborated in my forthcoming work, *Before God Died: The Rise and Fall of the Socialist Utopia*.

In the *Manifesto*, Marx and Engels made a successful effort to cover over these religious tracks and to set in their place a socio-economic genealogy appropriate to their new communist self-image. In fact, as this introduction will show, they not only wrote out the religious prehistory of communism, but also *any* form of intellectual prehistory. There was therefore no mention of the *Manifesto*'s intellectual debt to German classical historians, nor to the so-called 'German Historical School of Law' on the history of forms of ownership, to Adam Smith or Simonde de Sismondi on the operation of commercial society, to Proudhon's criticism of both property and community, to the development within the seventeenth-century natural law tradition of a historical conception, both of community and of private property. In the drafting of the *Manifesto*, any reference to these ideas, religious or secular, disappeared. Attention was deflected from socialist or communist ideas to the social forces supposedly represented by them. In this way, the history of socialism or communism appeared to become synonymous with the emergence of the industrial proletariat and the transition to modern society, starting from the industrial revolution in Britain and spreading to Europe and North America. Wars and revolutions became by-products of the social and political struggles engendered by the global industrializing process.

But despite the *Manifesto*, socialism or communism was never to become synonymous with the outlook of the 'proletariat'. The speculative or quasi-religious origins and character of socialist creeds, including that built upon the pronouncements of the *Manifesto* itself, continued to shine through the laboriously elaborated socio-economic façade. It was not the mere fact of proletarianization that generated the wars and revolutions of the twentieth century, but the experiences of social and political upheaval, shaped and articulated through the militant and apocalyptic languages of communism or revolutionary socialism. For this reason, historians have rightly likened the passions, intransigence and extremism of twentieth-century revolutions to the religious wars of the sixteenth and seventeenth centuries.

Similar reasoning also needs to be applied to the question of socialist decline in the second half of the twentieth century. Although the crises of socialist doctrine and the collapse of communist states were clearly hastened by political, military and socio-economic factors, the marked secularization of political beliefs in the decades after 1950 was equally important. The end of communism was not 'the end of history', but the end of an epoch in which criticism of global capitalism overlapped with the rise and fall of a powerful and organized post-Christian religion that, in the name of science, addressed itself to the oppressed.

The last general point to be made about the continuing historical importance of the *Manifesto* concerns its power as a text, its rhetorical force. Its claims and slogans were remembered even by those who had never read it – 'A spectre is haunting Europe – the spectre of Communism'. . . . 'The history of all hitherto existing society is the history of class struggles' . . . 'Proletarians have nothing to lose except their chains' . . . 'WORKING MEN OF ALL COUNTRIES, UNITE!'

But the power of the *Manifesto* did not simply consist of these memorable phrases. Nor could it be claimed that its impact derived from its overall design. The last section was hurriedly jotted down and looks unfinished, while the third section, despite its occasionally brilliant jibes, is arbitrary and sectarian. Undoubtedly, then, its power is concentrated in the first two sections. Propelled forward by the caustic and apparently undeviating logic of its argument, and enlivened by its startling rhetorical shifts, each paragraph still preserves the capacity to surprise and disconcert.

Even now – and certainly in the 1840s – readers of a 'manifesto' might have expected to find (as they would have found in an earlier draft composed by Frederick Engels) a declaration of 'The Principles of Communism', or even (in a yet earlier version proposed by another member of the Communist League, Moses Hess) 'A Communist Confession'.[3] In the 1840s, as will become clear, communism was overwhelmingly identified either with radical traditions of Christianity or

3. See F. Engels, 'Principles of Communism', in Karl Marx and Frederick Engels, *Collected Works*, London, 1976 – (hereafter *MECW*), vol. 1, pp. 341–58; Moses Hess, 'Kommunistisches Bekenntniss in Fragen und Antworten', in W. Mönke (ed.), *Moses Hess, Philosophische und Sozialistische Schriften 1837–1850*, Vaduz, 1980, pp. 359–71.

with the extremes of Jacobin rationalism deriving from the French Revolution. The starting point of the *Manifesto* is quite different. It opens with a sustained tribute to its declared antagonist – the very epitome of private property and egoism – the 'bourgeoisie' and 'modern bourgeois society'. The 'bourgeoisie' had 'accomplished wonders far surpassing Egyptian pyramids, Roman aqueducts, and Gothic cathedrals'. In a mere hundred years, it had 'created more massive and more colossal productive forces than have all preceding generations together'. If 'modern bourgeois society' were now approaching its end and about to yield to its opposite, communism, it was not because of the failings of the bourgeoisie, but because of its triumphs.

This end was nigh. 'Like the sorcerer, who is no longer able to control the powers of the nether world whom he has called up by his spells', the bourgeoisie, through the very magnitude of the material advance which it had accomplished, had 'forged the weapons that bring death to itself'. It had also 'called into existence the men who are to wield those weapons – the modern working class – the proletarians'. The first section then concludes with an account of the formation of the proletariat into a class. Modern industry or the industrial revolution, the great bourgeois achievement, had replaced the isolation of the labourers with their 'revolutionary combination' into a group. The fall of the bourgeoisie and the victory of the proletariat 'are equally inevitable'.

The second section is no less striking, though wholly different in tone. In a remarkable switch from epic to bathos, the scene shifts from the factory and the counting house to the bourgeois interior. There the bourgeois stands, no longer a herculean artificer, a world-transformer, rather a self-pitying paterfamilias, a wheedling householder, wiping the cold sweat of fear from his brow and wringing his pudgy hands in an entreaty to escape the retribution which communism is sure to bring.

Despite its title, 'proletarians and communists', this section mainly consists of an imaginary dialogue between the communist and the bourgeois, a dialogue in which the physiognomy of the communist 'spectre' is delineated in all its most lurid and flesh-creeping detail. The passage is both bitter and teasing. Most of the wild charges against communists – that they practised the community of women, the abolition of nationality, the destruction of property and civilization – are thrown back at the bourgeois' feet. A few, the communists cheerfully accept. If, therefore, the 'spectre' is exorcized, it is in a wholly unreassuring manner. For the bourgeois is invited to cast away his childish fears only to confront the real and grown-up terrors of a coming revolution.

The playful sadism of this passage is in turn only made possible by a third and equally arresting feature of the *Manifesto*, the changed identity of 'the communist'. It is no longer 'the communist' who threatens the bourgeois. Communists take no personal responsibility for the imminent expropriation of the bourgeoisie and even the proletariat will only be playing the role which history has assigned to it. Communists are no longer those who espouse a particular set of 'ideas or principles', they 'merely express, in general terms, actual relations springing from an existing class struggle, from a historical movement going on under our very eyes'. This 'historical movement' is an expression of

the revolt of modern productive forces against modern conditions of production, against the property relations that are the conditions for the existence of the bourgeoisie and of its rule.

The sole defining feature of the communist is a clear awareness of this fact.

The communist, therefore, is one who has the advantage of 'clearly understanding the line of march, the conditions, and the ultimate general results of the proletarian movement'. Among these 'ultimate general results' are the disappearance of 'class distinctions' and the concentration of all production in the hands of 'the associated individuals' or, as the later English version termed it, of 'a vast association of the whole nation'. Eventually, 'the public power will lose its political character' and in place of 'the old bourgeois society, with its classes and class antagonisms' there will arise 'an association, in which the free development of each is the condition for the free development of all'.

*

Were these audacious claims the product of a single process of reasoning, or did a semblance of theoretical unity conceal a more contingent and ad-hoc assemblage of propositions derived from different sources? Why should a declaration of communism have placed such emphasis upon the world-transforming achievements of the 'bourgeoisie'? Why should it have been imagined that existing social and political systems were unreformable or that periodic economic crises were signs of the impending end of the property system as a whole? Why should it have been assumed that there was a particular affinity between the grievances of workers and the goals of communism? Finally, why should it have been believed that a historical process, governed not by ideals but by the clash of materially contending interests ('the class struggle'), would nevertheless deliver such a morally desirable result?

2. *The Reception of the Manifesto*

Until recently, straightforward answers to these rather obvious questions would have been hard to find. A history of the reception of the *Manifesto*, both of its changing political uses and of the changing meaning attached to its theory, will help to explain why these questions were so rarely put.

From the very beginning, interest in promotion of the *Manifesto* seems to have been governed by a concern with its immediate political goals rather than its ultimate communist ends. Hurriedly written up by Marx on the basis of earlier drafts by Engels in the first few weeks of 1848, the *Manifesto* appeared within days of a general European revolution stretching from the Baltic to the Balkans. But despite, or perhaps because of, this accident of timing, its immediate impact was muffled. Written in German, only one edition appeared in 1848.[4] Amid the uncertainties of revolutionary upheaval, plans to

4. Two other editions of the *Manifesto* exist, dated 1848 and printed in London. One of these like the original edition was supposedly printed by J. E. Burghard of 46 Liverpool St, Bishopsgate; the other by R. von Hirschfeld, 'English and Foreign Printer, 48 Clifton Street, Finsbury Square'. It was therefore supposed that three editions appeared in 1848. In the light of recent research, however, it appears that neither of the latter editions belonged to that year. The first was published illegally in Cologne around the end of 1850; the second could not have appeared before 1856 and more likely in 1861. See *Das Kommunistische Manifest (Manifest der Kommunistischen Partei) von Karl Marx und Friedrich Engels*, Internet-Version, Bearbeitet und mit Vor- und Nachbemerkung sowie editorischen Anmerkungen versehen von Thomas Kuczynski, 1996, http://www.fes.de/marx/km/vesper.html. This text was originally published as No. 49 der Schriften aus dem Karl-Marx-Haus Trier in 1995.

translate the document into five languages announced at the beginning of the text were soon abandoned, and in Germany the authors
themselves found good reason to downplay both the proposals of
the *Manifesto* and the 'party' it was supposed to represent.[5] Indeed,
almost as soon as the revolutions of 1848 had broken out – in Paris
in February, in Vienna and Berlin in March – the Communist
League, the organization that had commissioned the *Manifesto*, was
disbanded.

It was the newly chosen head of the Central Committee of the
Communist League, Marx himself, who took this step. For once the
revolution had spread to Germany and Marx was able to return
from exile in Brussels and Paris, his first aim was to resume his
political career as editor of the radical Cologne-based *Rheinische
Zeitung* (Rhenish Gazette), broken off five years earlier in 1843 by the
forced closure of the newspaper by the Prussian government. Now,
once more editor of the renamed *Neue Rheinische Zeitung* (New Rhenish
Gazette), Marx considered that in Germany the political aims outlined in the *Manifesto* – 'formation of the proletariat into a class,
overthrow of the bourgeois supremacy, conquest of political power
by the proletariat' – were premature. The subtitle of the new paper

5. An English translation of the first section of the *Manifesto* by Helen McFarlane,
writing under the pseudonym, 'Howard Morton', did appear in *The Red Republican*,
edited by the Chartist G. J. Harney. See *The Red Republican*, vol. 1, no. 21 (9 November
1850), pp. 161–2; vol. 1, no. 22 (16 November), pp. 170–72. In the introduction, it was
stated that 'the turmoil' following the February Revolution of 1848 in France 'made
it impossible to carry out, at that time, the intention of translating it into all the
languages of civilized Europe' and also that two French translations existed in
manuscript, but that it was 'impracticable' to publish them under 'the present
oppressive laws of France', ibid. p. 161. Some notice was taken of the English version
of the *Manifesto* in the press. The *Manifesto* was cited without being named in a leading
article in *The Times*, 3 September 1851, bemoaning 'the number and infamy' of cheap
publications in which 'disorganising and demoralising principles' were preached to
the people. Further notice was taken in a review of 'revolutionary literature' which
appeared in *The Quarterly Review* of September 1851, vol. lxxxix, p. 523. The anonymous
author picked out passages proclaiming 'the destruction of *your* property' and
denouncing '*middle class marriage*' as '*in reality, a community of wives*', as particularly
horrible instances of the genre. I am grateful to Chimen Abramsky for drawing my
attention to these passages.

was 'organ of democracy', its aim to represent the radical flank of a 'bourgeois revolution', comparable to the French Revolution of 1789. Even if the *Manifesto* had confidently predicted that 'the bourgeois revolution in Germany will be but the prelude to an immediately following proletarian revolution', Marx considered that in these new circumstances it would be quite inappropriate to follow the *Manifesto*'s injunction 'to instil into the working class the clearest possible recognition of the hostile antagonism between bourgeoisie and proletariat'. The goal was to establish representative government and the liberal freedoms associated with the French Revolution of 1789. Only then would it be possible to proceed to a further revolution that would abolish private property. Marx, therefore, opposed the separate workers' programme proposed by another member of the Communist League, the leader of the Cologne Workers' Society, Andreas Gottschalk. But since it proved impossible to stifle this untimely display of working-class independence, Marx dissolved the League itself as a means of marginalizing Gottschalk and his supporters.

By December 1848 however, Marx was forced to concede the failure of his strategy of supporting a 'bourgeois' revolution and blocking the development of an independent proletarian party. Representative institutions had not overcome the entrenched powers of autocracy embedded in the armies and aristocracies of the principal German states. The German bourgeoisie had proved incapable of accomplishing its revolution, was primarily fearful of the threat from below and was sliding into reaction. In early 1849, Marx accordingly changed his position and began actively to encourage the development of proletarian independence. But by that time the main concern was no longer to proceed from a 'bourgeois' to 'proletarian' revolution. It was rather to save what little had been gained during the spring of 1848 in the face of the increasingly certain victory of reaction.

Between 1850 and 1870, the *Manifesto* was remembered by no more than a few hundred German-speaking veterans of the 1848 revolutions. It was first republished in significant numbers in Bismarck's newly constituted German empire as a result of the trial for treason in 1872 of the Social-Democratic leaders August Bebel and Wilhelm Liebknecht (another veteran of the Communist League) for their opposition to the war with France. In search of treasonable evidence, the prosecution entered into the records of the court the hitherto forgotten *Manifesto*, hoping to make the most out of its anti-patriotic claim that 'the working men have no country'. The unintended effect of this initiative was to enable socialist publishers to evade the censorship laws and embark upon the *Manifesto*'s republication. Hence the new German edition of 1872.

Thereafter, with the extraordinary growth of socialist and social-democratic parties across much of the world, numbers of translations and new editions rapidly increased. By 1914 these had amounted to several hundred, including translations into Japanese, Yiddish, Esperanto, Tartar and all the other major languages of the Russian empire.[6]

At first sight, the political crisis in France following the defeat and abdication of Napoleon III in 1870–71 looked as if it might bring about another round of revolutions similar to that of 1848. The first attempts in the 1840s to establish international associations of radicals, democrats or socialists had been followed in 1864 by the formation in London of the International Working Men's Association. Its secretary was Karl Marx. This association, now known in history books as the First International, began as a modest collaboration between English and French trade unionists designed to prevent the use by employers of foreign workmen in trade disputes in the building trades.[7] Marx attempted to use his position as secretary to mould the association into a vehicle of international working-class solidarity. Although never much more than a paper-organization, an increase in its geographical reach and an enlargement of its

6. For a comprehensive catalogue of editions and translations, see B. Andréas, *Le Manifeste Communiste de Marx et Engels: Histoire et Bibliographie 1848–1918*, Milan, 1963; for a discussion of the diffusion of the *Manifesto* in the years before 1914, see Eric Hobsbawm, 'Introduction', in Karl Marx and Frederick Engels, *The Communist Manifesto: A Modern Edition* (Verso), London, 1998.
7. On the origins of the First International, see H. Collins and C. Abramsky, *Karl Marx and the British Labour Movement: Years of the First International*, London, 1965. The First International was formally disbanded at a Congress in Philadelphia in 1876, but was effectively defunct from the time that Marx and Engels moved its headquarters to New York after the Hague Congress of 1872.

political aspirations through a series of well-publicized congresses had by the end of the 1860s ensured the International worldwide fame. In the unstable period that followed the Franco-Prussian war and the collapse of the Second Empire, many in Europe thought that it had masterminded the six-week radical and 'working class' takeover of Paris – the Paris Commune – in the spring of 1871. In the industrializing regions of Western Europe it was thought to have been responsible for a large strike wave, while in Germany it was believed to have been behind the emergence of the first mass working-class parties committed, in part at least, to a socialist programme. Not surprisingly, this string of events brought Marx international notoriety. His defence of the Commune, *The Civil War in France*, written in London in 1871 in his capacity as Secretary of the International Working Men's Association, led the conservative press everywhere to denounce him as leader of a secret communist international workers' conspiracy. Coming on top of his growing reputation as the author of *Capital*, first published in 1867, Marx became established almost overnight as the great revolutionary architect of 'scientific' socialism.

But the political circumstances in which the *Manifesto* had been republished were very different from those in which it had been written. In the period between the 1870s and 1914 the significance attached to the *Manifesto* among the mainstream socialist parties of Western and Central Europe was mainly emblematic. Critical questions about the larger ideas of the *Manifesto*, about the viability of its conception of communism, and about the plausibility of a supposed transition from all-powerful socialist state to stateless communist society had been raised in the debates of the First International in the mid 1860s. But Marx's success in expelling the Russian revolutionary Mikhail Bakunin and his followers from the International in 1872 meant that preoccupation with such issues was henceforth mainly confined to 'anarchists'.[8] Furthermore, by the

8. The term 'anarchist' was used in France in 1840 by P.-J. Proudhon. See P.-J. Proudhon, *What is Property?*, eds. D. R. Kelley and B. G. Smith, Cambridge, 1994, p. 205. On Proudhon, see below. Mikhail Bakunin (1814–76), from the Russian landed nobility, went to Berlin in 1840 to study philosophy, was a contemporary of Marx in

time of the formation of the Second International in 1889, the exclusion of anarchism, both at a doctrinal and at an institutional level, was becoming a defining feature of the new socialist orthodoxy.[9] The new European socialist parties of the 1870s and 1880s were based upon the participation of organized labour within the existing political system.

In these circumstances the political programme outlined in the *Manifesto* could no longer be accepted as relevant. Speculation about the world after the supersession of private property now appeared increasingly remote, while an insistence upon 'the forcible overthrow of all existing social conditions' seemed positively dangerous. Similarly, the notion of a party bore little relation to those current in the 1840s.[10] The language of the *Manifesto* had pointed back to the

---

Paris in the 1840s and a participant alongside the composer Richard Wagner in the Dresden revolution of 1849. Captured by the royalist forces, he was sent back for a long spell of prison in Russia and exile in Siberia. Having joined the International in 1864, he built up a following based mainly in Switzerland and was increasingly opposed to Marx's direction of the Association. Anarchists believed the state was as great an oppressor as private property. They were therefore strongly opposed both to 'state Socialism' and to participation within the existing political system. In opposition to Marx and his supporters, whose aim to transform the proletariat into a political party and gain power as a prelude to 'the withering away of the state', anarchists urged abstention from electoral politics. For Bakunin's objections to Marxian socialism, see M. Bakunin, *Statism and Anarchy* (1873), ed. M. Schatz, Cambridge, 1990.

9. The Second International was founded at a congress in Paris in 1889. It was a mainly European confederation of parties and trade unions, dominated by the German Social-Democratic Party. It was much larger than its predecessor and by 1914 incorporated 4 million members and 12 million parliamentary votes. Issues were debated at congresses, held every two to four years. Its effective existence was brought to an end by the outbreak of the First World War, which it was unable to prevent. But it was reconstituted in various successor organizations down to the Socialist International (founded 1951), which still exists today. Anarchists unsuccessfully challenged its position on political participation in 1893 and 1896, after which they were excluded from its proceedings.

10. It was in response to these changes that Engels changed the title of the 1872 edition from 'The Manifesto of the Communist Party' to 'Communist Manifesto'. See Kuczynski, *Kommunistische Manifest*, footnote 1.

cosmopolitan, free masonic and illuminist associations of an invisible church: 'the Communists' did not form 'a separate party', they pointed out 'the common interests of the entire proletariat, independently of all nationality' and clearly understood 'the ultimate general results of the proletarian movement'.[11] Alternatively, the term had referred to a small group of like-minded spirits: for instance, 'our party' as it was used by Marx in the 1850s to refer to the former editorial team of the *Neue Rheinische Zeitung* in 1848.[12] By contrast, in the 1870s, 'party' was coming to mean a national organization, with a democratic constitution and policies decided at annual congresses, an organization geared towards elections and increasingly towards participation in representative institutions. It was mainly for these reasons that the new parties preferred to describe themselves as 'socialist' or, even better, 'social-democratic' rather than 'communist'.

Insofar as *The Communist Manifesto* was studied in the decades after 1870, it was mainly as a pioneering example of 'scientific' socialism. But here again, its approach appeared dated. It had been written as an intervention in an 1840s debate about 'communism'. Its specific point, as we shall see, had been the promise of a viable conception of communism on the basis of a historicization of the notion of private property. By the 1870s and 1880s, however, this text was beginning to be presented to a socialist readership as but one part of the creation of an ever more cosmic and gargantuan theory, whose ultimate point was no longer political, but methodological and ontological. This was a 'scientific' conception of the world, even of being itself, which was to acquire ever larger and more billowy dimensions in the following seventy years. From 'the materialist conception of history', through 'Marxism' to 'historical materialism' and 'dialectical materialism', the process reached a grandiloquent and banal climax in 1940 with the enunciation of Joseph Stalin's *Dialectical and Historical Materialism*: 'the world outlook of the Marxist-Leninist party'.

11. For the links between eighteenth-century freemasonry and nineteenth-century secret societies, see A. Lehning, 'Buonarroti and his international secret societies', *International Review of Social History*, vol. 1, 1956, pp. 112–40.
12. See R. N. Hunt, *The Political Ideas of Marx and Engels*, vol. 1, 'Marxism and Totalitarian Democracy 1818–1850', London, 1975, pp. 278–83.

The trend had been initiated in the late 1850s by Engels with collusion from Marx in an effort to present their work in fresh terms that might appeal to a new, post-1848 generation of secularist and positivist radicals. Marx's work was to be represented as a great scientific discovery, the beginning of a new and entirely unprecedented 'materialist conception of history'. 'Just as Darwin discovered the law of development of organic nature', Engels proclaimed at Marx's graveside in 1883, 'so Marx discovered the law of development of human history.'[13] This claim was not only remote from the issues at stake in the political debates of the 1840s, but it also effectively uncoupled the new 'science' from all that connected it with antecedent political and social thought.

For those particularly attracted by such claims, the first generation of 'Marxists' who entered political life in the 1870s, Marx's *Capital* or, even better, Engels' *Anti-Dühring* of 1877, were considered more reliable guides to the new world outlook than the *Manifesto*.[14] Thus, no longer the outline of a current political programme and not quite definitive as a résumé of 'scientific socialism', the status of the *Manifesto* in the late nineteenth century was increasingly that of an honoured political relic, the cherished but somewhat dusty birth certificate of revolutionary socialism and an early and abiding symbol of the political and intellectual independence of the working class. Mindful of the constraints placed upon socialists in Bismarck's new German Empire, Marx and Engels had themselves unintentionally reinforced this view in their Preface to the 1872 German Edition. 'The Manifesto', they wrote, 'has become a historical document that we have no longer any right to alter.'[15]

Strangely perhaps it was therefore in the twentieth century rather

13. F. Engels, 'Karl Marx's Funeral', *MECW*, vol. 24, p. 467.
14. Karl Kautsky, the most influential Marxist theorist of the 1880–1914 period, wrote, 'judging by the influence that *Anti-Dühring* had upon me, no other book can have contributed so much to the understanding of Marxism. Marx's *Capital* is the more powerful work, certainly. But it was only through *Anti-Dühring* that we learnt to understand *Capital* and read it properly.' *F. Engels Briefwechsel mit K. Kautsky*, Vienna, 1955, pp. 4, 77.
15. *MECW*, vol. 23, p. 175.

than the nineteenth that *The Communist Manifesto* acquired its greatest political importance. Only then, galvanized into motion by the upheaval of the First World War and the Bolshevik Revolution of 1917, was the *Manifesto* able to call up, as if from its own nether world, real 'communists' prepared to act out an apocalyptic scenario of world revolution to the letter.

Even back in the 1870s, there had been those prepared to follow the injunctions of *The Communist Manifesto* in more literal ways than those found acceptable by mainstream socialist parties. In an autocratic regime such as the tsarist empire, without a previous history of representative government, socialism or labour organization, 'the forcible overthrow of all existing social conditions' made far greater sense, while in western Europe and North America, a host of militant and intransigent break-away groups, frustrated by the apparent docility of the parliamentary socialist parties, minutely disputed the meanings and implications of the prescriptions of the *Manifesto*. The triumph of the Bolshevik-led revolution in Russia in 1917 transported these hardened sectaries from the periphery to the centre of socialist politics.[16]

The formation of the Third International established an unprecedented and global form of Marxist orthodoxy and imbued *The Communist Manifesto* with a quite novel canonical status.[17] Upon the

16. For a description of such groups in Britain at the beginning of the twentieth century, see W. Kendall, *The Revolutionary Movement in Britain 1900–1921*, London, 1969; S. Macintyre, *A Proletarian Science: Marxism in Britain 1917–1933*, Cambridge, 1980; J. Rée, *Proletarian Philosophers: Problems in Socialist Culture in Britain, 1900–1940*, Oxford, 1984.

17. The Third International (1919–43) was founded by Lenin and the Bolsheviks in Moscow in the aftermath of the October Revolution of 1917. Lenin defined its fundamental principles as 'recognition of the dictatorship of the proletariat and Soviet power in place of bourgeois democracy'. According to its 'Twenty-one Conditions of Affiliation', laid down in 1920, parties wishing to affiliate had to remove 'reformists and centrists' from their leaderships and combine legal and illegal work. These conditions were to form the basis for the foundation of Communist Parties throughout the world in a period that was defined as one of 'acute civil war' demanding 'iron discipline and the maximum degree of centralization'.

The Third International, otherwise known as the Comintern, remained throughout its existence the ideological creature of the Soviet Union. Its hostility towards social-democratic parties reached a height between 1928 and 1933, during which social-democracy was denounced as 'social Fascism', and the distinction between Fascism and 'bourgeois democracy' was abandoned. After this policy had helped to secure

philosophical *naïveté* of post-1870 'Marxism' was superimposed the leaden weight of a dogmatic and intolerant 'Marxism-Leninism'. The numerous but limited runs of *The Communist Manifesto* associated with the socialist parties and Marxist sects of the pre-1914 period were all but engulfed by the global editions of Marxist-Leninist classics that poured forth from Moscow's Foreign Languages Publishing House. The new parties, expressly formed to support the October revolution and apply its principles in all other countries, were to be called Communist Parties. *The Manifesto of the Communist Party*, to give it its full and original name, became a text whose propositions all communists were expected to learn, understand and accept. Orthodox glosses and manuals helpfully ironed out discrepancies. The only sanctioned change was that suggested by Marx and Engels in 1872. Their cursory observation, originally enunciated by Marx in relation to the Paris Commune – that the working class could not 'simply lay hold of the ready-made State machinery, and wield it for its own purposes' – was elevated to *ex-cathedra* status by Lenin and decreed to mark the frontier between socialism and communism. The opportunist socialist parties of the pre-1914 era, it was declared, had evaded the revolutionary consequence of this truth: communists must '*smash* the state'.[18]

In the struggle over communism, which dominated the world between 1917 and 1992, the *Manifesto* was treated as a wholly contemporary document. Obsessive importance was now attached to some of its formulations and its general interpretation was carefully

---

the victory of Nazism in Germany, it was abandoned in favour of a broad 'popular front' against Fascism. After the Hitler–Stalin pact of 1939, the Comintern once again dropped the distinction between parliamentary and Fascist regimes and denounced the war as imperialist and reactionary. But after the German attack on the Soviet Union in 1941, it reverted to support for the war against the Axis powers. In 1943, Stalin dissolved the Comintern in an effort to please his new-found allies in the West.

18. V. I. Lenin, 'The State and Revolution', in V. I. Lenin, *Selected Works*, London, 1969, p. 289 and *passim*.

policed. Pioneering research into its historical origins made a promising beginning in the 1920s, but then shrivelled.[19] As a result, large and rudimentary questions about the definition of communism and the position of the *Manifesto* disappeared beneath an ever denser overlay of Marxist-Leninist monologue.

As the history of the *Manifesto*'s reception demonstrates, attention to the text was always dominated by particular political circumstances. In 1848, political circumstances dictated that the prescriptions of the *Manifesto*, even its existence, be downplayed. After its republication in the 1870s it became a public document. But the way in which it was read always remained extremely selective. An insistent emphasis upon the supposedly critical condition of capitalism and bitter argument about the role of a political party in the revolution that would bring it to an end was accompanied by bland and unquestioning assumptions about the shape of post-capitalist society and the transition to communism. Virtually unanimous endorsement of Marx's dismissal of communist blueprints indicated a general unwillingness to probe the misty contours of what seemed a remote future.[20] But,

19. Notably, the work of The Marx-Engels Institute under the directorship of David Riazanov in Moscow in the 1920s and early 1930s. Riazanov was the first to publish a complete edition of the Marx–Engels correspondence and began a *Collected Edition* of Marx and Engels' works, the *Marx–Engels Gesamtausgabe*, generally abbreviated *MEGA*, which appeared between 1927 and 1932. Riazanov fell from favour and disappeared under Stalin.

20. The murkiness of what was called 'the final goal of socialism' was one of the criticisms raised by Eduard Bernstein in his criticisms of 'orthodox Marxism', which set off the so-called 'revisionist' controversy in Germany in 1896. Bernstein argued that Marx's empirical predictions of the progressive worsening of the condition of the proletariat (its so-called 'immiseration') and the increasing polarization between two great classes in modern capitalist society had not come to pass. He then pointed to the vagueness of the idea of communist society. 'It is meaningless to say that in the communist future, "society" will do this or that . . . "Society" is . . . an indeterminate concept . . . and yet this metaphysical entity, this infinite unit . . . brings into being and guarantees the most complete harmony and the most wonderful solidarity imaginable.' Bernstein remarked of this 'final goal', 'this goal, whatever it may be, is nothing to me, the movement is everything'. See H. and J. M. Tudor (eds.), *Marxism and Social Democracy: The Revisionist Debate 1896–1898*, Cambridge, 1988, pp. 85, 168–9.

as the twentieth century was to demonstrate, such questions were not academic.

With the fall of communism and the disintegration of Marxism, consideration of such questions is no longer obscured by deference to a sacred doctrinal tradition according to which capitalism and communism formed part of a single historical process, a zero-sum game in which the defeat of one was the triumph of the other. What was obscured by this idea was the possibility that socialism or communism formed only one strand of the criticism that has accompanied the growth of a world economy in the last three hundred years. To define socialism as the critique of political economy was to obscure the fact that socialism was one of a cluster of highly idiosyncratic forms of that criticism since it was directed not at the defects of an exchange economy but at the exchange economy itself. What was also obscured was the fact that most of the major economic criticisms of the exchange economy, even when taken over by socialists, emanated from outside the socialist or communist tradition. Therefore, if socialism or communism are to be understood, they must be located not in the history of the economy but in the broader history of political thought.

In the case of the *Manifesto*, this means starting out from the same place from which its authors had started – from the questions raised about communism as it emerged at the beginning of the 1840s. Was communism a justified inference from Christian theology, the true basis of a republic or the ultimate social form appropriate to the human species? What was the difference between socialism and communism? Did communism stand for absolute equality or allocation according to need? How could progressive taxation, the abolition of inheritance, the equalization of wages or the communal appropriation of the land lead to a stateless society? How could human need be defined outside or beyond what the market recognized as consumption or demand? How would the hegemony of private property eventually be overcome? By collective living and the community of goods? By collective ownership, equality of possession or some form of 'negative community' reminiscent of the period antecedent to the establishment of law, private property and the state? These were the questions posed about communism in the 1840s, questions to which the *Manifesto* offered a provocative and highly unstable answer.

3. *The 'Spectre of Communism'*

In the opening sentence of the *Manifesto*, Marx wrote nothing less than the truth when he stated, 'a spectre is haunting Europe – the spectre of Communism.' In Central Europe the image was almost commonplace in the late 1840s. For example, in the entry on 'Communism' written for the 1846 'Supplement' to the famous liberal encyclopedia of pre-1848 Germany, Rotteck and Welcker's *Staats-Lexikon*, the political economist Wilhelm Schulz noted that 'for a few years in Germany the talk has been about Communism. It has already become a threatening spectre that some fear and others use to strike fear.'[21] Communism's rise to prominence had been astonishingly rapid. In the first edition of the *Staats-Lexikon* in 1834 neither the word 'communism' nor the phenomenon had merited a mention.

The word communism first came into general use in France in the early 1840s as a term to describe an ultra-radical offshoot of the republican movement that had re-emerged during the July Revolution of 1830. 'Communists' were distinguished by their emphasis on equality and by their identification with the radical Jacobin phase of the first French Revolution. Even the differences between them reproduced those of the Revolution – between the followers of Robespierre, of Hébert and of Babeuf; especially of 'Gracchus' Babeuf, who in 1796 had attempted to organize an

21. W. Schulz, 'Communismus', in C. von Rotteck and C. Welcker, *Supplemente zur ersten Auflage des Staats-Lexikons*, Altona, 1846, vol. 2, p. 23.

uprising against the Directory (the French government that followed the fall of Robespierre). Hence, the initial identification between 'communism' and 'babouvism'. Memory of this event had been revived by the veteran revolutionary conspirator and survivor of the plot, Philippe Buonarroti, whose account, *Babeuf's Conspiracy for Equality*, had appeared in Brussels in 1828.[22] According to his version of events, the conspirators who called themselves 'the Equals' had believed that popular sovereignty and a virtuous republic could never be secured while inequality remained. The corrupt government of Thermidor was therefore to be overthrown and replaced by an emergency 'dictatorship' of 'wise men' – akin to the Committee for Public Safety that had presided over the Terror two years before. This body would expropriate the rich, take over the land and establish a community of goods before handing power back to the people as constituted within an egalitarian and democratic republic.

The doctrine reappeared within the radical republican societies formed in the aftermath of the July Revolution of 1830.[23] Proponents of an egalitarian republic, especially members of the *Société des Droits de l'Homme* (the Society for the Rights of Man), regarded the parliamentary monarchy, propertied franchise and laissez-faire economics

22. On Babeuf, see R. B. Rose, *Gracchus Babeuf, the First Revolutionary Communist*, London, 1978. During the twentieth century, there was prolonged discussion about whether it was right to characterize Babeuf and his followers as 'communist'. In the eighteenth century, invocation of 'the agrarian law', signified by the adoption of the name Gracchus, implied periodic redivision of the land in the name of the prevention of inequality (an assumption radically undermined by the historical and legal researches of Savigny and Niebuhr at the beginning of the nineteenth century. See ch. 11, section ii below). Some of the 'Equals' went further than this. They believed that the consumption, if not the production, of material goods must be regulated by the community on the basis of strict equality. But there is no evidence that they envisaged communal production on the land or aimed at what later socialists meant by 'the socialization of the means of production'. For a discussion of the issue, see G. Lichtheim, *The Origins of Socialism*, London, 1969, ch. 1. Buonarroti's account of Babeuf's conspiracy was translated into English by the Chartist leader, Bronterre O'Brien; see Bronterre O'Brien, *Buonarroti's History of Babeuf's Conspiracy for Equality*, London, 1836, repr. New York, 1965.
23. See A. Lehning, *From Buonarroti to Bakunin: Studies in International Socialism*, Leiden, 1970.

of the new 'citizen-king', Louis Philippe, as a 'betrayal'. The repeated efforts at insurrection of these mainly Paris-based societies, composed of students and disaffected artisans, provoked an increasingly repressive governmental response, and in 1835 not only were the republican societies outlawed, but all advocacy of a republic was henceforth forbidden.[24]

Faced with this crackdown, one part of the republican opposition went underground. Secret societies were formed, such as the *Société des Saisons* (the Society of the Seasons), which attempted a badly botched uprising in 1839 under the leadership of Armand Barbès and Auguste Blanqui. Other radical republicans, notably Etienne Cabet, preferred legality and at the end of the 1830s put forward 'communism' as an ostensibly peaceful and apolitical surrogate for the forbidden idea of an egalitarian republic.

An admirer of Robespierre, Cabet had been shocked by the unwillingness of the July regime to better the plight of the poor. In exile in London between 1834 and 1839, where he came under the spell of More's *Utopia*, Cabet moved towards 'communism', which he depicted in his 1840 *Voyage to Icaria*, a laborious imitation of More's masterpiece.[25] But most important in shaping his subsequent political outlook was the contact he made with Robert Owen. Like Owen, Cabet emphasized the environmental determination of character, peaceful change through the establishment of experimental communities and an alliance with an enlightened middle class. When he returned to France in 1839, he vainly pressed for a broad campaign for universal suffrage. This, he imagined, would be followed by the election of a dictator who would inaugurate a fifty-year transition to communism.[26]

Britain may also have shaped his economic vision. For while

24. See C. H. Johnson, *Utopian Communism in France: Cabet and the Icarians, 1839–1851*, Ithaca, 1974, p. 67.
25. According to the Preface, the cause of 'troubles and disorders, vices and crimes, wars and revolutions, torture and massacre, catastrophes and calamities' was 'the bad organization of society', and the 'radical vice' that served as the basis of this organization was 'inequality'. E. Cabet, *Voyage en Icarie*, 5th edn, Paris, 1848, p. 1.
26. Johnson, *Utopian Communism*, pp. 59–60.

Buonarroti still looked to a Spartan austerity and agrarian simplicity lauded by eighteenth-century writers (Rousseau, Mably or Morelly), Icaria was affluent and up to date. It possessed an extensive rail network, the latest in scientific farming, huge mechanized factories and a source of energy even more productive than steam.

But rival conceptions of communism converged in their understanding of what was needed to keep at bay the corrosive ethos of individualism. Shortly after the establishment of Icaria, all 'harmful books' would be burnt. Thereafter, although participatory Icarian democracy would replace the 'government of men' by the 'administration of things', continuing care would be taken to protect Icarians from the wrong ideas. Just as speaking out against equality would be a punishable offence in the republic of the 'Equals', so in Icaria all art and literature would be subject to communal approval. Education in Icarian schools would be supplemented by collective recitation and large gymnastic displays, while the morale of factory workers would be sustained by mass singing.[27]

'Communism' became the object of public attention in 1840. Opponents of Cabet's gradualism, the 'violents' Dézamy and Pillot, outflanked the growing banqueting campaign for suffrage reform by staging 'the first communist banquet' in Belleville, attended by 1,200 people.[28] Some connected this banquet with a strike wave that occurred in Paris a few weeks later. Finally, towards the end of the year, a communist worker, Darmès, a member of a secret society, attempted to assassinate the king.

If this was the reality of 'communism' in 1840, it hardly accounted for the dark and awesome dimensions of the 'spectre of communism' as it began to walk abroad in the German-speaking lands for the rest

27. Cabet, *Icarie*, p. 101.
28. Banqueting was a tactic employed in the campaign that began in 1839 to extend the suffrage under the July Monarchy. Since associations and demonstrations were forbidden, banquets by subscription, formerly used to honour a deputy, and followed by speeches and toasts, were employed in the cause of electoral reform. The reformist banquets, numerous throughout France in 1839–40, were mainly composed of local notables. The use of the banqueting tactic to advance communism was both a brilliant piece of publicity and a significant innovation in popular politics.

of the decade. But the adoption of this word in 1840 was just one sign of a changed political constellation, in particular the emergence of what contemporaries perceived as an overlap between older radical republican obsessions with equality and newer, predominantly socialist, concerns about 'association' as a solution to the 'labour' question.

Before the late 1830s, there was not much common ground between these two positions. Communism was political. It represented a revival of the revolutionary republican tradition, an extension of the cause of equality from the destruction of privilege into a generalized assault upon private property. By contrast, socialism – a cluster of doctrines inspired by Saint-Simon and Fourier – was negative about revolution, indifferent to political forms, hostile towards equality and more interested in Church than State. In the longer term, it was geared towards the advent of a harmony made possible by a new social science, in the interim towards 'association' or 'cooperation' as a solvent of the 'antagonism' generated by competition and 'egoism' in social life and the economy.

In 1840 two books appeared that in quite different ways gave shape to this new political landscape: Louis Blanc's *Organization of Labour* and P.-J. Proudhon's *What is Property?* Blanc's book attempted to merge socialism with republicanism. It focused upon the 'labour question': an 'exterminatory' system of competition accompanied by falling wages, the dissolution of the family and moral decline; its cause, bourgeois rule, English hegemony and the pervasiveness of egoism; its remedy, workers' associations under the aegis of a republican state.[29] Proudhon's position was also a form of socialism, and his practical proposals included a non-state form of 'association'. Yet in his major object of attack, he seemed closer to

29. Blanc pushed the socialist attack upon the effects of competition to a new melodramatic pitch by combining it with a form of Jacobin patriotism. France and England were the modern equivalents of Rome and Carthage. Competition had begun to corrode national life, when the French had fallen under 'bourgeois domination' and adopted 'the traditions of English political economy' in 1789. It would necessarily end with 'a war to the death' between the two countries. L. Blanc, *Organisation du Travail*, 5th edn, Paris, 1848, pp. 84–97.

the communists. For despite his vehement opposition to the asceticism and authoritarianism of the babouvists, he, like them, argued that 'if you want to enjoy political equality, abolish property'.[30] In these ways, socialism, communism and the discontents of labour were becoming increasingly intertwined in the public mind.

In German reactions to 'communism', this novel and uneasy conjunction of distinct or opposed positions in the face of the labour question was turned into an unproblematic starting point.[31] At the same time, however, while communism was associated with 'the rage for equality' it was more or less detached from its republican roots, repositioned as part of the 'social question' and identified with a primordial and extra-political force, 'the proletariat'. Thus in May 1841 the conservative *Preussische Staats-Zeitung* (Prussian national newspaper) linked communism with 'the industrial misery of modern society' and defined its ideas as 'the anguished cry of an unhappy and fanaticized class', while the poet and exile Heinrich Heine reported from Paris that communists possessed a simple and universal language comprehensible to all, whose basic elements were 'hunger', 'envy' and 'death'.[32]

The 1842 publication of Lorenz von Stein's substantial scholarly study *Socialism and Communism in contemporary France* greatly reinforced

30. Proudhon, *What is Property?*, p. 32.
31. The best general overviews of perceptions of communism in Germany in the 1840s are to be found in W. Schieder, 'Kommunismus', in *Geschichtliche Grundbegriffe*, Stuttgart, 1982–, vol. 3, pp. 455–529; J. Grandjonc, *Communisme/Kommunismus/Communism Origine et développement international de la terminologie communautaire preMarxiste des utopistes aux neo-babouvistes 1785–1842*, 2 vols., Trier, 1989. See also W. Schieder, 'Sozialismus', in *Geschichtliche Grundbegriffe*, Stuttgart, 1982–, vol. 5, pp. 923–96. Another important factor in perceptions of communism in Central Europe was the memory of communist experiments in community of goods associated with the Reformation. According to Bob Scribner, throughout the period between 1525 and 1622 there existed continually at least one or more communities practising community of goods. The most famous experiment was that of the Anabaptists in Münster, but the most long lasting were those of the Hutterites in Moravia. In the period in which they were freest from persecution, 1553–91, the total number of Hutterites may have reached 40,000. See B. Scribner, 'Practical Utopias: Pre-Modern Communism and the Reformation', *Comparative Studies of Society and History*, 1994, pp. 743–72.
32. Schieder, 'Kommunismus', pp. 474–5.

this simplistic chain of associations. Once more, the 'proletariat' took centre stage. In Stein's account socialism and communism were classed together as responses to the creation of the 'proletariat' by the French Revolution and its formation as a class. Socialism became the scientific response to the labour question, which would bring to an end the split between society and the state. 'Communism' was its instinctive and destructive counterpart, embodied in a proletariat both propelled by its ignorance and lack of property into the unrealizable pursuit of a once-and-for-all redistribution and unable to escape the circle of negation in which it found itself trapped.[33]

In Germany in the 1840s the associations of the word 'proletariat' were not with the world of modern industry, but with abject misery, pauperism and crime. In modern parlance the proletariat was an 'underclass'. As Marx defined it for the first time in 1843, it was not 'the *naturally arising* poor but the *artificially impoverished* . . . the masses resulting from the *drastic dissolution* of society'.[34] Despite enclaves of industrial development, overall population increase between 1815 and 1848 had substantially exceeded opportunities for employment, a situation that by the 1840s had reached crisis dimensions. This was a society in dissolution, in the sense that the old categories of rural estate society no longer described economic reality either in the towns or the countryside.[35]

Three-quarters of the German population were rural, but of these

33. L. Stein, *Der Sozialismus und Communismus des heutigen Frankreichs*, 2nd edn, Leipzig, 1848, vol. 1, pp. 447–8. Stein's research in Paris had been supported by the Prussian government. Stein built upon a Hegelian conception of the state. He put forward a political explanation of the emergence of the 'proletariat'. It was a consequence of the French Revolution, in which birth had been superseded by wealth as the criterion of political participation. The proletariat was therefore an estate composed of all those excluded from political life by their lack of property. His recommendation was of a monarchical government based upon manhood suffrage.

34. K. Marx, 'Contribution to the Critique of Hegel's *Philosophy of Law*: Introduction', *MECW*, vol. 3, pp. 186–7.

35. For general overviews of social and political conditions in the German Confederation between 1815 and 1848, see J. J. Sheehan, *German History 1770–1866*, Oxford, 1989, pt 3; D. Blackbourn, *Fontana History of Germany 1780–1918: The Nineteenth Century*, London, 1997, chs. 1–3; J. Sperber, *Rhineland Radicals: The Democratic Movement and the Revolution of 1848–1849*, Princeton, 1991, chs. 1–4.

half were landless day labourers and semi-pauperized outworkers. In Prussia, east of the river Elbe, the onerous terms of the emancipation of the serfs led to a growth of landlessness. In the north and west large numbers of poor peasants depended upon supplementary winter textile production, particularly linen, to make ends meet. But the home and overseas markets for linen goods were drastically reduced by English factory competition in cotton and flax. In the south-west of Germany a growing sub-division of peasant holdings and dependence upon the potato created a situation scarcely less serious than that in Ireland before the famine of 1846.

The livelihood of artisans, especially those in the overcrowded clothing and furniture trades, was as precarious as that of their poverty-stricken customers. In the first half of the nineteenth century there had been a rapid growth in their numbers, a phenomenon often blamed by contemporaries upon the removal of guild restrictions. Increasing numbers of small masters and journeymen were therefore obliged to tramp further and further in search of work. Even abroad: by the late 1830s there were estimated to be 20,000 of them resident in Paris, 10,000 in London and thousands more in cities stretching from Vienna and Zurich to Brussels and New York.

In German towns life was little better than in the countryside. In cities such as Cologne between 20 and 30 per cent of the population were on poor relief. Pauperism and underemployment went with crime. Another term for this city poor was 'the dangerous classes'. Statistics suggest that crime shot up in periods of distress such as 1840–41 and 1845–7.[36] There was nothing irrational, therefore, in the the contemporary preoccupations with crime and low life captured in the novels of the period from Dickens' *Oliver Twist* to Eugène Sue's *Mysteries of Paris*. During the worst years, the harvest crisis and industrial depression of 1844–5, Ernest Dronke estimated that 25 per cent of the population of Berlin were beggars, criminals and prostitutes.[37]

In the period before 1848 crime was assumed to be an expression both of need and of hatred of the rich, a sentiment shared by the whole

36. See Blackbourn, *Germany*, p. 113.
37. E. Dronke, *Berlin*, Frankfurt am Main, 1846, repr. Darmstadt, 1974, p. 238.

of 'the proletariat', not only paupers and casual labourers but factory workers as well. Inclusion of the still-tiny factory population within this underclass again reflected anxiety about the growth of a workforce outside the categories and expectations of estate society. According to Robert von Mohl in 1835, factory workers, unlike apprentices, could not expect to become masters; they would always remain dependent for their subsistence upon machinery which belonged to others. The proletarian was therefore condemned to remain 'a serf chained like Ixion to his wheel'.[38] This was a group with nothing to inherit, no skill to acquire, no reason to defer marriage, no hope of escaping beggary, a group 'condemned never to possess anything'. Who could doubt its bitterness? Proletarians, according to Sismondi (who had introduced the term in 1819), were 'a miserable and suffering population' that would always be 'restless' with 'no affection' for their country and 'no attachment to the established order'.[39]

Stein's 1842 association of communism with the proletariat was therefore alarming. But according to his argument communism was the specific product of post-revolutionary conditions in France. No threat was posed to Germany. It therefore caused considerable shock when a year later the arrest and imprisonment of the travelling tailor and communist author Wilhelm Weitling in Zurich revealed that 'communism' was already spreading among the German 'proletariat'. In an official report compiled from incriminating papers found

38. Cited in Sheehan, *German History*, p. 647.
39. J. C. L. Simonde de Sismondi, *Nouveaux Principes d'Economie Politique ou de la Richesse dans ses Rapports avec la Population* (New Principles), 2 vols., Paris, 1819, vol. 2, pp. 350, 368. Sismondi (1773–1842) was born in Geneva of a Protestant family, Simonde, claiming descent from the ancient Pisan aristocratic family of Sismondi. He first established himself as a follower of Adam Smith and as a member of the romantic circle around Madame de Staël at Coppet. He became famous for his 16-volume history of the Italian City Republics, begun in 1803 and completed 1818. Sismondi's *Nouveaux Principes* (New Principles) was the first major treatise to direct attention to the new system of production in textiles and its relationship to employment and the world market. It was written to explain the post-war glutting of markets and was one of the first to dramatize the social and economic effects of English factory production upon the traditional cotton-spinning industry of 'Hindoostan' (Bengal).

in Weitling's possession, the local Swiss magistrate and conservative politician J. C. Bluntschli appeared to confirm all the darkest fears about the association of communism with the angry, destructive and criminal desires of the proletariat. 'Communism' had been brought to Switzerland by Weitling and others who had fled after the failed Parisian uprising of 1839. Weitling called for a revolution that would bring about the community of goods and the abolition of the state 'since every state, even the most extensive democracy, requires subordination' and subordination was incompatible with equality.[40] According to Bluntschli, Weitling's argument had made little impression upon the Swiss but had made many converts among itinerant German workmen. Following Stein, Bluntschli used the material to associate communism above all with destruction. Thus although in Weitling's published work, *Guarantees of Harmony and Freedom*, the argument against private property appealed to reason, Bluntschli was able to demonstrate from the private correspondence that he also believed that the attainment of communism required 'wild', 'criminal' and 'gruesome' actions on the part of the misery-stricken poor of great cities, including theft, disorder and terror.[41]

From the time of the Bluntschli report through to 1848 and beyond, panic about communism continued unabated. Among the highly placed from Metternich to the Prussian king, Frederick William IV, communists were thought to be behind everything from the 1844 Silesian weavers' revolt and the German Catholic movement to the peasant uprising in Galicia and the new poor law in England.[42]

40. J. C. Bluntschli, *Die Kommunisten in der Schweiz nach den bei Weitling vorgefundenen Papieren* (Communists in Switzerland according to papers found in Weitling's possession), Zurich, 1843, repr. Glashütten im Taunus, 1973, p. 5.

41. Ibid., p. 99.

42. Prince Metternich (1773–1859) was the Austrian minister for foreign affairs between 1809 and 1821 and in addition Chancellor from 1821 to 1848. He was an organizer of the Holy Alliance, a pact of reactionary powers against further outbreaks of revolution after 1815. Within the German Confederation his was the dominant voice against liberal demands, popular disorder or intellectual dissent through to his fall from office in the revolution of 1848. Frederick William IV (1795–1861) ascended the Prussian throne in 1840. A romantic and a Christian fundamentalist, he was a determined opponent of Hegel and Young Hegelianism in the 1840–48 period. See below.

Behind every moderate demand for reform there lurked the looming shape of social revolution; or, in the gothic imagery of one anonymous pamphlet in 1848, 'in the lightning flashes that followed the thunder of discontent with the existing world was revealed the pale spectre of Communism'.[43]

It is clear that just as Stein had greatly exaggerated the extent of 'communism' in France, so Bluntschli had wildly overreacted to its modest appeal among itinerant German artisans. So far as 'communism' emerged *within* Germany before 1848, it was almost wholly confined to the drawing-room conversation of the more adventurous of bourgeois youth.[44] What really underlay the overreaction was not the phenomenon itself, but the fear that communism put into words the misery and anger of the 'proletariat', and that in some sense communism and the proletariat were the same thing. The identification of the proletariat with 'the dangerous classes', with a predatory antagonism towards private property, was all but universal in the 1840s; and what was communism but the expression of that antagonism? Even those who, like the liberal Wilhelm Schulz, mocked the 'spectre' and noted the systematic exaggeration of the communist threat in the reactionary press, did not doubt the existence of a 'real evil' of which this spectre was the symptom. This, according to Schulz, was the war between rich and poor, the growing material and spiritual inequality resulting from unbridled competition, and the hatred, envy and rage of 'the proletariat'.[45]

In *The Communist Manifesto*, as will be seen, a new image of the proletariat was presented, that developed by Engels from his account of Chartism and the industrial revolution in England. The proletariat was the product of industrialization, disciplined by the factories which gave them employment and the cities in which they were congregated. Proletarians were no longer put together with the miserable and rootless poor of large cities, invoked by Weitling. This

43. Schieder, 'Kommunismus', p. 486.
44. See for example the speeches on communism given by Frederick Engels and Moses Hess to the businessmen and commercial assistants of Elberfeld in February 1845. *MECW*, vol. 4, pp. 243–65.
45. Schulz, *Staats-Lexikons*, pp. 25–6.

city poor was now consigned to a separate and wholly negative moral category, the '*Lumpenproletariat*', defined as criminal and ready for anything.

But the *Manifesto* only partially abandoned the earlier image of the predatory and instinctively communist proletarian. The proletariat still lacked a country; 'law, morality and religion' were still to him 'so many bourgeois prejudices'. The task of the proletariat was still destructive. The bourgeois fear of the spectre of communism was derided, but the threat to his property remained. Communists continued to stress the 'forcible overthrow of all existing social conditions', and the proletariat became the executioner who carried out the sentence. The association of the proletariat with violence and 'larcenous desires' was not denied. Instead, it was turned into a dialectical progression whose higher stage would be the proletarian revolution and the attainment of the aims of communism.

But whatever its literary or philosophical merits, as a political tactic this line of argument backfired. The artful shifting between actual and spectral communism frightened not only the bourgeoisie but the workers as well, and a generation later when a social democratic movement emerged in Germany in the 1860s and 1870s, its leaders, Ferdinand Lassalle and August Bebel, took great care that the word communist was never mentioned.[46]

46. Schieder, 'Kommunismus', p. 507.

4. *The Communist League*

The notion of the 'spectre of Communism' was a product of the mounting fear of mobs, of beggars and of violence during a decade of endemic economic crisis. But its modest reality – a movement of little more than a thousand people operating almost entirely beyond the frontiers of Germany – was an ironic tribute to the success of Metternich and his allies in blocking even the most moderate movements for reform within the Germanic Confederation and in preventing any overlap between middle-class and plebeian discontent. The reform banquets of notables took place behind closed doors, popular protest on the streets. There was not even the convergence of forms of protest witnessed in the English Reform Bill in 1832 or the banqueting campaign, both inside and outdoors, in 1840s France. There were years between 1815 and 1848 – 1816–17, 1830–34, 1841–3 – in which nationalist, liberal and radical hopes were raised. At such times there were demands for a national assembly, for representative government, for the separation of Church and State and a free press – or even, among radicals, for a republic and manhood suffrage. But any possibility in these brief periods of liberal advance of moving beyond Welcker's assumption that the mob was 'a more savage enemy of the common good than any other' was immediately stifled in the energetic conservative counter-attacks that followed.[47] In the face of

47. Cited in Sheehan, *German History*, p. 602. Carl Welcker together with Carl Rotteck edited the *Staats-Lexikons*, which became 'a basic reference work for the political opposition' during the years before 1848 (see note 21). Street riots in Leipzig in 1830 occasioned by news of the fall of the Bourbon monarchy in France were condemned

such harassment, the leaders of the opposition movements – mainly journalists or academics – found themselves reduced to silence or forced into exile. It was for this reason that the radical writers Heinrich Heine and Ludwig Börne had moved to Paris in 1830, and the radical Hegelian editors Arnold Ruge and Karl Marx followed them towards the end of 1843.

Exile, whether political or economic, formed the common basis of the German secret societies that grew up abroad after 1830. Political exiles forced to find a livelihood usually as teachers or journalists found themselves thrown together with journeymen willing to tramp to foreign cities in search of employment. Working in isolation in Paris, London, Brussels, Zurich or Geneva, often with only a rudimentary grasp of the local language, journeymen were understandably attracted by the social events, teaching, lectures and debates organized by German-speaking cultural associations that had sprung up in the towns where migrants tended to cluster. It was in this way in London in 1840 that Karl Schapper, Joseph Moll and five others founded the German Workers' Education Association, an organization situated just off Tottenham Court Road that survived until 1914.[48]

These associations also provided the perfect cover for the organization of secret societies. The Workers' Education Association, known to an inner group as the Communist Workers' Association, was also to act as the London branch of the League of the Just, the organization that under its revised name, the Communist League, was to commission Marx and Engels to write its manifesto in the winter of 1847.

The League of the Just had been founded in Paris in September 1837. Its aims included 'the liberation of Germany from the yoke of disgraceful oppression, cooperation to free mankind and realization

by Rotteck as 'crimes against the community without concern for the fatherland and constitution that have as their impulse and expression the mob's personal passions, crude energy, irrationality, and larcenous desires'. Ibid. pp. 606, 616.

48. The best account of the German Workers' Education Association and of London activities of the League of the Just and the Communist League is to be found in Christine Lattek, *Revolutionary Refugees: German Socialism in Britain, 1840–1860*, London, 2002.

of the principles contained in the declaration of human and civil rights'.[49] In his 1885 essay 'On the History of the Communist League', Engels maintained that the League was a breakaway of 'the most extreme, chiefly proletarian elements' of the preceding League of the Outlaws whose one 'very great defect' was that its members were 'almost exclusively artisans'.[50] But the records suggest that disagreements were more political and religious than social in nature. The original 1834 League of the Outlaws was a republican secret society inspired by Buonarroti and organized along strictly hierarchical lines. The split seems to have been occasioned by the arrival in Paris of members of a rival society, Young Germany, expelled from Switzerland in 1836 at the behest of Metternich. This organization was more democratic in its structure and committed not to Buonarroti's 'European republic', but to Mazzini's 'Europe of Republics'.[51]

During the 1830s both these republican societies began to make reference to social questions and to include social aims. Greater attention was paid to the agrarian problem and to the danger that a republic based upon equality could be undermined by the machinations of a 'money-aristocracy'. But this was not a progression towards 'communism', nor is it likely that it would have become so, but for

49. Cited in Lattek, *Revolutionary Refugees*, p. 34.
50. See F. Engels, 'On the History of the Communist League', *MECW*, vol. 26, p. 313.
51. See W. Schieder, *Anfänge der deutschen Arbeiterbewegung*, Stuttgart, 1963, pp. 29–60, 222–4. Buonarroti's ideas derived from the French revolutionary war of 1792. The Jacobin model of the French Republic was to be established everywhere. The vision was not national but cosmopolitan. Europe would be transformed through an international conspiracy led by a secret hierarchical leadership, entitled the Carbonaria or Charbonnerie réformée. Giuseppe Mazzini (1805–72) left the Carbonaria after the failure of its Italian rising of 1831–2 and founded the radical secret society Young Italy. Young Germany and Young Poland followed and were loosely coordinated in Young Europe. In contrast to the Carbonaria model, these movements possessed democratically elected leaderships and were primarily focused upon the 'fraternity' and 'association' of democratic peoples. Mazzini's programme appealed not just to the French Revolution, but also to a religious principle. Christ was the first prophet of freedom, equality, humanity and the emancipation of the common people. Catholicism betrayed this message by selling itself to monarchy. Mazzini remained the dominant figure in Italian republican politics from the 1830s to the 1870s.

the impact in France of a revived Christian radicalism that reached its peak in the years between 1835 and 1843. This change was largely inspired by the works of Félicité de Lamennais, in particular *Words of a Believer* (1834) and *The Book of the People* (1838).[52] The impact of these books on the European mainland can probably only be compared with that once made by Tom Paine in the English-speaking world. Furthermore, unlike the works of Buonarroti or Cabet, Lamennais was immediately translated into German.[53]

Lamennais announced the advent of paradise on earth promised by Christ and heralded in the principles of 1789. Christianity meant justice and the love of neighbour. Through its imminent realization, Satan's reign, which had introduced poverty and misery into the world, would be brought to an end and all would soon live as brothers in freedom and equality. Although Lamennais wrote of universal suffrage, association and the end of privilege and monopoly, his was a vision of moral renewal rather than political transformation. But in the writings of his German disciples, in particular William Weitling, this became the basis of an aggressive physical force argument for 'communism', for a return to the Christian principle of community of goods. The Bible was a revolutionary document, its message – 'hope lies only in your sword'.[54]

---

52. Abbé Félicité de Lamennais (1782–1854) in the 1820s had been associated with the counter-revolutionary, ultramontane and theocratic thinkers Joseph de Maistre and Louis de Bonald. But he moved towards liberalism and, after 1830, to democracy. He argued that the democratic cause should be championed by the Roman Catholic Church. The Pope responded in 1832 with a condemnation ('Mirari vos'). As a result Lamennais turned his back upon the hierarchy of the church and argued for an alliance between radical democracy and a renewed Christianity based upon the principles of 'love thy neighbour' and justice. He constantly invoked association and fraternity but did not endorse explicitly socialist proposals.

53. *Words of a Believer* went through seven editions in a few months and sold 100,000 copies. It was translated into German by the radical German Jewish émigré Ludwig Börne and quickly sold out. Weitling was among the translators of *The Book of the People*, which also made a large impact, particularly upon wandering artisans. See Schieder, *Anfänge*, pp. 232–40.

54. Cited in Schieder, *Anfänge*, p. 268. Wilhelm Weitling (1808–71) was an itinerant tailor, born in Magdeburg. He was the most important theorist of early German socialism. He joined the League of the Outlaws in Paris in 1836.

Discussions about 'community of goods' took place within the League of the Just in 1837 and culminated in a resolution mandating Weitling to prepare a report on its practicability. The resulting document, *Mankind as it is and as it ought to be*, finished in the winter of 1838–9, was adopted as the league's official programme and turned Weitling into the uncontested doctrinal leader of the league until 1843.

Weitling argued that the unequal distribution of work and wealth in society was the result of the 'money system'.[55] Community of goods, therefore, was not simply a means to preserve equality in a democratic republic, but the basis of a wholly different social order premissed upon the universal duty to work and consisting of a centralized economy, 'family associations' of around one thousand each and a senate elected from these family associations. For a number of details of his economy, Weitling borrowed from the writings of the French socialist Charles Fourier: work was divided into two-hour periods and unpleasant tasks were undertaken by a teenage industrial army.[56]

But the spirit of Weitling's system was quite different from Fourier's picture of 'harmony'. Its guiding passion was equality with limited concessions to freedom such as a much discussed system of tradeable hours (*Commerzstunden*) through which extra luxuries in

---

55. W. Weitling, *Das Evangelium des armen Sünders, Die Menschheit, wie sie ist und wie sie sein sollte*, ed. W. Schäfer, Hamburg, 1971, p. 151.

56. Charles Fourier (1772–1837) constructed a theory of society in the aftermath of the French Revolution. It was based upon 'the science of passionate attraction'. According to Fourier, 'civilization' produced poverty and misery because it was based upon the repression of the passions. In the approaching era of 'harmony', humanity would live in 'phalansteries'; elaborately designed communities of around 1,620 persons in which all passions could be expressed and combined. In place of the monotony of marriage and waged work, all forms of sexuality would be fully expressed. Work would become 'attractive'; it would be combined with the acting out of specific forms of desire. Among the passions not recognized by 'civilization' was 'the butterfly' – the need for variety and change, felt 'moderately' every hour and 'acutely' every two hours. It was for this reason that the different activities which made up a day in Fourier's phalanstery were divided into two-hour periods. See note 2 and see also C. Fourier, *The Theory of the Four Movements*, ed. G. Stedman Jones and I. Patterson, Cambridge, 1996.

kind, travel or holidays for example, might be acquired in return for extra work.[57]

Weitling's position gained enthusiastic support in the League, but began to unravel in the face of hostile criticism from the reconstituted Young Germany group in Switzerland. In response to his Swiss critics, Weitling underlined his anti-nationalism, asserted the necessity of dictatorship as the means of transition to community and, even more contentiously, attempted to prove the Christian foundation to his argument by arguing that the words 'communion' and 'communism' stemmed from an identical etymological root.[58] When this latter argument was quickly demolished by his opponents, Weitling did a volte-face and attempted to develop a purely secular theory of communism in his *Guarantees of Harmony and Freedom* in 1842. Under the impact of Proudhon, Weitling now ascribed evil to private property rather than the money system and drew again on Fourier to develop a theory of progress based upon the unchangeableness of human desires. Marx praised this book enthusiastically, but it did not strike the same chord as his previous work.[59] Exasperated by the sluggish response within the League and suspecting that this might derive from the absence of a Christian dimension, Weitling attempted to reinsert a religious argument in a third work hurriedly composed in 1843, *The Gospel of a Poor Sinner*. But imprisonment and a delay in publication meant that this work only appeared in 1845, too late to make any further impact on the ongoing discussions of the League.

In London and Paris Weitling's original position remained in the ascendant until 1842.[60] Thereafter, the different branches of the League began to diverge. In Paris, under the leadership of Dr

57. Weitling, *Die Menschheit*, ch. 7. Fourier believed harmony and equality to be incompatible.

58. See W. Weitling, 'Die Kommunion und die Kommunisten', *Der Hülferuf der deutschen Jugend*, No. 3 (Nov. 1841), pp. 33–9; Schulz, *Staats-Lexikons*, pp. 47–8; Schieder, 'Kommunismus', p. 478.

59. K. Marx, 'Critical Marginal Notes on the Article, "The King of Prussia and social reform", by a Prussian' (10 August 1844), *MECW*, vol. 3, pp. 201–2.

60. Schieder, *Anfänge*, pp. 53–4.

Ewerbeck, the League became increasingly Cabetist. In London, as late as March 1845 the leaders, Schapper, Bauer and Moll, declared that communism was the realization of Christianity, but already from 1841–2 their position had become increasingly blended with pacific and rationalist assumptions drawn from Owenism.[61]

Led by Schapper in a series of debates around 1843–4, the League's London leaders had rejected the communist settlements proposed by Cabet on the grounds that mankind was not yet ready for such experiments. During the following two years they were to search for a new basis for communism.[62]

In September 1844 Weitling arrived in London and pressed the League to discuss his theory. In a series of discussions ending in January 1846, Weitling's position was considered and rejected. Schapper agreed with Weitling that Man needed only to live according to the laws of nature – that is, without private property – in order to become good. But such a change could only come about gradually and through the progress of enlightenment, rather than through

61. Karl Schapper (1812–70) was the dominant figure in the London branch of the League. Schapper had been a forestry student at the University of Giessen, and had joined the radical student organization, the *Burschenschaft*, in whose name he acquired duelling scars. He became involved in the 'Young Germany' group in Switzerland and took part in Mazzini's expedition to Savoy in 1834. He joined the League of the Just in Paris and in 1838 submitted a rival document to Weitling setting out the aims of the League. Schapper found asylum in London after the failed 1839 uprising of the Parisian secret society, the *Société des Saisons*, in which the League of the Just was suspected to be involved.

Heinrich Bauer (1813–?) was a shoemaker and had also been a member of the Parisian branch of the League of the Just. He was expelled from France in 1842 for distributing Weitling's journal, *Der Hülferuf*.

Joseph Moll (1812–49), a watchmaker from Cologne, was, like Schapper, a republican nationalist. He also came to London from Paris after the failure of the 1839 uprising. He was killed in battle during the Baden-Palatinate rising of 1849.

For Engels' memories of the League and its leaders, see his 1885 essay, 'On the History of the Communist League', *MECW*, vol. 26, pp. 312–31.

62. See Lattek, *Revolutionary Refugees*, ch. 2; and see also A. Lehning, 'Discussions à Londres sur le Communisme Icarien', in Lehning, *From Buonarroti to Bakunin*, pp. 123–43; 'Diskussionen im Kommunistischen Arbeiterbildungsverein, 18 Feb. 1845–14 Jan. 1846', *Der Bund der Kommunisten: Dokumente und Materialien*, 3 vols., Berlin, Dietz, 1982–4, vol. 1, pp. 214–38.

Weitling's immediate and violent revolution. The details of Weitling's polity were also examined, but overall his proposals were rejected as 'too military'.

The general move made within the London group away from a Christian-based communism was equally important during this period. Schapper argued for a strict separation of political and religious questions, and in 1846 he proposed that the League discuss the Young Hegelian position on religion.[63] By the end of 1845, partly under the influence of Owenism, an increasing number of League members declared themselves atheists. Positively, the new position of the leading members seemed closest to the communist 'humanism' of Moses Hess. According to the section on religion in Hess's 'Communist Confession', God was the human species or 'mankind united in love'. God had seemed outside humanity, because humanity had itself lived in a state of separation and antagonism. But with the coming of communism, hell would no longer exist on earth, nor heaven beyond it; rather, everything that in Christianity had been represented prophetically and fantastically would come to pass in a truly human society founded upon the eternal laws of love and reason.[64]

Lastly, what is most noticeable in the discussions of 1845–6 is the concern, particularly expressed by Schapper, that communism should above all enable the free self-development of individuals. Like Cabet's, Weitling's communism would stultify mankind; equality should mean equal opportunity, not equal consumption or equal enjoyment. Communism and individual self-realization must go together. It was probably the result of Schapper's preoccupations that the *Manifesto* speaks of 'an association, in which the free development of each is the condition for the free development of all'.[65]

63. See Lattek, *Revolutionary Refugees*, ch. 2.
64. M. Hess, 'Kommunistisches Bekenntniss in Fragen und Antworten', in Mönke (ed.), *Moses Hess*, pp. 367–8. Hess's ideas are discussed further below, pp. 55–9, 122–3.
65. This comes out clearly in Schapper's objections to Weitling in the League's discussions in 1845–6, in which he insisted that each must have full freedom, but not at the expense of the personal freedom of others. See *Der Bund der Kommunisten*, vol. 1, p. 235.

In the summer of 1846 the headquarters of the League were moved from Paris to London. In February of that year, Marx and Engels had set up the Brussels Communist Correspondence Committee to organize propaganda internationally. In need of an English contact, they wrote to the editor of the Chartist journal the *Northern Star*, G. J. Harney. Harney in turn suggested Karl Schapper of the London branch of the League. Initial contact between the two groups was attended by considerable suspicion. Marx and Engels wrongly believed that the London League was still dominated by Weitling. The Londoners had half-believed the Brussels committee to be a scholarly clique with no time for workers, a story spread by Weitling after his argument with Marx in Brussels in March 1846.[66] Once direct contact was established, however, hostility towards the religious and conspiratorial positions of Weitling formed the basis for joint work. Support for Chartism and for the Polish uprising

66. In the spring of 1846, Marx, together with Engels and a Belgian friend, Philippe Gigot, set up a Communist Correspondence Committee in Brussels. The aim was to organize correspondence with German socialists and communists 'on scientific questions', to 'supervise' popular writing and socialist propaganda in Germany and to keep German, French and English socialists in contact with each other. See Marx's letter to Proudhon inviting him to join (5 May 1846), *MECW*, vol. 38, pp. 38–40. (Proudhon declined the invitation.) Weitling had passed through Brussels and met the Marx group on 30 March 1846. He also had been invited to collaborate with Marx's committee. But the meeting was stormy and unfriendly. Marx asked him to defend his form of social-revolutionary agitation. According to the account of the Russian, Annenkov, who was present, before Weitling finished Marx interrupted impatiently, arguing that there could be no talk of the immediate realization of communism, that first there must be a period of bourgeois rule and that communism would never be achieved on the basis of Weitling's 40,000 bandits or the building of a new society on the basis of Christian virtue. There is a graphic account of Marx's confrontation with Weitling, based on the testimony of Annenkov, in B. Nicolaievsky and Otto Maenchen-Helfen (eds.), *Karl Marx: Man and Fighter*, London, 1973, pp. 121–8.

Marx did not publicly denounce Weitling but insisted that there must be a 'sifting' of the Communist or Socialist Party. It was therefore decided to circulate a public attack on Hermann Kriege, a close friend and follower of Weitling. It was argued that Kriege was not 'a communist' and that his line was 'compromising in the highest degree to the Communist Party', an extraordinary claim, given that there was no 'Communist Party'. See *MECW*, vol. 6, p. 35. This action was judged as harsh and sectarian by many in the League of the Just.

provided other reasons for cooperation. Furthermore, even Schapper now believed a revolution to be inevitable. After alluding to this point in answer to a letter from Marx, Schapper and the London committee continued:

... our task is to enlighten the people and to make propaganda for community of goods; you want the same, therefore let us join hands and work with combined strength for a better future.[67]

In the year that followed, collaboration between London and Brussels grew to the point where Marx and the Brussels committee agreed to join a refashioned League. The relationship did not begin smoothly. Without consulting the Brussels committee, the Londoners called for a conference to clarify 'relations with the religious party' and with 'the radical bourgeoisie'. For their part, Marx and Engels talked about the London League with barely concealed contempt. It was only after the League sent Joseph Moll to negotiate with Marx in February 1847 that an agreed plan for reform took shape. Marx and Moll agreed that the League should cease to be a secret society and that it should draw up a new programme. A congress was to be held 2–9 June 1847, new statutes were to be issued and a 'communist catechism' was to be discussed. At this congress it was agreed to change the name to the League of Communists, to draw up new statutes and to adopt Engels' 'Draft of the Communist Confession of Faith' as its new programme.

Collaboration between London and Brussels was not based upon adherence to 'Marxism' as it was later understood. There is little to suggest that the Londoners tied communism to an industrial working class or to a particular stage in production. More relevent was a shared commitment to 'community of property' to be achieved through an 'attack on the existing social order and on private property' combined with a rejection of the 'barrack-room communism' and conspiratorial tactics of those who still followed Weitling. The London leaders of the League were prepared to make large concessions to Marx and his supporters if only to find a new basis of

67. Schapper to Marx, 6 June 1846, in *Der Bund der Kommunisten*, vol. 1, p. 348.

consensus comparable to that once built upon Weitling's *Mankind as it is and as it ought to be*. Since 1843 the League had been divided between three groups, supporting Weitling, Cabet and Proudhon respectively. In 1846 it had 'almost collapsed entirely'. It was in response to this 'crisis' that the Londoners had 'taken steps to draw into the league other elements of the Communist movement who until then had stood aside from it'.[68] Maybe the new conception of communism proposed by Marx and Engels could reunite the League.

A depiction of the role of the League of the Just and Communist League in the formulation of the *Manifesto* is important because standard accounts still present the story as a confrontation between the scientific outlook of Marx and Engels and the primitive mentality of the League, represented by the artisan communism of Weitling. That approach not only ignores the debates which occurred within the League after 1842, but misses the yet more significant point that the very few sentences devoted to the compatibility between communism and freedom of individual development most probably were contributed by the League rather than by Marx and Engels themselves.

68. See anon. (W. Wolff and K. Schapper), 'A Circular of the First Congress of the Communist League to the League Members, 9 June 1847', *MECW*, vol. 6, p. 594.

5. *Engels' Contribution*

Frederick Engels was a vital intermediary between London and Brussels in the process of devising the new 'communist credo'. As eldest son and presumptive heir to his father's textile firm, Ermen and Engels, Engels had begun his lifelong collaboration with Marx in Paris in the summer of 1844. Both had been active among the Young Hegelians, the radical philosophical grouping that had grown up in Prussia during the preceding eight years. But during the preceding two years any semblance of unity within this movement had disappeared. At their meeting in Paris, Engels and Marx had agreed to write a joint work, *The Holy Family*, setting out their disagreement with other Young Hegelians. Engels had stopped off in Paris on his way back to the parental home in Barmen after a two-year stay in Manchester representing the family firm. Back in Barmen, he spent six months writing up his famous study, *The Condition of the Working Class in England*, and then in April 1845 left for Brussels to join Marx.

Engels' main role during the years between 1845 and 1848 was political and journalistic. Ostensibly travelling for the purpose of research and continuing to rely upon an uncertain allowance from his father, Engels wrote extensively in the political press and worked among German artisan and communist groups in Brussels, Paris and London. Unlike Marx, who had been banished from Paris, Engels could move freely between these cities and act as a roving advocate of their shared position. It was therefore as an emissary from the Brussels Communist Correspondence Committee that

Engels put forward the original 'Draft of a Communist Confession of Faith' at the first congress of the newly named Communist League, held in London in June 1847. In September of that year he almost certainly contributed to the first and only number of the League's intended newspaper – *Die kommunistische Zeitschrift* (the Communist Newspaper) – and it is likely that he suggested the new watchword of the League, 'Workers of the World, Unite!', in place of 'All men are brothers'.

Later, at a meeting of the Paris branch of the league on 22 October 1847, Engels proposed a second draft of the credo, the so-called 'Principles of Communism', which was accepted in preference to an alternative put forward by Moses Hess. At the second congress of the League, which met in London between 28 November and 8 December 1847 and was attended by both Marx and Engels, this draft appears to have been accepted as the basis of a final version. In a letter written to Marx a week before, Engels provided a brief summary of the 'Principles' and suggested that since 'a certain amount of history has to be narrated in it', they 'abandon the catechetical form and call the thing Communist *Manifesto*'. On the congress itself, he assured Marx, 'THIS TIME WE SHALL HAVE IT ALL OUR OWN WAY'.[69]

After the congress, Marx and Engels spent a few days in London and then a further ten days together in Brussels before Engels returned to Paris. He did not go back to Brussels until 29 January 1848 and the manuscript of the *Manifesto* was apparently delivered before 1 February. Only one page of preparatory notes survives, a plan of section two, probably dating from December 1847.[70] It seems likely therefore that Marx wrote up the final version alone in January 1848.

The order of the *Manifesto* closely followed Engels' 'Principles'. The *Manifesto*'s first two historical sections correspond to questions 1–23 of the 'Principles'. Section three, on communist literature, elaborates question 24 of the 'Principles'; section four, on communists and

69. Engels to Marx, 23–4 November 1847, *MECW*, vol. 38, pp. 146–9.
70. *MECW*, vol. 6, p. 576.

opposition parties, relates to question 25. In substance as well, the *Manifesto* drew heavily on the previous writing of the two men, especially their jointly written 'The German Ideology' (1845–7); Marx's first critique of political economy (1844); his polemic against Proudhon, *The Poverty of Philosophy* (1846); Engels' 'Outlines of a critique of Political Economy' (1843–4); and his *Condition of the Working Class in England* (1845), together with a number of shorter pieces written in 1846–7. Marx either paraphrased or simply lifted usable sentences or phrases from these writings.[71]

In communist literature Engels was presented as the ever-ready loyal lieutenant to Marx, always willing to play second fiddle to the man of genius. The writings of the two men were treated as indistinguishable and attempts to discriminate between them were treated as acts of political hostility. In reaction, the opponents of Soviet communism strained to find points of possible divergence. In these somewhat forced accounts, Marx was presented as the champion of a noble and impassioned humanism, while the determinism, positivism and mechanistic thinking associated with 'orthodox Marxism' were assigned to Engels.[72]

Since the *Manifesto* devoted little space to these humanist themes, its stance was largely ascribed to Engels. Many of its central themes – the transition from 'feudal' to 'bourgeois' society, the growth of free trade and the world market, the industrial revolution, the end of 'patriarchal idyllic relations' and the formation of the proletariat – were to be found four years earlier in 1844 in Engels' writings about England at a time when his collaboration with Marx had not yet begun.[73]

There is a moment of truth in this argument but overall it is misleading. What is certainly true is that the historical case for 'communism' made by the *Manifesto* placed at its centre a barely concealed account of English social and economic development that

71. For the details of borrowings, see Andréas, *Le Manifeste Communiste*, pp. 1–4.
72. For a useful delineation of the main strands within this approach, see J. D. Hunley, *The Life and Thought of Friedrich Engels*, New Haven, 1991, ch. 3.
73. These similarities are set out in T. Carver, *Marx and Engels: The Intellectual Relationship*, Brighton, 1983, pp. 80–83.

closely followed what Engels had already sketched out in 1844. But, as will be seen, the significance now accorded to this history was wholly different.

Frederick Engels was born in 1820 in Barmen, Westphalia, originally in the Grand Duchy of Berg, but in Engels' time part of the enlarged Prussian state. Brought up in a strongly Calvinist household, Frederick attended the Elberfeld Gymnasium before being sent to Bremen to learn the skills of a merchant. But from school onwards Engels developed radical literary ambitions. Unlike Marx, his first political attitudes were strongly shaped by the liberal nationalist movement of the 1830s. His earliest heroes had been drawn from Teutonic mythology, and in Bremen the legend of Siegfried remained important to him as a symbol of the courageous qualities of young German manhood in struggle against the petty servile Germany of the princes. Contributing to the press and writing pamphlets under the pseudonym Frederick Oswald, he was initially drawn to Young Germany, a short-lived literary group that had arisen in the wake of the 1830 revolution. His particular hero was Ludwig Börne, the Jewish radical – already encountered as the translator of Lamennais – who had gone into exile in Paris at the time of the revolution. What attracted Engels to him were his radical republican denunciations of German princes and aristocrats combined with an equally sharp polemic against the Francophobe tendencies of German nationalism.

Engels gravitated towards the Young Hegelians after reading David Strauss's *Life of Jesus* in Bremen towards the end of 1839. This led him finally to abandon his childhood Christian faith, first in favour of a vaguely pantheist reading of Hegel and then, in 1841 after he had arrived in Berlin for a year's military service, of 'the secret atheist Hegel' espoused by the leading Berlin Young Hegelian Bruno Bauer.[74]

Young Hegelianism played a central role in Marx's development during his years in Berlin and Cologne. But less needs to be said of

74. On Strauss, Bruno Bauer and the Young Hegelians, see below, chapter 6.

the Hegelianism of the young 'Frederick Oswald'. For what became distinctive in Engels' outlook was formed not within Young Hegelian circles in Berlin, but in England, to which his father sent him between November 1842 and August 1844. In Berlin Engels was impulsive, intrepid and eclectic. Acting the soldier was a way of escaping the family firm for a time and was a move that his patriotic father could hardly refuse. It was also his first chance to get away from his small-town upbringing and savour life in a large city free from the moral surveillance of elders. But peacetime soldiering brought its own forms of tedium. Young Hegelianism offered a more bohemian diversion and a chance to engage with 'the ideas of the century'.[75]

As it happened, an important battle provoked by these ideas was just about to be fought out in the lecture halls of Berlin. Worried by the un-Christian tendency of Hegelianism, the new Prussian government of Frederick William IV had summoned to Hegel's chair in Berlin the aged philosopher Schelling, with instructions to 'root out the dragon's seeds of Hegelianism'. Engels attended Schelling's first course of lectures and within weeks of his arrival was publishing pseudonymous pamphlets against Schelling's 'philosophy of revelation'.[76]

Engels had no contact with the university and no philosophical training. Disagreements between Young Hegelians appear to have made little impression upon him. Until he joined forces with Marx in Paris in the summer of 1844, his journalistic writings showed no awareness of the differences between the views of Bauer and those

75. Engels to his schoolfriend Friedrich Graeber, 8 April 1839, *MECW*, vol. 2, p. 422.
76. See 'Schelling on Hegel', 'Schelling and Revelation' and 'Schelling, Philosopher in Christ, or the Transfiguration of Worldly Wisdom into Divine Wisdom', *MECW*, vol. 2, pp. 180–264. F. J. W. von Schelling (1775–1854) had once been a fellow student and friend of Hegel and it was from Schelling that Hegel had first adopted a notion of the 'absolute'. It was through Schelling that Hegel first secured a position as a Privatdozent (unsalaried lecturer) in the University of Jena in 1801. Thereafter a rift developed between them, made permanent when Hegel publicly broke with Schelling's notion of the absolute in his *Phenomenology of the Spirit*, published in 1807.
   Engels captured the drama, but did not grasp the seriousness of Schelling's challenge to Hegel's philosophical starting point. On Schelling's philosophical importance to the Young Hegelians, see footnote 135 below.

of Feuerbach (see chapter 7 below). They were simply grouped together as part of a common assault upon Christianity, leading to the replacement of theology by anthropology. In politics too, Engels was barely touched by Hegel. Unlike most of the other Berlin Young Hegelians, he had already become a republican and a revolutionary democrat before he became a Hegelian. During his time in Berlin, he still believed he could combine Hegel's philosophy of history with Börne's republican view of politics.[77] In 1842, in a mock epic poem about Bauer's dismissal from his university post co-written with Bruno's younger brother, Edgar, Engels referred to himself as 'Oswald the montagnard':

> A radical is he, dyed in the wool and hard.
> Day in, day out, he plays the guillotine a
> single, solitary tune and that's a
> cavatina.[78]

Jacobinism and the vehement rejection of Louis Philippe's '*juste milieu*' liberal constitutionalism in France was one way of expressing his off-the-record delight in shocking the respectable. Another was joining in the anti-Christian excesses of the 'Free', an informal coterie of radical freethinkers formed to champion the atheism of the dismissed Bauer. The publication of these unrestrained diatribes greatly irritated Marx, at a time when as editor of the *Rheinische Zeitung* he was trying to build a broad front of liberal and constitutional opposition to the absolutist policies of the monarchy. No doubt this helps to explain why Engels' first encounter with Marx in the newspaper's offices in Cologne was said to have been cool.

More important was a meeting with the paper's Parisian correspondent, Moses Hess. Hess claimed that as a result Engels shifted his position from Jacobinism to a form of socialism inspired by an activist vision of Young Hegelianism and Feuerbach's humanism. Hess, the prime proponent of this position, was another philosophical

77. See F. Engels, 'Alexander Jung, "Lectures on Modern German Literature"', *MECW*, vol. 2, p. 289.
78. 'The insolently threatened yet miraculously rescued Bible or the Triumph of Faith', *MECW*, vol. 2, p. 335.

outsider like himself. In the following three years, his part in the political and intellectual development of German socialism was central. In different ways it shaped the positions both of Engels and of Marx. Something must, therefore, be said about Hess's own formation.[79]

Like Engels, Hess was the rebellious son of a manufacturer – a sugar refiner in Cologne – and again like Engels he was drawn enthusiastically towards communism and humanism as a replacement for a strong family faith, in his case Judaism. In the mid 1830s, Hess had travelled to France and in 1837 brought out a radical millenarian work, entitled *The Sacred History of Mankind by a disciple of Spinoza*, effectively the first philosophical espousal of communism in Germany.[80] According to *The Sacred History*, during the childhood of mankind there had been community of goods and an unconscious harmony between God and Man; in the second period, inaugurated by Christ, this harmony had gradually broken down with the coming of private property and the hereditary principle. The third epoch would witness the restoration of harmony both between God and Man and between man and man. The first restoration was heralded by Spinoza's declaration of the unity of nature and spirit, the second by the principle of social equality championed by Rousseau and extended by the French Revolution and the communism of Babeuf.

Hess was not a Young Hegelian, but in his second book, *The*

79. As will also be seen in the case of Proudhon, the crucial role played by Moses Hess (1812–75) in the genesis of Marx's theory of communism was often discounted in the twentieth-century Marxist tradition. It was convenient, but not historically accurate, to associate Hess with the doctrines of 'True Socialism', attacked in the third section of *The Communist Manifesto*. Hess remained a communist and at the beginning of the 1860s, collaborated with Lassalle in the formation of his new General Federation of German Workers, the foundation of all organized social democracy in Europe. Inspired by Mazzini and the struggle for Italian unification around the same time, Hess wrote his most famous book, *Rom und Jerusalem, die Nationalitätsfrage* (Rome and Jerusalem, the question of nationality), Leipzig, 1862, in which he made a pioneering argument for a national homeland for the Jews. See Isaiah Berlin's essay, 'The life and opinions of Moses Hess', I. Berlin, *Against the Current Essays in the History of Ideas*, Oxford, 1981, pp. 213–52.
80. See Mönke (ed.), *Moses Hess*, pp. 6–66.

European Triarchy of 1841, he tried to articulate his position in Hegelian terms. Hess was attracted not so much to Hegel himself as to a book that reformulated his philosophy in 1838, *Prolegomena to Historiosophy*, which turned Hegelianism into an activist and future-oriented creed. Its author, an exiled Polish count named August Cieszkowski, argued that history should be considered an organism, a unity of rationally developing and independent elements governed by dialectical laws.[81] On this basis, history could be understood as a science that could encompass the future. Hegel himself had not pursued his discoveries and wrongly maintained that history had reached its conclusion. In Cieszkowski's view, after antiquity and middle ages, history was now entering a third age of synthesis.

Cieszkowski maintained that Hegel had considered human activity only in the form of thought and had produced a philosophy of 'contemplation'. By combining thought with a more activist notion of will derived from Fichte, Hegelianism could be refashioned into an action-oriented philosophy of the future. The coming third period of humanity would be governed by this unity of knowledge and action, which Cieszkowski called 'praxis' or 'the deed'. Now that humanity could understand its own history and the laws of its historical development, it could act in full knowledge of its vocation. As an admirer of Fourier and follower of the ex-Saint-Simonian Christian Socialist Philippe Buchez, Cieszkowski defined this

81. August Cieszkowski (1814–94), heir to a wealthy, cultivated and aristocratic Polish family, was educated at Cracow and then Berlin, where he was particularly influenced by the liberal Hegelians Eduard Gans and Carl-Ludwig Michelet. Apart from the *Prolegomena*, Cieszkowski participated in (old) Hegelian debates about the nature of God and immortality and in resistance to Schelling's 'philosophy of revelation'. In the decade before 1848, however, he spent most of his time in Paris, where his book on money, *Du crédit et de la circulation* (1839), became one of the sources of Proudhon's *Philosophie de la Misère*. After 1848 he returned to Posen in the Prussian province of Poland, where he was active in local politics. His life work, *Our Father*, an attempt to build an utopian vision of the future upon an esoteric reading of the Lord's Prayer inspired by Joachimite prophecy, a millenarian reading of Hegel and Lessing's *Education of the Human Race*, remained unfinished at his death. An abbreviated translation of Cieszkowski's *Prolegomena* and an account of his life and work is to be found in A. Liebich (ed.), *Selected Writings of August Cieszkowski*, Cambridge, 1979, pp. 49–82 and *passim*.

vocation in the language of socialism and the new, socially oriented millenarian Christianity of post-1830 France.

Cieszkowski's book made a strong impression on Hess, particularly in its insistence upon the need to move from 'the philosophy of the spirit' to the 'action of the spirit' and upon the primacy of the social dimension in the harmony to be realized in the third epoch.[82] Hess argued against Hegel that Man was not yet in a position to become 'at one with himself', nor could this act of reconciliation be confined to thought. In the coming epoch, oppositions would fade away in every sphere of human activity. Thus the reconciliation of which Hegel wrote could only be realized within a socialist society and under the aegis of a new humanist creed. As Hess conceived it, the movements towards spiritual and social harmony proceeded in parallel.

In *The European Triarchy*, progress towards this ultimate harmony was embodied in an emancipatory movement borne by three European nations each in its characteristic way. The task of Germany, the land of the Reformation, was to realize spiritual freedom; that of France, embodied in its great revolution, was to attain political freedom. The task of England, now on the verge of social revolution as a result of the mounting contradiction between 'pauperism' and 'the money aristocracy', was to bring about social equality.[83]

In November 1842, when Engels left for England, Hess's prophecy of 1841 seemed literally to be coming true. In the summer, at the height of Chartist agitation and the plug-plot riots around Manchester, Hess, acting as foreign editor of the *Rheinische Zeitung*, had discerned the final onset of 'the approaching catastrophe'. Within days of his arrival in England, Engels was writing in the same terms.[84] This was the point at which Hess converted Engels to communism.

Engels himself defined his communism as a consequence of Young

---

82. See M. Hess, 'The Philosophy of the Act', in A. Fried and R. Sanders (eds.), *Socialist Thought, A Documentary History*, Edinburgh, 1964, pp. 249–75.
83. 'Die europäische Triarchie', in Mönke (ed.), *Moses Hess*, pp. 159–60.
84. 'Über eine in England bevorstehende Katastrophe' (*Rheinische Zeitung*, no. 177, 26 June 1842) in Mönke (ed.), *Moses Hess*, pp. 183–5; F. Engels, 'The internal crises' (*Rheinische Zeitung*, no. 343, 9 Dec. 1842) in *MECW*, vol. 2, pp. 370–72.

Hegelianism. In an article written in 1843, he stated that by 1842 the Young Hegelians were 'atheist and republican', but that by the autumn of that year,

some of the party contended for the insufficiency of political change and declared their opinion to be that a *social* revolution based upon common property, was the only state of mankind agreeing with their abstract principles.

He described Hess as 'the first communist of the party'.[85]

During his stay in England, Engels continued his double life. Just as in Berlin, as 'Frederick Oswald', he had written polemical attacks on the philosopher Schelling, so now he wrote frequently for the English and German radical press and began to collect materials for his book, *The Condition of the Working Class in England*, which appeared in 1845. A businessman in office hours, outside them Engels developed a relationship with a radical Irish millhand, Mary Burns, and got to know some of the leading Owenites and Chartists around Manchester. Much of the enduring strength of his work derived from these encounters and from the first-hand observation that resulted from them.

Engels followed Hess in believing that in each of the three European nations 'a thorough revolution of social arrangements based on community of property' was an 'urgent and unavoidable necessity'. The English had arrived at this conclusion 'practically', the French 'politically' and the Germans 'philosophically, by reasoning on first principles'. During his stay, Engels was particularly impressed by the practical perspectives of the Owenites. In the autumn of 1843 he wrote that, 'in everything bearing on practice, upon the *facts* of the present state of society, we find that the English Socialists are a long way before us'.[86] Around the same time he wrote his 'Outlines of a Critique of Political Economy'. Starting from Owenite criticisms of political economy, Engels was the first of the Young Hegelians to

85. F. Engels, 'Progress of Social Reform on the Continent' (*New Moral World*, 18 Nov. 1843), *MECW*, vol. 3, p. 406.
86. Engels, 'The Progress of Social Reform', *MECW*, vol. 3, pp. 393, 407.

make the connection with Proudhon's critique of private property. In this essay, the contradictions of political economy were ascribed to the corrosive logic of private property itself, which, after its victory over previous social forms and the triumph of free trade, was now propelling England towards its final social crisis.[87]

In subsequent essays Engels went on to enlarge upon this crisis and its historical causes. The starting point of his diagnosis resembled that of Thomas Carlyle: individualism was dissolving all social ties.[88] After the dissolution of the feudal system, mankind was no longer to 'be held together by force, by *political* means, but by *self interest*, that is, by *social* means' ... 'The abolition of feudal servitude has made "cash payment the sole relation between human beings".' Mercantilists had acknowledged the antagonism that underlay buying cheap and selling dear. But Adam Smith had praised commerce as 'a bond of union and friendship'. This 'hypocritical way of misusing morality for immoral purposes' was 'the pride of the free-trade system'. All small monopolies were abolished 'so that the *one* great basic monopoly, property, may function the more freely and unrestrictedly'.

By 'dissolving nationalities', the liberal economic system had intensified 'to the utmost the enmity between individuals, the ignominious war of competition'. 'Commerce absorbed industry into itself and thereby became omnipotent.' Through industrialization and the factory system, the last step had been reached, 'the dissolution of the family'. 'What else can result from the separation of interests, such as forms the basis of the free-trade system?' Money, 'the alienated empty abstraction of property', had become the master of the world. Man had ceased to be the slave of man and had become 'the

---

87. See F. Engels, 'Outlines of a Critique of Political Economy', *MECW*, vol. 3, pp. 418–44; this essay, together with a review essay on Thomas Carlyle's *Past and Present*, appeared in the single number of the *Deutsch-Französische Jahrbücher* (the German–French Annals), edited by Marx and Arnold Ruge, and made a deep impression on Marx; see chapter 8 below.

88. Thomas Carlyle (1795–1881) was the most important social critic writing in Britain in the 1830s and 1840s. Through his essay 'Chartism' (1839), and his book *Past and Present*, London, 1843, he provoked a debate on what contemporaries called 'the condition of England question'. Carlyle drew heavily upon Goethe, Herder and German romantic literature.

slave of *things*. 'The disintegration of mankind into a mass of isolated mutually repelling atoms in itself means the destruction of all corporate, national and indeed of any particular interests and is the last necessary step towards the free and spontaneous association of men.'[89]

The framework within which Engels developed this picture was that of the crisis and last days of Christianity. 'The Christian world order cannot be taken any further than this.' The setting was England because 'only England has a social history ... only here have principles been turned into interests before they were able to influence history'. Following Hegel's *Philosophy of History*, the origin of the present crisis was to be traced back to 'the Christian-Germanic view of the world' whose essential principle was individualistic – 'abstract subjectivity'.[90] After the disintegration of feudalism, this idea had culminated politically in 'the Christian state'. 'Subjective and egotistical ... interestedness' had been elevated into 'a general principle' resulting in 'universal fragmentation' and 'the domination of property'.[91]

In eighteenth-century England the social upheaval of the industrial revolution and the expansion of trade were portents of

the assembling, the gathering of mankind from the fragmentation and isolation into which it had been driven by Christianity, it was the penultimate step towards the self-understanding and self-liberation of mankind.

Engels was confident of the 'irresistible progress' of the human species through history, 'its ever certain victory over the unreason of the individual'. He wrote in 1844:

89. See Engels, 'Outlines', *MECW*, vol. 3, pp. 423–4; 'The Condition of England. 1. The Eighteenth Century' (31 August 1844), *MECW*, vol. 3, pp. 475–6, 485.
90. See G. W. F. Hegel, *The Philosophy of History*, New York, 1956, Pt. IV, Section 1, The Elements of the Christian German World, pp. 347–411. These lectures began an expansion of the section on world history in *Elements of the Philosophy of Right*, Cambridge, 1991, pp. 371–80. Hegel published *The Philosophy of Right* in 1821. *The Philosophy of History*, taken from students' lecture notes, was published after Hegel's death by Eduard Gans. On Gans see below, pp. 157–8.
91. F. Engels, 'The eighteenth century', *MECW*, vol. 3, pp. 475–6.

Man has only to understand himself [, and] to organize the world in a truly human manner according to the demands of his own nature, and he will have solved the riddle of our time.[92]

In the following year Engels somewhat modified his position on England. In *The Condition of the Working Class in England*, written up in the winter of 1844–5, the focus was no longer simply upon private property, individualism and social dissolution. This was now counter-balanced by an emphasis upon the redemptive role of the proletariat, a theme he had probably derived from a reading of Marx's essay in the *Deutsch-Französische Jahrbücher* (German-French Annals), and from his discussions with Marx in Paris in August 1844.

The story told in *The Condition of the Working Class in England* derived from the categories of Feuerbach.[93] Starting from an account of the bucolic innocence of English pre-industrial textile workers, Engels recounted how industrialization had dragged these workers into the mainstream of world history and progressively reduced them to the horrific animal conditions detailed in his description of Manchester. But pauperization and dehumanization formed the essential prelude to their recovery of humanity through proletarian revolt, beginning with crude acts of individual violence and culminating in an organized labour movement, Chartism and social revolution.

Engels still aligned himself with the Owenites, but his view was now more critical. In the summer of 1844, he had still believed like the Owenites that 'social evils cannot be cured by People's Charters'. But in *The Condition of the Working Class in England*, he criticized the Owenites for their disapproval of 'class hatred' and for not discerning 'the element of progress in this dissolution of the old social order'. Their ambition 'to place the nation in a state of Communism at once, overnight not by the unavoidable march of its political development', he now considered naive. They should 'condescend to return for a moment to the Chartist standpoint'. This might enable them to conquer 'the brutal element' in what would other-

92. F. Engels, 'The Condition of England. *Past and Present* by Thomas Carlyle, London, 1843' (*Deutsch-Französische Jahrbücher*), *MECW*, vol. 3, p. 464.
93. On Feuerbach's ideas, see chapter 7 below.

wise be the 'bloodiest' war of the poor against the rich ever waged.[94]

The basic assumption behind Engels' approach, both in his early months in England and at the point at which he was writing up his book, was of the parallel development of theology and economics. Man's 'fear of himself' expressed itself both in the 'Christian-Germanic conception of subjectivity' and in private property. While philosophers had destroyed 'the abstraction of a God', the economic sequence which followed from private property 'unconsciously' served 'the reconciliation of mankind with nature and itself'. In championing the virtues of free trade, Adam Smith was the 'economic Luther' who had replaced 'the Catholic candour' of mercantilism by 'Protestant hypocrisy'. Just as it was necessary to overthrow Catholicism,

so it was necessary to overthrow the mercantile system with its monopolies and hindrances to trade, so that the true consequences of private property would have come to light [and] the struggle of our time could become a universal human struggle . . . [for] just as theology must either regress to blind faith or progress towards free philosophy, free trade must produce the restoration of monopolies on the one hand and the abolition of private property on the other . . . Once a principle is set in motion, it works by its own impetus through all its consequences, whether the economists like it or not.[95]

Only England, however, was destined to experience this apocalyptic social revolution. In Germany, Engels still hoped for a peaceful change inaugurated by the philosophers. In March 1845 he was delighted to report to the readers of the Owenite *New Moral World* 'the most important fact' that 'Dr Feuerbach has declared himself a communist' and that 'communism was in fact only the *practice* of what he had proclaimed long before theoretically.' Other Young Hegelians were denounced because they refused to draw 'practical inferences' from their theories.[96] In speeches which he made around

94. F. Engels, 'The Condition of the Working Class in England. From Personal Observation and Authentic Sources', *MECW*, vol. 4, p. 526.
95. F. Engels, 'Outlines', *MECW*, vol. 3, pp. 421, 424.
96. F. Engels, 'Rapid Progress of Communism in Germany', *MECW*, vol. 4, p. 235.

the same time to 'the respectables' of Barmen and Elberfeld together with Moses Hess, Engels also argued that the transition to communism in Germany ought to be a peaceful one. Middle-class audiences were urged to embrace communism on prudential grounds. Their position, he warned, was being undermined by the polarization between rich and poor, by the impact of competition and by the chaos resulting from periodic trade crises. As an alternative to revolution, he argued for the benefits of planning and for the gradual introduction of the community system. Interim measures might include free education, the reorganization of poor relief and a progressive income tax.[97]

On these questions, Engels' position changed markedly after April 1845, when he joined Marx in Brussels. In Brussels they worked at length together on their unpublished and never completed manuscript 'The German Ideology'. This was a second attempt on the part of the 26-year-old Marx and the 24-year-old Engels to clarify what distinguished their position from that of other Young Hegelians. A new view of history built upon the relationship between class struggle, the property system ('relations of production') and the development of human productive power ('forces of production') dated from this time and provided the *Manifesto*'s point of departure. It had largely been developed by Marx and this was why Engels insisted that the *Manifesto* was essentially Marx's work.

But although this new approach to history clearly represented an important shift in position, it did not amount to a general repudiation of the two men's earlier writings. In particular, arguments first put forward in Engels' 1843 essay on political economy, and taken up in Marx's writings of 1844, together with Engels' study of English 'social history' and the formation of the proletariat, continued to provide the starting point of the *Manifesto*. This position at its simplest was that the claims of political economy depended upon the existence of private property, that private property was in a state of terminal crisis and that 'Communism', as the negation of private property, was the rapidly approaching goal of history.

97. F. Engels, 'Speeches in Elberfeld', *MECW*, vol. 4, pp. 243–65.

It is true, therefore, that the *Manifesto*'s accounts of the transition from feudal to bourgeois property, of the development of free trade, the world market and the formation of the proletariat, remained those first sketched out by Engels in 1844–5. What changed was the overall theoretical framework within which this history was placed.

A teleological picture of inexorable crisis and global transformation remained. But what it depicted had changed. It was no longer a vision of the decline and fall of 'the Christian world order'. It was now the analysis of an ostensibly secular socio-economic process. The notion of a final crisis had first emerged in Berlin in Young Hegelian discussions about the end of the 'Christian state'. Subsequently, religion had been assigned a more limited role. The advent of socialism had still been tied to the end of 'the Christian world order', but only as part of a larger process. Religion and economics had jointly expressed the alienation of Man's true 'species' or 'communal' being. Religion had represented the alienation of Man's thought, private property the alienation of his practical activity.

Now the development of 'bourgeois property' (formerly, 'egoism'), originally no more than a signifier of cosmic disorder, had become a single self-sufficient causal mechanism of self-destruction. 'Bourgeois property' was destined for imminent collapse because it could no longer ensure its own continued reproduction. The stark and melodramatic imagery of apocalypse was now concealed within a deliberately prosaic and colourless economic phraseology. Despite the growing wealth of society, the worker was sinking into pauperism. As the *Manifesto* put it, drawing this time much more on Marx's earlier ideas on immiseration from 1844, the bourgeoisie was unfit to rule because it was 'incompetent to assure an existence to its slave within his slavery'.

If, then, it is clear that the leading ideas in the *Manifesto* had a very complicated cross-parentage, is there any point in distinguishing between the ideas of its two authors? The answer to this question is emphatically yes. Communism and the Cold War led to a search for divergence in the wrong places, while large and obvious differences, tangential to the twentieth-century battle of ideas, were ignored or missed. As a result it largely passed unnoticed that two quite different conceptions of communism were buried beneath the formulations of the *Manifesto*. These differences did not point forward to the battles of the twentieth century, but back to the differing notions of communism or socialism that the two authors had acquired before they began to collaborate. But they are not for that reason solely of antiquarian interest. For the fact that these differences were not made explicit, not explored and not resolved, may help to account for the strange obscurity, even vacancy, of the notion of communism at the heart of the subsequent Marxist tradition.

Engels lacked a formal training in philosophy or the history of law. In his reading outside office hours, whether in Barmen, Bremen, Berlin or Manchester, he followed his enthusiasms, spurred on by his linguistic facility and his reading of the radical and socialist press. As a result, he was and was to remain much closer to the optimistic expectations and beliefs of what in the *Manifesto* Marx was to call 'critical-utopian Socialism'. During his stay in England Engels became strongly attracted to the Owenites and regularly attended their meetings.[98] Around the same time, he also read Fourier, for whom he retained a lifelong enthusiasm. He was drawn, it seems, both by the wit of Fourier's attack on commerce and by his sexual unorthodoxy.[99]

Evidence of these loyalties, quite distinct from those of Marx, were still visible in areas of detectable divergence between the preparatory drafts of the *Manifesto* and Marx's final version. On the question of democracy, for example, Engels still reproduced the scepticism about political forms that he had acquired from the Owenites. In 1843 he denounced democracy as 'a contradiction in itself', an 'untruth'.[100]

98. For Engels' contacts with Owenites in Manchester, see G. Stedman Jones, 'Frederick Engels', *Dictionary of National Biography*, forthcoming; G. Claeys, *Machinery, Money and the Millennium: From Moral Economy to Socialism, 1815-1860*, Princeton, 1987, pp. 166–84.
99. For Engels' appreciation of Fourier, see F. Engels, 'A Fragment of Fourier's on Trade' (1845–6), *MECW*, vol. 4, pp. 613–45; and for his later appreciation, F. Engels, 'Socialism: Utopian and Scientific' (1880), *MECW*, vol. 24, pp. 292–3.
100. F. Engels, 'Progress of Social Reform on the Continent', *MECW*, vol. 3, p. 393.

But even in 'The Principles of Communism', his attitude remained grudging. 'Democracy would be quite useless to the proletariat if it were not immediately used to carry through further measures directly attacking private ownership.'[101] The *Manifesto* itself spoke more positively about the need 'to win the battle of democracy'.

Conversely, Engels' 'Principles' straightforwardly advocated communism on the grounds that it abolished private property and educated children communally. It thus destroyed

the twin foundations of hitherto existing marriage – the dependence through private property of the wife upon the husband and of the children upon the parents.[102]

In the *Manifesto*, the point about abolishing the dependence of the wife upon the husband disappeared.

But perhaps the most obvious point of divergence concerned the status of socialist communities. In Engels' writings there was the repeated advocacy of such communities, both before and after he had decided to join forces with Marx. In *The Condition* he agreed with Owenite proposals of home colonies of 2,000 to 3,000 people, which would combine agriculture and industry. In his 1845 communist speech in Elberfeld he advocated 'large palaces built in the form of a square' to house such settlements. In the same year, he wrote an extraordinarily sanguine essay on the success of socialist communities in the United States, drawing his evidence almost entirely from the Owenite press. Finally, the penultimate draft of the *Manifesto* in the autumn of 1847 once again proposed

the erection of large palaces on national estates as common dwellings for communities of citizens engaged in industry as well as agriculture and combining the advantages of both urban and rural life without the one-sidedness and disadvantages of either.[103]

101. F. Engels, 'The Principles of Communism', *MECW*, vol. 6, p. 350.
102. F. Engels, 'The Principles of Communism', *MECW*, vol. 6, p. 350.
103. F. Engels, 'The Condition', *MECW*, vol. 4, p. 525; F. Engels, 'Speeches in Elberfeld' (8 Feb. 1845), *MECW*, vol. 4, p. 252; F. Engels, 'Description of Recently Founded Communist Colonies still in Existence' (1844–5), *MECW*, vol. 4, pp. 214–28; F. Engels, 'Principles of Communism', *MECW*, vol. 6, p. 351.

No hint of this proposal survived into the final version of the *Manifesto*, nor was there a single explicit mention of socialist communities in any of Marx's writings between 1844 and 1848. How different would 'Communism' have looked, had that proposal remained!

In part, the reason for this divergence was to be found in the different types of socialism that they had encountered before they began to work together. Unlike Engels, Marx's first acquaintance with socialism had been with that of Saint-Simon and the Saint-Simonians and had dated back to teenage discussions in the early to mid 1830s with his neighbour and future father-in-law, Ludwig Westphalen. Saint-Simon never mentioned socialist communities and, aside from the brief, divisive and ill-starred commune of 'Father' Enfantin in Menilmontant in 1831, there had been no Saint-Simonian equivalent of Fourier's 'Phalanstery' or Owen's 'village of cooperation'.[104]

But this divergence went deeper than a simple accident of personal

---

104. Barthélemy Prosper Enfantin (1796–1864), a former student of engineering at the École Polytechnique, became one of the two 'Fathers' of the Saint-Simonian church founded after Saint-Simon's death in 1825. In 1828–9 the Saint-Simonians produced a systematic statement of teachings of the master in the form of biweekly lectures, known as *Doctrine of Saint-Simon. An Exposition. First Year, 1828–1829*, tr. G. Iggers, Boston, 1958. The Saint-Simonian church saw itself as a successor of the Catholic Church and imitated its hierarchical organization. In addition to its scientific and socio-economic teachings, under Enfantin's leadership a new sexual doctrine (mainly inspired in fact by Fourier) – 'the rehabilitation of the flesh' – was enunciated. This led to a schism and Bazard, the other 'Father' of the Church, withdrew. With the remaining Saint-Simonian 'family' Enfantin retreated to his property at Menilmontant, where life was to be conducted along communal lines until a 'Mother' of the Church was found to sit beside the 'Father'. The scandal and notoriety associated with this experiment received international coverage. Enfantin and the economist Michel Chevalier were sent to prison for offending against public decency. But after their release, a search for the 'Mother' resumed, taking Enfantin and his followers to Turkey and Egypt, where they also attempted to interest the authorities in the building of a Suez canal. Later in the 1830s, after a spell in Algeria, Enfantin became a promoter of railway amalgamation and a director of the Paris–Lyon–Mediterranean line. He continued to promulgate the Saint-Simonian doctrine, both in its practical and its spiritual dimensions, until his death. It was the *Doctrine of Saint-Simon* and Enfantin's community at Menilmontant that first brought socialism to the attention of educated Europe.

biography. For in Marx's writings, the absence of model socialist communities as experimental proof of socialist claims about human nature also went together with a quite different set of historically based assumptions about the historical imminence of communism throughout the world. This Marxian communism would require neither state, commune nor juridical framework to enforce it. It drew nothing from communist egalitarians and very little from Engels or the utopian socialists. Instead, it attempted to infer the advent of a future society beyond private property from the history of property itself.

6. *Marx's Contribution: Prologue*

What then was Marx's contribution? Some impression of the distinctiveness of Marx's communism emerges straightaway from a comparison between Engels' 'Principles of Communism' and the final version of the *Manifesto*.[105]

First, Marx introduced a forceful and unequivocal tribute to the material achievements of the 'bourgeoisie'.

The bourgeoisie, during its rule of scarce one hundred years, has created more massive and more colossal productive forces than have all preceding generations together.

This transformation was no longer purely technological. It was also cultural. 'All fixed, fast-frozen relations . . . are swept away . . . All that is solid melts into air, all that is holy is profaned.' Marx did not merely note these changes, he welcomed them: 'Man is at last compelled to face with sober senses, his real conditions of life, and his relations with his kind.'

Other changes were equally marked. Marx removed the residual Owenite scruples of Schapper or perhaps even Engels about the

105. Evidence for the distinctiveness of Marx's approach to communism is drawn not only from the *Manifesto*, but from a comparison of the writings of the two authors in the preceding five years. It is possible that Engels' 'Principles' accommodated the views of the League of the Just to a greater extent than the final draft. Equally, Engels may have participated in the composition of the final draft. These are matters of surmise. What cannot be maintained is that the differences between the 'Principles' and the *Manifesto* are purely matters of form.

violence of revolutionary overthrow. Communist aims, according to the *Manifesto*, could 'be attained only by the forcible overthrow of all existing conditions'. Similarly, while the *Manifesto* followed the 'Principles' in identifying communism with the abolition of private property – the task of communists was always to bring to the fore 'the property question' – it was no longer even implicitly associated with 'community of goods', 'palaces of industry', 'social levelling' or 'universal asceticism'. Lastly, while the *Manifesto*'s overall depiction of communism was far less explicit than that found in the 'Principles', in one area it was more clear cut. The 'Principles' had detailed the end of classes, of the division of labour, even of the antagonism between town and country, but it had said nothing about the state or its putative successor, 'the general association of all members of society'. Here, the *Manifesto* ventured one terse prediction, 'the public power will lose its political character.'

It might be tempting to ascribe some of these changes – especially perhaps the characterization of the bourgeoisie – to an underlying difference of character and temperament between the two men. Engels was more open, more gregarious, more pleased with life, a lover of good wines and attractive women, a fluent and prolific journalist and an able businessman, as much at home in his bourgeois as in his revolutionary persona. Marx, on the other hand, was more obsessive, more thin-skinned, unable to compromise, an altogether more liminal figure – the grandchild of rabbis, son of a lawyer who had converted to Christianity as the Prussian state began to have second thoughts about Jewish emancipation. Brought up in the aristocratic quarter of Trier and married into its echelons, he was guiltily concerned with family appearances even when unable to maintain them. He was impassioned, single-minded, less original in creating new ideas than some of his elders and contemporaries – Feuerbach, Proudhon, Heine, Hess or Engels – but infinitely more tenacious, rigorous and uncompromising in following through their logic, once he had taken them into his possession.[106]

106. On Marx's personality and abilities, the early judgement of Moses Hess is often cited: 'Imagine Rousseau, Voltaire, Holbach, Lessing, Heine and Hegel fused into one person – I say fused, not juxtaposed – and you have Dr Marx' (Moses Hess to

These differences are clearly important, but precisely how important in shaping the distinctive features of Marx's communism cannot be decided unless the provenance of his ideas and their systematic interconnection are examined in their own right. Too often, insights derived from psychological speculation turn out to be unfounded or else to be what the French utopian socialist Charles Fourier described as 'the fifth wheel on the cart' – an assumption that adds nothing to an explanation reached more securely by a different route. Serious attention to the history of ideas can lessen these dangers by distinguishing more sharply between those propositions or modes of expression peculiar to a particular author and those that derived from a shared genre or theoretical system. And so in Marx's case, whatever the place of personal preoccupations in shaping his hatred and admiration for the bourgeoisie or the mirthlessly sardonic judgement passed upon them in the *Manifesto*, they cannot in themselves be made to account for the distinctive features of Marx's communism. These features can only be identified after first re-establishing Marx's starting point and that means tracing his intellectual formation.

This point is elementary, but crucial. Unlike Engels, Marx received a systematic university education, initially in Bonn and then in Berlin, over the six years 1835–41. Berlin was probably the foremost university in the world at the time: especially in law and philosophy, the subjects which interested Marx. Originally destined for law, the young Marx attended the lectures of the great conserva-

---

Berthold Auerbach, 2 September 1841); less often mentioned, though not necessarily incompatible, are the later and more disenchanted judgements of Heine. To Moritz Carriere he remarked in 1851, when Marx's name came up in conversation: 'When all is said and done, a man is very little if he is nothing but a razor.' His public judgement, recorded in 1854 in his *Confessions*, was respectful, but scarcely warmer: 'The more or less occult leaders of the German communists are great logicians, the most powerful of which have come from the school of Hegel; and they are, without doubt, Germany's most capable thinkers and most energetic characters. These revolutionary doctors and their pitilessly determined disciples are the only men in Germany who have any life; and it is to them, I fear, that the future belongs.' It is only fair to add, however, that the Marx–Heine relationship had been poisoned by the revelation that Heine had secretly taken money from the government of Louis Philippe. See S. Prawer, *Karl Marx and World Literature*, Oxford, 1976, pp. 25, 150–51.

tive champion of the German Historical School of Law Karl von Savigny, as well as those of his opponent, the Hegelian Eduard Gans. Marx took law seriously, even as an undergraduate writing a 300-page manuscript on the philosophy of law before abandoning the project. These studies were to provide an indispensable basis for his later work on the development of property relations.[107]

107. On the importance of Marx's studies as a law student, see D. R. Kelley, 'The Metaphysics of Law: an Essay on the very young Marx', *American Historical Review*, 83 (1978), pp. 350–67. The dispute between Savigny and Gans and its importance in the shaping of Marx's conception of communism is discussed in chapter 9.

7. *The Young Hegelians*

(i) Hegel and Hegelianism

From the beginning, Marx showed much less interest in the practice of law than in its underlying theory. It is not therefore surprising that by the autumn of 1837, his real interests had turned to philosophy, the philosophy of Hegel. Hegel had died in the cholera epidemic of 1831. His appeal to a radical and intellectually questing student in the 1830s is not difficult to imagine. As Marx explained to his understandably anxious father, 'from . . . the idealism of Kant and Fichte, I arrived at the point of seeking the idea in reality itself.'[108]

To be a Hegelian was to accept some large claims, but a willingness to take seriously the claims of communism was not one of them. Hegel himself in the *Philosophy of Right*, his theory of the modern state, had condemned communism in unequivocal terms. Property was the means by which the 'will' acquired existence, so it therefore had to possess the characteristic 'of being mine'. Hegel called this 'the important doctrine of the necessity of *private property*'. The idea of 'a pious or friendly or even compulsory brotherhood of men with *communal property* and a ban on the principle of private property', Hegel thought, could only suggest itself to 'that disposition which misjudges the nature of the freedom of spirit and right'.[109] Why,

108. K. Marx, 'Letter from Marx to his father' (10–11 November 1837), *MECW*, vol. 1, p. 18.
109. G. W. F. Hegel, *Elements of the Philosophy of Right*, ed., A. W. Wood, Cambridge, 1991, paras. 45, 46, pp. 76–8.

therefore, should a serious and philosophically trained follower of Hegel come to espouse the communist cause?

The short answer is that after the 1830 revolutions, as Prussia increasingly turned its back upon the lengthy period of liberal reform forced upon it after defeat by Napoleon in 1806, it also became increasingly difficult to remain a Hegelian.[110]

Like the Prussian reforms, Hegel's philosophy had been a product of the tumultuous years between 1789 and 1819 – the years of the French Revolution, of a world war, of Napoleon's abolition of the Holy Roman Empire and transformation of central Europe, and finally of the establishment of an entirely new European state system at the Congress of Vienna.[111]

This turmoil had not been simply political. Before it had become engulfed in war and revolution, German-speaking Europe – or at least its educated classes – had already entered a period of religious crisis engendered by the new critical philosophy of Kant and the rehabilitation of the 'atheist' or 'pantheist' doctrine of Spinoza. The fall of the *ancien régime* in France, succeeded by the collapse across Europe of so many forms of ancient authority, spiritual as well as temporal, had only added to a fear of the imminence of 'nihilism' – a term invented in the 1780s to describe this crisis of faith.[112] Hegel's idea of the 'absolute spirit' and of world history as the progress of

---

110. The Prussian 'reform era' (1807–19), associated with the ministries of Stein and Hardenberg, was set in motion by the catastrophic defeat of Prussia by Napoleon at the battles of Jena and Auerstadt in 1806. The main aims were to increase the effectiveness of the army and to strengthen the machinery of government. The reforms included the introduction of conscription, the emancipation of the peasantry, the removal of corporate distinctions and privileges, the emancipation of the Jews, the liberalization of economic life, the introduction of municipal self-government, a complete reform of the education system and the foundation of the University of Berlin.

The best study of Hegel and the Hegelian movement is J. E. Toews, *Hegelianism: The Path Toward Dialectical Humanism, 1805–1841*, Cambridge, 1980.

111. It was as a result of the Congress of Vienna that the Rhineland and Trier, the town in which Marx grew up, became part of Prussia.

112. On the reception of Kant's philosophy in Germany in the 1780s and 1790s, see F. Beiser, *The Fate of Reason, German Philosophy from Kant to Fichte*, Cambridge, 1987; on the emergence of Spinozism and idea of 'nihilism', ibid. chs. 1 and 2, pp. 30–31.

reason and freedom, his famous doctrine of the identity of reason and actuality embodied in his depiction of the modern state and his insistence that religion and philosophy only differed in form, were all part of his response to this multifaceted crisis.

The centre-point of conservative criticism of the French Revolution, starting from Edmund Burke's 1790 *Reflections on the Revolution in France* (which had rapidly been translated into German), had been the portrayal of revolutionaries as fanatical adherents of a disembodied reason, deaf to the lessons of history and experience. By embedding reason in history, Hegel had been able to steer a middle course in the battle between rationalists and traditionalists. He had endorsed the criticism of the abstractness of the notion of reason espoused by the French Jacobins and the followers of Kant – the placing of reason outside space and time. But he turned this conservative attack on its head by arguing that reason was itself a historical product and therefore that the revolution, far from being an arbitrary event, had been prepared by the whole course of previous history.

It was true, Hegel believed, that no belief or institution would survive unless justified by reason. But he did not think that such an idea had been an invention of the French Revolution. Ever since Luther, this assumption had been implicit in Protestant Christianity, just as it now formed the foundation of the modern state.[113] It was only because the state was based upon reason and freedom that it

113. The equation between reason and Protestantism was derived from the Lutheran idea of the priesthood of all believers. Catholics believed that the relationship between God and the individual believer was mediated through the authority of the Church and the priesthood. Protestants believed that the relationship between God and the individual was direct. Believers were to be guided solely by Scripture – one of the reasons why philosophical and historical criticism of the Bible made its greatest impact in Protestant countries. But this doctrine, *sola scriptura*, was itself not free from ambiguity, since texts must be interpreted. Therefore, from Luther's time onwards, Protestants had differed on the relative importance of textual authority, reason and purity of heart in forming the judgement of the individual believer. Hegel's Christianity contained a millenarian streak that he probably acquired from the Pietist Protestantism of his native Württemberg. See L. Dickey, *Hegel, Religion, Economics and the Politics of Spirit 1770–1807*, Cambridge, 1987.

could be recognized as a legal and political community, a *we*, in which the individual could self-consciously will the common will as his or her own will. Such a principle presupposed freedom of opinion, religious toleration and the separation of Church and State together with the elimination of the residues of feudalism, civil inequality and arbitrary privilege.

But Hegel had also agreed with those critics such as Hamann who objected to the disembodied character of reason as it had been deployed by Kant.[114] Reason could not be treated as if it existed beyond the constraints of time and space. Reason had a history. It was embodied in language and culture. Languages and cultures changed over time and differed across space. Thus reason should not be considered a formal criterion of judgement, a mere 'ought', but rather as something embodied in more or less developed form in the spirit of a particular people. It was for this reason that the future of freedom appeared to Hegel more secure in the Germanic Protestant areas of Northern Europe than it had been in Catholic and Jacobin France.[115]

From its necessarily embodied character it also followed that reason was part of nature. One of the reasons for the crisis of belief engendered by Kant in the 1780s had been the impossibility of coupling an immaterial notion of freedom to a wholly determinist picture of nature (including Man himself, so far as he was a natural being). Following the lead of his friend Schelling, therefore, Hegel had abandoned this 'mechanical' idea of nature and adopted a vitalistic conception drawing upon recent advances in the life sciences. Both Man and the whole of existence now belonged to a single substance, an 'absolute' whose form was organic. Body and

---

114. J. G. Hamann (1730–88) attacked Kant's conception of reason in 1783. Reason, he argued, had no autonomous existence except insofar as it was embodied in language and action. Since its major embodiment was language, it was specific to particular cultures and particular times.

115. In Hegel's view, the mistake in the French Revolution was to imagine that political reform was possible without the reform of religion; it proved impossible to reconcile a constitution based upon reason with a church based on authority. See, for instance, *Hegel's Philosophy of Mind (Encyclopedia Part III)*, tr. W. Wallace, Oxford, 1971, para. 552, p. 287.

mind, reason and nature, being and consciousness then became different degrees of organization of a single living force. In place of the static and mechanically contrived seventeenth-century system of 'God or Nature' worked out by Spinoza, what had been devised was a new interactive notion of the whole, as a self-engendering organic process or activity.

The defect of this romantic conception of 'absolute life' was that it abstracted from all specific differences and could only be grasped through religious or artistic intuition. Hegel soon became dissatisfied with this ineffable construct and proposed instead a transparent and unmysterious idea of 'the absolute', which could be grasped by philosophy as the self-moving embodiment of reason. To grasp this process was to gain access to 'absolute knowledge', in which ultimate reality could be seen as the activity of an infinite rational subject that exteriorized itself through its embodiment in nature, and then came to know itself through human history as absolute self-consciousness or absolute spirit. Hegel claimed that this process captured the basic Christian truth of the incarnation and was the speculative translation of the doctrine of the Trinity.

Although Hegel's approach presupposed some of the political gains of the French Revolution, the crises that his philosophy had aimed to resolve had been primarily spiritual. His early followers recorded their euphoria at learning that Man's spirit was no different from God's spirit or that Man carried the consciousness of God within himself, and they often interpreted this blissful sense as the fulfilment of the redemptive promise of the Christian faith. But speculative philosophy was not intended as a transformation of Man's existence as a whole. As Hegel himself emphasized, Man could achieve identity with the absolute *only* in the activity of speculative thought.[116]

Similarly, even the freedom that Hegel had celebrated as the goal of history possessed less tangible political content than it at first seemed to promise. If the essence of Man was freedom, and freedom that could only be achieved in the state, then the goal of history was to achieve a state in which freedom was realized. By freedom,

116. See Toews, *Hegelianism*, p. 66.

however, Hegel understood not a set of demands, but a form of wisdom. Freedom was a condition in which the *alien* character of the external world disappeared and individuals came to understand themselves as 'being at home' within it. History as the realization of freedom, therefore, did not simply describe the strivings of limited and finite beings, but rather the process of re-unification between the spirit of these limited and finite beings and that of absolute or infinite spirit.

In a more mundane sense as well, the plausibility of Hegel's politics depended upon an acceptance of his optimistic belief that reason *was* being actualized in the world, that its forward march was not merely a subjective wish but an objective process. Hegel's prestige had been at its height when he had been invited to Berlin in the years following the fall of Napoleon, a time during which the reasonable gains of the revolution had been written into the constitutions and legal systems of France and the newly formed states of the Germanic Confederation. In Germany, these gains had been secured not by the mobilization of patriotic passions by romantic nationalists in the 1813 uprising, but through the agency of the rationally based legal and political institutions of the reformed state. This was also the political message of the *Philosophy of Right*. Hegel stated that his aim was not to declare how the world ought to be changed, since ethical life was already being achieved in the post-revolutionary modern state, at least in broad outline. His aim was rather to demonstrate the rationality of the change that he and his contemporaries had experienced.

From 1819, however, there was a marked change in the political atmosphere.[117] In the Germanic Confederation, the reactionary

117. Hegel's initial optimism about the progressive character of the post-war settlement was expressed in the first set of lectures he gave in Heidelberg in 1817–18. See Hegel, *Lectures on Natural Right and Political Science*, eds. M. Stewart and P. C. Hodgson, Berkeley, 1996. The shift towards reaction was sparked off by the assassination of the reactionary poet, August von Kotzebue, by a radical student who believed him to be a tsarist agent. Metternich, who was worried by the progress of liberalism in Prussia, used the occasion to summon a meeting of continental powers in Carlsbad in August 1819. This meeting resulted in the Carlsbad Decree, which imposed severe censorship upon academics and academic publications. Hegel had just completed a draft of his *Philosophy of Right*, but withdrew it and revised it in order to escape censorship.

stance of Metternich was gaining sway, while in Prussia the advocates of reform found themselves increasingly opposed by a conservative and religious backlash. Members of the old aristocracy, for the most part ex-soldiers still stunned by the humiliating defeat of Prussia by Napoleon in 1806, had been swept up in a fundamentalist religious revival opposed to all forms of liberalism and rationalism, whether political or religious. Therefore, despite the king's 1815 promise to summon a representative assembly, hopes that Prussia might become a constitutional monarchy receded.

Hegel and his supporters had found themselves on the defensive and, politically, his tactic had been to retreat into a wilful obscurity. In his 1821 preface to the *Philosophy of Right*, with its notorious dictum that what is rational is actual and what is actual is rational, Hegel appeared to have dissociated himself from the cause of reform. But ambiguity remained. If the poet Heinrich Heine is to be believed, he listened to Hegel's lectures and was shocked by the claim of the identity of the 'rational' and the 'actual', so he went up to Hegel and asked him to explain the meaning of this statement. Hegel is alleged to have smiled furtively and said quietly, 'it may also be expressed thus: all that is rational must be'.[118] This was the interpretation built upon by Hegel's more liberal supporters. Eduard Gans, for instance, embraced popular sovereignty and welcomed the 1830 revolutions as a new chapter in the history of world spirit. Hegel himself, however, became more fearful of political change in the course of the 1820s and shared the frightened official reaction to 1830.[119]

118. See G. Nicolin, *Hegel in Berichten seiner Zeitgenossen* (Hegel seen in the Reports of his Contemporaries), Hamburg, 1970, p. 235. Heine probably picked the story up from his friend, Eduard Gans, rather than hearing it himself as he claimed.

119. In a series of articles on the English Reform Bill crisis, written in 1831 in the official Prussian State Gazette, Hegel began by agreeing that reform was needed to bring 'justice and fairness' into Parliamentary representation in place of 'the most bizarre and haphazard anomalies and inequalities that prevail at present'. But he became increasingly anxious about the constitutional weakness of the English monarch in contrast to the rational guidance provided by the Crown in Prussia and he ended up by fearing the attempt to reform would usher in a revolution. See G. W. F. Hegel, 'The English Reform Bill', in Z. A. Pelczynski (ed.), *Hegel's Political Writings*, Oxford, 1964, pp. 295–330. Within days of writing the last instalment of this essay, Hegel collapsed and died of cholera.

Generally, the reawakening of a revolutionary spirit abroad lessened the chances of further state-led political liberalization in Prussia. What pressure there was for reform increasingly came from outside or below.

Religion rather than politics was the arena in which Hegel looked most vulnerable. In the 1820s, his idea that 'absolute spirit' was the rational kernel of Christian belief was anathema to fundamentalists; his claim that religion and philosophy differed only in 'form' was also regarded with deep suspicion. But in this area Hegelians could continue to count on official protection. For on questions of church government and higher education, the policy of the king, Frederick William III, and of his minister for 'Church, Health and Educational Affairs', Karl von Altenstein, remained quite at odds with the conservative anti-rationalist reaction of the post-war years. In 1817, without prior consultation, Frederick William had proclaimed the union of the Lutheran and Calvinist churches, and in the 1820s he had devised for the United Church a new liturgy cobbled together from the German, Swedish, Huguenot and Anglican prayer books. This royal policy of 'aggressive confessional statism' not only aroused Pietist and conservative opposition, but also provoked the breakaway and emigration of several thousand 'old Lutherans' in Silesia.[120] A similar policy of centralization and rationalization was pursued in the newly acquired Rhineland, where in addition to an unpopular attempt to introduce the Prussian legal code, aggressive support was given to Protestant forces in what was an overwhelmingly Catholic province. This policy culminated in 1837 in the imprisonment of the Archbishop of Cologne for enforcing Catholic teaching on the upbringing of children of mixed marriages.

But together with these expansionist ambitions, the royal administration made every effort to preserve Prussia's eighteenth-century reputation as a state of toleration and free enquiry in matters of

120. On the confessional policy of Frederick William III and Altenstein see C. Clark, 'Confessional policy and the limits of State action: Frederick William III and the Prussian Church Union 1817–40', *Historical Journal*, 39:4 (1996), pp. 985–1004.

religion. Altenstein's viewpoint remained that which was once imputed by Kant to Frederick the Great: 'argue as much as you like and about whatever you like, but obey.' It was Altenstein who had originally invited Hegel to Berlin, and throughout his long period of office, he continued to push for appointments and preferment for Hegelians. Hegelianism remained attractive because of its support for religious toleration, for spiritual freedom, for a rationalized Protestantism, for Prussian leadership in the German Confederation and for the unambiguous subordination of church to state.[121]

(ii) The Battle over Christianity and the Emergence of the Young Hegelians

In 1835, David Friedrich Strauss published his epoch-making study *The Life of Jesus critically examined*.[122] Strauss was from Württemberg like Hegel himself and, also like Hegel, educated for the Protestant pastorate in the Tübingen Theological Seminary. Initially drawn to romanticism, by the time of his graduation in 1829 Strauss had become a Hegelian. During the following two years as an assistant vicar in the Swabian village of Klein Ingersheim, he had adequate time to ponder the Hegelian claim of identity between dogmas of faith and the truths of philosophy. In the autumn of 1831 he left for one year in Berlin, where he met Hegel one week before the latter succumbed to cholera. Strauss returned to Tübingen and lectured at the university, but was forced to resign his teaching position following the publication of his book.

Conservatives and evangelicals believed that Strauss's book con-

---

121. For Hegel's position on these questions, see in particular *Elements of the Philosophy of Right*, para. 270, pp. 290–304.

122. D. F. Strauss (1808–74), *Das Leben Jesu kritisch bearbeitet*, 2 vols., Tübingen, 1835–6. Strauss was the son of a retailer to the royal court of Württemberg. On Strauss, see Toews, *Hegelianism*, pp. 165–75, 255–88; H. Harris, *David Friedrich Strauss and his Theology*, Cambridge, 1973; M. C. Massey, *Christ Unmasked: The Meaning of the Life of Jesus in German Politics*, Chapel Hill, 1983.

firmed all their darkest suspicions about the supposed Hegelian identity between religion and philosophy. But in fact, Strauss's mythological approach owed nothing to Hegel.[123]

Nevertheless Strauss set his conclusions firmly within a Hegelian framework. If religious representation were to accord with philosophical truth, he argued, the Gospels must first be freed from the superstitious and supernatural setting in which they had originally been placed. The rational truth contained in Christianity was that of the incarnation, the union of human and divine. But the Gospels had concealed this truth behind an archaic form of representation, in which the 'idea' was embodied in a narrative about the life and activity of a single individual. If modern 'critical scientific consciousness' were to restore Christian truth it would have to replace the Jesus of the Gospels by the idea of humanity in the whole course of its development. For only the infinite spirit of the human race could bring about the union of finite and infinite implied in the Christian story of incarnation and translated into conceptual form in Hegel's notion of 'absolute spirit'.

Altenstein allowed the free circulation of the book in Prussia, despite its denial of the supernatural and miraculous elements of the Christian story and despite a fierce campaign to ban the book led

123. Before Strauss, it had generally been assumed that the Gospels possessed a factual basis. Primitive Man ascribed to supernatural forces the natural phenomena he did not understand – an approach popularized by Hume. The problem for rationalists had been to sift out the factual from the supernatural and to provide naturalistic explanations of the miraculous. But Strauss argued that even as a historical account, the Gospel life of Jesus was impossible. The Evangelists were 'eyewitnesses, not to outer facts, but ideas'. The Gospel stories were therefore the product of 'an unconscious mythologizing process': speech and action were substituted for thought; religious and philosophical ideas were presented in historical form. The myths arose slowly and were set down in the thirty years after Jesus' death. Their content was shaped by a picture of the Messiah based upon the Old Testament and already accepted by the people. It was for this reason that so many of the miracles performed by Jesus matched those of Moses, Elisha and Elijah. In Strauss's account, the Gospels were composite structures created by a later tradition out of sayings that originally belonged to different times and circumstances. Their purpose was to portray a Messiah who matched the apocalyptic expectations present among the Jewish people at the time.

by Hengstenberg and the evangelicals. But the publication of Strauss did mark a turning point. Thereafter, Altenstein found it increasingly difficult to find Hegelians university positions, and the moderate reforming consensus which had characterized the first generation of Hegel's followers broke up into what came to be known as 'right', 'left' and 'centre.'[124]

It was through the debate over Strauss and the imprisonment of the Archbishop of Cologne that the term 'Young Hegelian' came into being. The Cologne affair provoked a major pamphlet battle, led on the Catholic side by the ultramontane publicist Joseph Görres, and among Protestants by the orthodox Lutheran Hegelian Heinrich Leo. But both were then attacked by a radical lecturer from the university of Halle, Arnold Ruge, soon to become the main publicist of the Young Hegelian movement. Ruge had recently set up the *Hallische Jahrbücher* (the Annals of Halle), originally intended as a literary feuilleton garnering contributions from the whole spectrum of Hegelian opinion, but now also standing for 'the independence of scientific enquiry' (i.e. Strauss) and the supremacy of state over church. Ruge attacked Görres and Leo for their hostility to 'rationalism', which he claimed to be the essence of the Prussian state. Leo's reply was entitled *Die Hegelingen* (the little Hegelians). It accused the *Hallische Jahrbücher* and the defenders of Strauss of being enemies of

---

124. Strauss himself, after a crisis in confidence in 1837–8 in which he attempted to strike a more accommodationist stance, reiterated his original arguments in 1838–9. In that year he was appointed Professor of Theology at Zurich, but after a crisis over his appointment he retired on half-pay. Although he wrote prolifically for the remainder of his career, he was never to receive another academic appointment.

In *Die christhiche Glaubenslehre in ihrer geschichtlichen Entwicklung und im Kampfe mit der modernen Wissenschaft* (Christian faith in its historical development and in struggle with modern science), 2 vols., Tübingen, 1840–41 and subsequent works, Strauss attempted to replace Christianity by a form of humanism appropriate to a cultural elite. Despite his anti-Christian stance and his central place in the formation of Young Hegelianism, Strauss's politics remained conservative. He was soon criticized from the left by Ruge, Feuerbach and the *Hallische Jahrbücher*, while Bruno Bauer criticized his work first as an orthodox Hegelian and then, after 1840, as the standard-bearer of the Young Hegelian left. In 1841, therefore, Strauss broke off further relations with the Young Hegelians, complaining that in the radical critique of Christianity he was a Columbus displaced by an Amerigo Vespucci.

religion and the state, while Hengstenberg denounced Ruge as a fomenter of atheism and revolution.[125]

Alarmed by this exchange, moderates deserted the *Hallische Jahrbücher* and Altenstein backed away from promoting Ruge to a chair. As a result, Ruge retired from the university and began to write articles directly critical of the government. The essence of Prussia, he now claimed, was liberty established by the Reformation and the Enlightenment. But the state was in danger. It had fallen under the sway of 'Catholicism' and 'romantic reaction' and would provoke revolution unless it returned to its true mission.

Ruge also made contact with the other nucleus of 'Young Hegelianism', the so-called Doctors' Club in Berlin, founded in 1837. The style of this Club was bohemian, with meetings in favoured cafés and wine cellars. Its original purpose had been academic, but in the wake of the Cologne affair it too had become drawn into religious and political controversy. Members of the club included academics, schoolteachers, journalists, freelance writers and students, notably Marx. The acknowledged intellectual leader of the club was the Berlin university lecturer, Bruno Bauer.[126] Bauer had originally been chosen to defend the orthodox reconciliation between religion and philosophy against Strauss. But in 1838 he had

125. Arnold Ruge (1802–80) was an activist in the student movement, the *Burschenschaft*, in the early 1820s, for which he was imprisoned for six years. In the 1830s, he taught as a Privatdozent at the University of Halle, where in 1837 he set up the *Hallische Jahrbücher*, the main journal of the Young Hegelian movement, followed from 1841 to 1843 by the *Deutsche Jahrbücher*, once censorship had forced him to move the journal to Saxony. With the enforced closure of this journal in 1843 at the behest of the Prussian government, he moved to Paris. He broke with Marx over the question of socialism. In 1848 he was a radical member of the Frankfurt assembly, after which he stayed in exile in England, settling in Brighton. In later years, however, he was a strong supporter of the Bismarckian unification of Germany.

126. Bruno Bauer (1809–82) was one of four sons of a porcelain painter at the royal workshops at Charlottenburg. He entered Berlin University to read theology in 1828, was a brilliant student, winning a prize for an essay on aesthetics. During the years 1834–9, he taught as a Privatdozent at Berlin and was counted as one of the most gifted of the orthodox Hegelians, firmly attached to the harmony between Hegel and Christianity. He was appointed to edit Hegel's lectures on religion against the objections of Hegel's son who thought him too conservative.

shifted his position and launched a sharp attack on his former supporter, Hengstenberg, the leader of the evangelical Christians.

The controversy surrounding Ruge soon encompassed Bauer. In 1839, in an effort to keep him out of trouble, Altenstein had moved Bauer from Berlin to the theology faculty at Bonn. But this transfer only pushed him further towards heterodoxy. Bauer never accepted Strauss's mythological approach. Not only did it lack a credible account of the character or composition of the Gospels, but also – in contrast to Hegel – it equated the Gospels with the apocalyptic expectations of the Old Testament, thus missing the distinctiveness of Christianity as a new stage in the development of the 'absolute idea'. Bauer's starting point was the match between the Bible and the Hegelian idea. In his original answer to Strauss, he had attempted to establish a concordance between reason and the Biblical narrative, a task he began in detail in relation to the Old Testament in 1838.[127] In his next major work, *The Criticism of the Gospel History of John*, which appeared in 1840, his position had shifted considerably. He had demonstrated that the Gospel of John was a purely literary creation and that its graphic character was that of a fiction. But the ultimate direction was still not entirely clear. For it still left open the possibility that the other three Gospels might contain the history that John lacked. Finally, however, in *The Criticism of the Gospel Story of the Synoptists*, which appeared in 1841–2, Bauer moved towards a position even more destructive of the factual claims of the Gospel narrative than that originally presented by Strauss.

What this study showed was that the distinction between John and the Synoptic Gospels (Matthew, Mark and Luke) was not one of kind, but only of degree. Bauer's approach built upon a discovery established in orthodox Biblical commentary during the 1830s: that the original evangelist had been Mark. Mark had set down the original connection between events; the other Gospel writers had supposedly elaborated and supplemented Mark's account by recourse to sayings

---

127. Bauer's approach, in which every detail of the Gospel was in accord with the 'absolute idea', drew him into insoluble conundrums such as the need to demonstrate the metaphysical necessity of the virgin birth, and was dismissed by Strauss as 'a foolish piece of pen-pushing'.

and anecdotes taken from a broader tradition.[128] Bauer, however, gave this argument a radical and unanticipated twist. For if John could no longer count as an eyewitness and if two of the Synoptic Gospels were expansions of the first and the third also an elaboration of the second, this suggested that the original Gospel story went back to a single author. Furthermore, the only evidence for the 'broader tradition' supposedly drawn upon by the other evangelists came from the Gospel stories themselves. In other words, 'the broader tradition' might also have been the creation of the original evangelist. This would mean that the idea of messiahship and its association with the ministry of Jesus had not been a matter of common knowledge before being set down in writing. More likely, it had been a way of discussing the experience of the early Christian community through the creation of a literary tradition built out of the general ideas of the time.[129]

By the time the study of the Synoptists had appeared, Bauer had

128. The argument about Mark was associated with the findings of two German Biblical scholars in the late 1830s, C. H. Weisse, *Die evangelische Geschichte kritisch und philosophisch bearbeitet* (A Critical and Philosophical Study of the Gospel History), 2 vols., Leipzig, 1838, and C. G. Wilke, *Der Urevangelist* (The Original Evangelist), Dresden and Leipzig, 1838. For an evaluation of their arguments, see A. Schweitzer, *The Quest of the Historical Jesus* (1906), London, 2000, ch. 10.

129. The weak point in the radical use of the Mark approach (that the Gospel story was the literary creation of a single author) was the existence of the many inexplicable repetitions in the text. The only way of getting around this problem was to distinguish between a supposed Ur-Mark and later interpolations. In 1841, Bauer left open the question whether there had been a historical Jesus, to whom the subsequent early Christian church had ascribed messiahship. The issue would be settled by examining the Epistles of Paul. But in the following decade, he became increasingly seized by the idea that Jesus was a purely literary invention, a product of the imagination of the early Christian church. He argued this in *Kritik der Evangelien* (Criticism of the Gospels), 2 vols., Berlin, 1850–52, but without serious historical substantiation. But this account itself was stated to be no more than preliminary. The use of historical and textual scholarship was even more cavalier in Bauer's final account, *Christus und die Cäsaren. Der Ursprung des Christentums aus dem römischen Griechentum* (Christ and the Caesars: The Origin of Christianity from Graeco-Roman Civilization), published in Berlin in 1877. In this work, Bauer maintained that the Christian stance towards the world, outlined in the utterances of Paul, was the invention of the Stoic Seneca. This stoicism had been born out of despair for the possibility of thought making any impact on the world of Nero and Domitian. It was deepened by the introduction of Neoplatonic elements mixed with the Graeco-Roman Judaism of Philo and Josephus.

already lost any chance of university employment. In 1840, both Altenstein and the old king had died, and although the first actions of the new king, Frederick William IV, had been greeted with general enthusiasm, he soon revealed himself as a romantic reactionary. Frederick William believed in a personal God and in his own grace as a monarch. He also believed that all social order would disappear, if the belief in revelation were undermined. Far from standing above the parties, as some of the Young Hegelians had hoped, he openly expressed his dislike of Hegelianism and invited Schelling to Berlin to propose his 'philosophy of revelation' in its place.

In the spring of 1841, Ruge's *Hallische Jahrbücher* was forbidden in Prussia and even the *Athenaeum*, the tiny journal of the Doctors' Club, was closed down. In Bauer's case, the new minister for church and education, Eichhorn, sent out a questionnaire to Prussian Theology Faculties asking whether Bauer's licence to teach should be revoked for denying the divine inspiration of the Gospels. The Theological Faculties did not recommend dismissal, but a minor affair in Berlin on 28 September 1841 – Bauer's speech at a festive dinner of the Doctors' Club to honour a visit by the South German liberal editor of the *Staats-Lexikons*, Carl Welcker – led the king personally to insist that Bauer not be allowed to resume his post in Bonn. Bauer's dismissal from Bonn was finally confirmed in March 1842. Before he left Bonn, he and Marx 'rented a pair of asses' to ride through the city. 'The Bonn society was astonished. We shouted with joy, the asses brayed.'

Between 1840 and 1842, in response to government hostility, the Young Hegelians elaborated a wholesale attack on Christianity and conjoined it with a republican critique of the Prussian state. The attack on Christianity was led by Bauer. Christianity was not, as Strauss thought, grounded in the substance of tradition, of Jewish apocalyptic expectation or of the Old Testament God of Spinoza.[130] It was a

130. In 1864, in the wake of the runaway success of Ernest Renan's 1863 *Life of Jesus* in France, Strauss brought out *Das leben Jesu für das deutsche Volk bearbeitet* (A Life of Jesus for the German People), Leipzig, 1861, a work in which he both dropped any remnant of Hegelianism and the close connection he had earlier made between Jesus and Old Testament Jewish eschatology. In other respects, he reiterated his former positions and adopted a hostile stance to much subsequent scholarship. In particular, he

response to the new universal conditions of the Roman Empire. It marked the 'death of nature' and the beginning of self-consciousness, but unfortunately only a false beginning. For Christianity did not represent a true victory over nature achieved through knowledge of nature's laws. It was rather the projection of an individual self-consciousness that withdraws from the world, of a personality that grasps itself in antithesis to the world, but feels helpless to overcome it except through the false medium of miracles. Similarly, in its portrayal of the Christ of the Gospels, Christianity had created not a true man but an ego alien to actual humanity. The historical Jesus had overcome the separation between human and divine only at the cost of creating a new form of religious division and alienation. Christianity therefore did not provide Man with knowledge of himself, but only of a parody of himself. Reform, as Bauer went on to insist in 1843, would require not merely the elimination of God, but an end to Christian culture with all its age-old assumptions about human incapacity.

In place, therefore, of Hegel's identity between religion and philosophy, Bauer presented an antithesis. He also alleged – though he knew it not to be true – that secretly this had also been Hegel's own position. In the spring of 1841, in a pseudonymous pamphlet, *The Trumpet of the Last Judgement against Hegel the Atheist and Anti-Christ* (hereafter *The Trumpet*), purportedly written by an outraged Pietist pastor, Bauer assembled all the passages that pointed to an 'esoteric' Hegel, who was not only an atheist but also a friend of subversion, disorder and revolution. The pastor exclaimed:

If one looks into what Hegel means by the reconciliation of reason and religion, it is that there is no God and the Ego has only to deal with itself in religion, whereas in religion it means to deal with a living personal God.

---

dismissed all the work (including that of his old enemy Bruno Bauer) that built upon chronological priority of the Gospel of Mark. He compared this idea with contemporary nonsense about 'the music of the future' (Wagner) and the anti-vaccination movement. This helps to explain Nietzsche's attack, 'David Strauss the Confessor and the Writer' (*Unfashionable Observations*, Stanford, 1995, pp. 1–83), which presented Strauss as the epitome of 'the cultivated philistine'. Nietzsche conceived the essay as a birthday present for Wagner on 22 May 1873.

Realized self-consciousness is that play in which the Ego is doubled as in a mirror, and which, after holding its image for thousands of years to be God, discovers the picture in the mirror to be itself . . . Religion takes that mirror image for God, philosophy casts off the illusion and shows Man that no one stands behind the mirror.[131]

(iii) The Young Hegelians against the 'Christian State'

Combined with this radical rejection of religious consciousness went a republican-inspired revision of Hegel's political philosophy. Bauer was provoked by the Cologne affair and the growing conservative clamour led by the reactionary philosopher F. J. Stahl to dismantle the Church Union of 1817 and restore ecclesiastical independence. He therefore published an anonymous pamphlet in 1840 pushing the case for state supremacy over the church far beyond anything dreamt of by Altenstein. He said that during the Enlightenment subjective consciousness had first risen to universality; in place of the mutilated picture of human essence found in religion, the Enlightenment had put forward a true idea of humankind. In this way, religious consciousness had given way to self-consciousness. Thereafter, the churches had lost any reason for independent existence. They were now no longer expressions of 'absolute spirit', but purely 'positive' institutions without rational justification.

The true location of 'free subjectivity' had changed from the church to the state. The state, as Hegel taught, was 'the actuality of the ethical idea'; reason and freedom constituted its essence and this meant that the state must stand with science and philosophy against all forms of 'positivity'. But Hegel's fear of popular sovereignty had led him to an unsatisfactory compromise between a state based on 'free subjectivity' and the tutelage represented by absolutism. His picture had been of an universal suspended above particulars without a reciprocal

131. B. Bauer, *The Trumpet of the Last Judgement against Hegel the Atheist and Anti-Christ: An Ultimatum*, tr. L. Stepelevich, Lewiston, New York, 1989, pp. 189–90.

relationship between them and, in practical terms, of the restriction of the capacity to make universal judgements to an official class.

The Young Hegelians therefore recast this state in republican form. In Bauer's case, this meant a new way of interpreting the capacity of subjects to withdraw their will from any particular object and to place it in another. Hegel had confined his discussion of this 'negative' moment of universality of the will to the sphere of 'abstract right', in effect the acquisition and exchange of property by individuals. Bauer, however, identified it with the general political activity of the state. The citizens of such a state consisted of those capable of 'autonomy', in other words, of those capable of action according to universal principles. What prevented the state from acting according to universal norms were particular forms of religious consciousness and private economic interests.

Prussia, therefore, would not only have to abandon the irrational role of 'Christian State' imposed upon it by the new king. It would also have to move beyond the liberal constitutionalist form of the state. As Bauer outlined his position at the famous Doctors' Club dinner (see p. 88), to which the king took such offence, Hegel was to be commended because he had identified freedom with universality and it was this association of the state with true universality that had made such large strides during the Enlightenment and the French Revolution. By contrast, the defect both of Stahl's conservatism and of Rotteck's liberalism was that freedom was identified as a private interest. If Stahl prevailed, there would be a return to the Reformation with the state as no more than an external 'police' force. But liberal constitutionalists also identified freedom with private right. By protecting religious particularism and economic individualism, these political philosophies held back the state as a vehicle of progress and free self-consciousness.[132]

132. Most accounts focus almost exclusively upon Bauer's religious radicalism and assume that he lacked a coherent political philosophy. For an important corrective to this approach, see D. Moggach, 'Bruno Bauer's Political Critique 1840–1841', *Owl of Minerva*, 27:2 (Spring 1996), pp. 138–54.

Bauer remained a committed republican if not a democrat until after the failure of the 1848 revolutions.

Arnold Ruge also developed a republican critique. He noted a growing interest in Prussian domestic politics, which he connected with a new-found sense of citizenship in the state. Such a development highlighted one of the principal defects of the *Philosophy of Right*, its lack of any notion of 'public virtue'. Hegel had been deeply aware that the Germans had not yet achieved 'a state in the form of a state'. But his treatise had been a child of a time 'that totally lacked public discussion and public life'. He implicitly recognized the inadequacy of this position by distinguishing the dynastic familial state and 'the state of need' (Notstaat) corresponding to civil society from the 'free state' as 'the actuality of the ethical idea'. This 'free state', as Hegel had implied in 1817, presupposed national representation, juries and freedom of the press, which the Germans almost totally lacked: institutions that raised 'humans in their total worth and in the full light of public consciousness to creators of their own freedom'.[133]

But both Kant and Hegel had been 'diplomats'. In Kant's case, 'Protestant narrowness' had led to a conception of freedom only as 'freedom of conscience', a position that recognized no other virtue than 'the private virtue of inward self-congratulation', a virtue of 'moralistic self-directed subjects, not state-citizens'. Hegel as well had not escaped 'the abstract inwardness of Protestantism'. In his case, it led to the illusion that one could be 'theoretically free without being politically free'. Hegel had also been ready to 'tolerate appearances'. From his theoretical standpoint of 'Olympian repose', 'he had looked at everything that reason had made and it was good'. He veered away from the 'nasty should of praxis'.[134]

After Strauss, this stance had become impossible. Now the times

133. See A. Ruge, 'Hegel's *Philosophy of Right* and the Politics of our Times' (1842), in L. S. Stepelevich (ed.), *The Young Hegelians: an Anthology*, Cambridge, 1983, pp. 211–37.
134. The tone of Ruge's attacks upon the political accommodation of Kant and Hegel had already been set in the 1830s by the Young German attack upon Goethe and Weimar. Heine ironized at the expense of 'the German Jupiter' who 'if he were suddenly to stand erect', 'would shatter the dome of the Temple' and 'so remained calmly seated, and permitted himself to be tranquilly adored and perfumed with incense'.

were political. Hegel had started from logic, but logic did not confront the problem of existence. It was impossible to grasp the state 'absolutely' by detaching it from history. 'Only with the entry of history into the realm of science does existence assume relevance.' Yet history had not been discussed in the *Philosophy of Right*. In a clear summary of the Young Hegelian position, Ruge wrote, 'the *historical process* is the relating of theory to the historical existences of the spirit; this relationship is critique'. Conversely, 'the *Philosophy of Right* raises existences or historical determinations to logical determinations'. By failing to distinguish between the historical and metaphysical, Hegel had become engaged in 'a foolish juggling act' in which the hereditary monarch and the bicameral system were turned into logical necessities.[135] The net result had been that while in Catholic countries, such as France, spiritual freedom had been hindered, in Germany political freedom had been hindered by 'Protestant abstraction', which had reached its highest point in Hegel.

One probable, if unmentioned, source of Ruge's line of criticism was the lecture series on 'positive philosophy' delivered by Schelling in Berlin in 1841. Schelling started from the premiss that the structure of thought was not identical to that of reality. Schelling claimed that Hegel's philosophy and the 'absolute idealism', which he himself had also once espoused, were only 'negative'. It could only explain what happened once there was a world, but had nothing to say

---

135. Schelling's emphasis in his critique of Hegel upon the primacy of existence over reason and upon the facticity of world did make some impact. It has been claimed that some aspects of his approach anticipated Nietzsche, Wittgenstein and Heidegger. More immediately, it was an unacknowledged source of the growing criticism of Hegel among the Young Hegelians themselves in 1842–3. Not only Ruge, but Marx as well in 1843 attacked Hegel for his 'logical pantheistic mysticism . . . not the philosophy of law, but logic is the real centre of interest'.

But whatever the appeal of Schelling's criticism, its effect was muffled by almost unanimous hostility towards the details of his 'positive philosophy' and its official promotion by the circle around the new Prussian king. Kierkegaard's reaction was characteristic. Initially enthusiastic, he was soon commenting, 'Schelling drivels intolerably'. See K. Marx, 'Contribution to the Critique of Hegel's Philosophy of Law', *MECW*, vol. 3, pp. 7, 17; A. Dru (ed.), S. Kierkegaard, *Journals*, London, 1938, p. 102; K. Löwith, *From Hegel to Nietzsche: The Revolution in Nineteenth-century Thought*, New York, 1964, pp. 115–21.

about the *fact* that there was a world. Hegel had removed this problem of the facticity of the world by treating being as part of a structure of reflection, rather than the ground of that structure. But if reason could not account for the fact of its own existence, it would therefore be necessary to begin, not with reason, but with the contingency of being. Hegel's dialectic could say nothing about existence, nor could existence be absorbed into Hegel's system. There was thus a 'wide ugly moat' between Hegel's *Logic* and his *Philosophy of Nature* or what Lessing had earlier called 'necessary truths of reason' and 'contingent truths of history'. According to Schelling, existence and idea, the world and God, could not be synthesized in thought, but they could be conjoined through will. Free will and existence conjoined in a theistic metaphysics would then form the basis of Schelling's 'positive philosophy'.

Marx had gravitated towards the Young Hegelian circle in Berlin in the summer of 1837.[136] His particular mentor was Bruno Bauer, whose lectures on the prophet Isaiah Marx was recorded as attending in 1839. Bauer remained the dominant force in Marx's intellectual development through to the beginning of 1843. Not only was he probably the supervisor of Marx's doctorate, but a close intellectual and political collaboration developed between them. In 1841, they had jointly planned a new journal to be called *The Archives of Atheism*, and Marx followed Bauer to Bonn after his transfer from Berlin.

The impact of Bauer was clear in Marx's doctorate, *Difference between the Democritean and the Epicurean Philosophy of Nature*. Philosophy, Marx declared, took its stand against 'all heavenly and earthly Gods who do not acknowledge human self-consciousness as the highest divinity'. Epicurus rather than the materialist and determinist, Democritus, was the hero of the dissertation because he stood for 'the absoluteness and freedom of self-consciousness'. The choice of topic was also politically relevant. For the relationship of the Epicureans, Stoics and Sceptics to Aristotle could be compared with that of the Young Hegelians to Hegel. These were 'unhappy and

136. On the Young Hegelians, see Toews, *Hegelianism*; D. McLellan, *The Young Hegelians and Karl Marx*, London, 1969.

iron epochs', in which the old Gods had died and the new Gods still lacked 'the colours of day'. Unity created by a great system became discord and philosophy turned once more against the world of appearance. Like other Young Hegelians, Marx believed that the crucial means by which to secure transition to a new epoch was 'the will' in the form of 'criticism'. Philosophy was 'the critique that measures the individual existence by the essence, the particular reality by the idea'. In this epoch, 'what was inner light has become consuming flame . . . The result is that as the world becomes philosophical, philosophy also becomes worldly.'[137]

Marx could scarcely have been surprised by the final dismissal of Bauer from his post at Bonn in April 1842 and he would already have known that this would mean the end of his own chances of academic employment. If he expressed no regret, it was no doubt because interesting opportunities had opened up in journalism, just as those in academia were closing down. At the end of 1841, a liberalization of the Prussian press laws had led a group of leading liberals from Cologne to found the *Rheinische Zeitung* (the Rhenish Newspaper).[138] Marx had been involved in the discussions which led to the launching of the newspaper from the start. He became its editor in the autumn of 1842 and remained so until it was closed down in the spring of the following year. From a Young Hegelian perspective, his move could hardly have been better timed. 'Criticism' had dismantled the claims of Christianity; the next task was 'public enlightenment'.

On the *Rheinische Zeitung*, Marx appears to have remained close to

137. K. Marx, 'Difference between the Democritean and Epicurean Philosophy of Nature', *MECW*, vol. 1, pp. 30, 72, 85, 492.
138. Promoters of the *Rheinische Zeitung* included Ludwig Camphausen and Gustav Mevissen, prominent leaders of liberal reforming ministries in 1848. Initially, the government was pleased at the prospect of a new Rhineland newspaper, backed by Protestant businessmen, and pro-Zollverein (the customs union), pro-Prussian leadership in Germany and pro-Prussian policies in the province. The businessmen, who set up the newspaper in the form of a joint-stock company, invited as its first editor, Friedrich List, the famous promoter of railways and German protectionism. But List backed down and the editorship went to Young Hegelians, first Adolf Rutenberg and then Karl Marx.

the positions voiced by Bauer and Ruge. Religious particularism and private material interests in combination with 'the Christian state' were contrasted with the state as a 'moral and rational commonwealth'. Bauer had argued that the state was 'the only form in which the infinity of reason and freedom, the highest goods of the human spirit, exist in reality'.[139] Marx, as editor of the *Rheinische Zeitung*, emphasized the same point: the state was 'the great organism, in which legal, moral and political freedom must be realized'.[140]

Marx also shared Bauer's view that 'the religious party' was 'the most dangerous in the Rhine area'. But the peculiar situation of the newspaper as a liberal, Protestant and pro-Prussian outpost in a heavily Catholic province meant that the religious issue had to be treated with kid gloves. For this reason Marx as editor rejected atheist 'scribblings' from the successors to the Doctors' Club in Berlin, now calling themselves the 'Free'. He also published his only personal contribution on theology, a short defence of Bauer's interpretation of the Synoptic Gospels, in Ruge's journal.[141]

Instead, he concentrated upon the other major obstacle to the emergence of a republican state, the dominance of private interests. Debates in the Rhine Province Assembly about freedom of the press and about revisions to the law concerning the collection of dead wood by peasants in the forests provided him with ample opportunity to elaborate on the theme. Delegates were ridiculed for attempting to treat press freedom as a form of freedom of trade. In the case of the forest laws, there should not have been 'a moment's delay in sacrificing the representation of particular interest to representation of the interests of the province'. But delegates wavered between 'the deliberate obduracy of privilege and the natural impotence of

139. See Toews, *Hegelianism*, p. 314.
140. K. Marx, 'The leading article in No. 179 of the *Kölnische Zeitung*' (*Rheinische Zeitung*, 10 July 1842), *MECW*, vol. 1, p. 202.
141. On 'the religious party' see Marx to Ruge, 27 April 1842, *MECW*, vol. 1, p. 390; on the 'Free', see Marx to Ruge, 30 November 1842, *MECW*, vol. 1, pp. 393–5; on Bauer's *Synoptiker*, see K. Marx, 'Yet another word on *Bruno Bauer und die Akademische Lehrfreiheit*, by Dr O. F. Gruppe, Berlin, 1842' (*Deutsche Jahrbücher für Wissenschaft und Kunst*, 16 November 1842), *MECW*, vol. 1, pp. 210–14.

half-hearted liberalism'. In sum, it showed 'what is to be expected from an Assembly of the Estates of particular interests if it were ever seriously called upon to make laws'.[142]

For obvious reasons, Marx avoided a direct attack upon 'the Christian State', but it was implicit in his 'concept of the state as the realization of rational freedom'. The bedrock of this rational state was the law. The law comprised 'the positive, clear, universal norms in which freedom has acquired an impersonal theoretical existence'. Censorship, on the other hand, was not part of the law, it belonged to 'unfreedom' and 'the world outlook of semblance'. In the light of the hostility of 'the Christian state' of Frederick William IV, the current danger was of sacrificing 'the immortality of the law' to 'finite private interests' or the arbitrariness of censorship. For this reason, the immediate priority was to champion a 'free press'. The free press was 'the ubiquitous vigilant eye of a people's soul'. It would recall the state to its inner principle as the embodiment of reason and freedom. Behind Marx's confidence lay the assumption common to most of the Young Hegelians that 'criticism' was only making conscious the real desires of the people. Through the activity of the free press, reason and freedom would rapidly triumph over the 'Christian state'.[143]

It therefore came as a considerable shock when, in the first few months of 1843, the government closed down the *Rheinische Zeitung* and other opposition publications.

The political strategy of the Young Hegelians was now in tatters. How now could Germany change, if all public means of expression were denied to philosophy? How could it still be maintained that the inner principle of the modern state was the actualization of reason and freedom, when it was the state that had abolished the free press?

142. K. Marx, 'Debates on the Freedom of the Press and Publication of the Proceedings of the Assembly of the Estates' (*Rheinische Zeitung*, 19 May 1842), *MECW*, vol. 1, pp. 171, 175, 180; K. Marx, 'Debates on the Law on Thefts of Wood' (*Rheinische Zeitung*, 3 November 1842), *MECW*, vol. 1, p. 262.
143. K. Marx, 'Debates on Freedom of the Press' (*Rheinische Zeitung*, 12, 15 May 1842), *MECW*, vol. 1, pp. 154, 165; K Marx, 'The Leading Article in No. 179 of the *Kölnische Zeitung*' (*Rheinische Zeitung*, 10 July 1842), *MECW*, vol. 1, pp. 195. 200.

Finally, why had there been so little opposition to the government suppression of the free press? In 1842, the Young Hegelians had believed themselves part of a broader Prussian reform movement campaigning for representative government and liberal freedoms. The *Rheinische Zeitung* had been set up by the leading liberals of the Rhineland. Surely they would not now accept its summary closure? In France in 1830, when the last Bourbon king, Charles X, had attempted to close down the liberal press, he had provoked the July Revolution. Why then in Prussia had the action of the government been accepted with hardly a murmur of protest? It was in an attempt to find answers to these questions that, in the course of 1843, Marx moved from a republican position shared by all the leading Young Hegelians towards his own highly individual version of communism.

8. *From Republicanism to Communism*

Immediately after the end of the newspaper, newly married and secluded for a few months in the spring of 1843 in the village of Kreuznach, Marx still remained optimistic. He continued to expect the imminent return of 'the self confidence of the human being, freedom', which had 'vanished from the world with the Greeks and under Christianity disappeared into the blue mists of the heavens'. Marx planned a new paper to confront 'the old regime of Germany, which is decaying and destroying itself' and he managed to convince a more sceptical Arnold Ruge, whose *Deutsche Jahrbücher* had also been suppressed, to join the scheme. The plan was to draw together German philosophic radicalism and French politics.[144] Reports coming from France about 'the system of industry and trade, of ownership and exploitation of the people' offered hope of 'a rupture within present day society'. But political and religious reform remained important. He rejected the 'communism' identified with Cabet, Dézamy and Weitling as 'a dogmatic abstraction'.[145] Reform should begin from present realities.

144. This was the *Deutsch-Französische Jahrbücher* (the German–French Annals) whose first and only number appeared in Paris at the beginning of 1844.
145. Theodore Dézamy (1803–50) was one of the principal babouvist communists in France at the beginning of the 1840s. He appealed to the proletarians to struggle against their 'oppressors' and was known at the time as one of the 'violents', 'material-ists' or 'immediates'. He was one of the organizers of the first communist banquet at Belleville on 1 July 1840.

The reform of consciousness [consisted] *only* in enabling the world to clarify its consciousness, in waking it from its dreams about itself, in explaining to it the meaning of its actions.[146]

But in the course of the summer Marx's position changed. 'Criticism' had got nowhere. The less-than-heroic reaction of the German middle class to the return of censorship, and its 'modest egoism' as 'the general representative of the philistine mediocrity of all the other classes', meant that little could be expected of it.[147] Marx came to doubt that there could be a political solution to Germany's problems. In October, he concluded that 'there was no scope for free activity in Germany', and left for Paris.

For all the Young Hegelians 1843 was to prove a year of disorientation and disenchantment. In 1842, Bruno Bauer had thought his dismissal would be treated as a 'world historical event' in the battle between Christianity and modern consciousness. Certainly, his followers among the 'Free' had thought so and recorded their reaction in the mock-epic poem by Frederick Engels and Edgar Bauer. But such expectations were soon disappointed. Bauer was not destined to become another Luther or Voltaire. His self-defence, which Marx considered his best writing so far, passed almost unnoticed.[148] Nor, more generally, was

146. K. Marx, 'Letters from the *Deutsch-Französische Jahrbücher*' (March, May, September 1843), *MECW*, vol. 3, pp. 137, 143, 144.

147. At this stage, Marx's model of middle-class radicalism was derived primarily from the famous pamphlet by the Abbé Sieyès, *What is the Third Estate?*, which had set France on an unambiguously revolutionary course in 1789 with the answer (in Marx's words): 'I am nothing and I shall be everything.' The other, more recent, precedent for middle-class involvement in revolution related to July 1830 in which general resistance to the press decree of Charles X led to his abdication and flight. The three-day uprising in Paris that provoked Charles X's downfall was commemorated in Delacroix's famous painting of Liberty leading a bourgeois and a worker over a barricade. Records of the dead and wounded, however, suggest that the fighting was primarily done by artisans. In Germany, quite apart from the generally loyalist viewpoint of the North German small-town middle classes, the suppression of the anti-Christian *Rheinische Zeitung* was never likely to provoke widespread indignation in the overwhelmingly Catholic Rhineland.

148. Anon. (E. Bauer and F. Engels), 'The Insolently Threatened Yet Miraculously Rescued Bible', *MECW*, vol. 2, pp. 313–52; Marx to Ruge, 13 March 1843, *MECW*, vol. 1, p. 400.

the outcome of the liberal challenge to the romantic absolutism of Frederick William IV any more reassuring. In the face of government repression, whether in the Rhineland or in East Prussia, the liberal opposition of 1842 simply appeared to fade away. 'Criticism' had been defeated in its bid to turn the world 'philosophical'. This was the setting in which unity among the Young Hegelians disintegrated and the conflict between republicanism and socialism was acted out.

Although in many ways the hardest hit, Bauer was politically the best equipped to deal with the new situation. He had assumed from the beginning that 'a new principle always comes to consciousness in relatively few minds' and only finally encounters 'a mass that it stirs only dully and that can scarcely be raised from its indifference'.[149] In Bauer's theory, the achievement of autonomy was an individual attainment. Therefore, although like Marx he believed in social liberation, his emphasis upon universality and equal rights was incompatible with any conception of the proletariat as a special class. Socialism meant a new form of the privileging of particular and heteronomous interests.

Defeat, therefore, sharpened but did not create his distrust of popular movements. The mass remained wedded to religion and their private material interests. Bauer's sense of its credulity was strongly conveyed in his later history of the epoch in which he dwelt with gloomy resignation upon the million who came to view the display of the Holy Robe of Trier between August and October 1844. Only in the 1850s did Bauer finally despair of the cause of reform; in 1848 he had stood for the Prussian Parliament as a supporter of popular sovereignty. But like his later ally, Nietzsche, Bauer never placed any reliance upon the capacities of the people.[150]

149. Cited in Moggach, 'Bruno Bauer's Political Critique 1840–1841', p. 149.
150. On the Holy Robe of Trier, see B. Bauer, *Vollständige Geschichte der Parteikämpfe in Deutschland während der Jahre 1842–1846* (A Comprehensive History of the Party Battles in Germany during the Years 1842–1846), Charlottenburg, 1847, vol. 3, p. 229 et seq., cited in Stepelevich (tr.), *The Trumpet*, p. 48.

In the 1850s Bauer became increasingly preoccupied with the growing power of Russia, seen from a German nationalist perspective. Germany was presented as the predestined yet scorned leader of the West. At the same time his contempt for democracy and his hostility to Judaism became increasingly prominent and

The year 1843 was more disconcerting for those like Ruge and Marx, who had been committed to a more democratic form of republicanism. Ruge expressed the deepest disappointment. As an ex-*Burschenschaftler* (student radical), he considered it 'the discovery of our century' that the masses could be witnesses to truth and bearers of 'the spirit of the age'. But in 1843, like the poet Hölderlin, he could only see Germany as a space without human beings, without whole persons but only their severed limbs strewn across a desolate battlefield, a country with nothing to show except fifty years of shame and humiliation.[151]

Marx was more hopeful, but could not but agree with much of Ruge's diagnosis. While at the *Rheinische Zeitung* Marx's republicanism had been scarcely less pedagogic than Bauer's. 'True liberalism', he had written, meant striving for 'a completely new form of state corresponding to a more profound, more thoroughly educated and freer popular consciousness'.[152] Hope for philosophy and the cause of freedom was no longer to be found in Germany, but only across the Rhine. In the light of Germany's debased past there was no reason to expect the imminent arrival of representative government, and no

---

unrestrained, particularly once he became assistant to Hermann Wagener, editor of the ultra-conservative *Kreuzzeitung* (Journal of the Cross), between 1859 and 1866.

During the years between 1866 and his death in 1882, Bauer took up farming in the Berlin suburb of Rixdorf, mainly to support the orphaned daughters of his brother. Despite this miserable existence in 'a wasteland, a scenic stupidity, that could only be invented by the most daring phantasies of a Gogol', he remained intellectually engaged. According to Nietzsche's retrospect in *Ecce Homo*, after his 1873 attack on Strauss Bauer was Nietzsche's 'most attentive reader', even 'his entire public'. In a stall converted into a rude study, a series of works on late antiquity and the beginnings of Christianity testified to his continued ambition to become the nineteenth-century Gibbon. Bauer's last essay, in 1882, an article on the classicist Karl Philipp Moritz, was to the *Internationale Monatsschrift* (the International Monthly), a journal combining Wagnerian aesthetics, Nietzschean philosophy, nationalism, atheism and anti-Semitism. On Bauer's later life see Stepelevich's introduction to Bauer's *The Trumpet*.

151. Ruge to Marx, March 1843; A. Ruge and K. Marx (eds.), *Deutsch-Französische Jahrbücher*, Paris, 1844 (repr. Leipzig, 1973), pp. 102–3.
152. K. Marx, 'In Connection with the Article "Failures of the Liberal Opposition in Hanover"' (*Rheinische Zeitung*, 8 November 1842), *MECW*, vol. 1, p. 265.

reason to expect a real transformation of the condition of Germany even if such government did materialize. In the course of 1843 Marx came to agree with French socialists about the 'bourgeois' character of modern representative government. Its nature was summed up by the 'bourgeois monarchy' of Louis Philippe. By the end of the year, therefore, the political hopes of 1842 were beginning to be eclipsed by a 'radical' vision of 'the dissolution of the hitherto existing world order' and 'the negation of private property' based upon 'the theory which proclaims Man to be the highest being for Man'.[153]

The new position was spelled out in a re-examination of Hegel's political thought, 'Contribution to the Critique of Hegel's *Philosophy of Right*'. This manuscript drew upon a mixture of German and French sources: from Germany, the radical 'humanist' attack both upon Christianity and Hegel, launched by Ludwig Feuerbach; from France, Proudhon's *What is Property?* fleshed out by the social and historical criticism of Louis Blanc, Pierre Leroux and Victor Considerant.[154]

153. K. Marx, 'Contribution to Critique of Hegel's *Philosophy of Law*: Introduction', *MECW*, vol. 3, p. 187. It is confusing that *Elements of the Philosophy of Law* and *Elements of the Philosophy of Right* are different translations of the title of the same work by Hegel. Marx's shift to communism was, according to Arnold Ruge, the main reason for the split between the two editors and the folding of the *Deutsch-Französische Jahrbücher* after one number. Ruge claimed that between September 1843 and the spring of 1844 Marx had resisted 'crass socialism' and effectively criticized it in their published correspondence of 1843. In March 1844, Marx had declared himself a communist and no longer able to work with Ruge. See A. Ruge, *Zwei Jahre in Paris: Studien und Erinnerungen* (Leipzig, 1846), Hildesheim, 1977, vol. 1, pp. 139–40; 'Ein Briefwechsel von 1843', *Deutsch-Französische Jahrbücher* (1844), Leipzig, 1973, pp. 101–28. Although there is no reason to doubt this account as far as it goes, the dispute between the two men was as much personal and financial. Ruge paid Marx's salary and became irritated by Marx's unreliability as a journalist. The Marxes and the Ruges lived in adjoining apartments. Ruge was ill and unable to take his share of editing. The Prussian government confiscated many of the copies of the journal and Ruge attempted to pay Marx in unsold copies.

154. The views of Louis Blanc (1811–82) have been described above (p. 31). As well as his pamphlet on the organization of labour Marx evidently read his *Histoire de dix Ans. 1830–1840*, 1841–4 (English translation, *History of Ten Years*, London, 1845), a text that, more than any other single work, set the tone of the radical interpretation of the July Monarchy and its 'bourgeois' character.

Pierre Leroux (1797–1871) was editor of *The Globe* around 1830 and originally a member of the Saint-Simonians. He rejected the Saint-Simonian church as a new

Feuerbach was particularly important since his writings fuelled Marx's growing disenchantment with *political* emancipation and shaped his break with Hegel.[155] Human emancipation was not a question of political forms, but of social relationships. Early in 1844, Marx praised Feuerbach for 'the establishment of *true materialism* and of *real science*, by making the social relationship of "man to man" the

---

form of papal despotism, counterposing to it what he called 'religious democracy'. He became close to the novelist George Sand and appears to have been well respected by Marx throughout his subsequent life. He claimed to have invented the word 'socialism' in its modern meaning.

Victor Considerant (1808–93), a former student of the École Polytechnique, became the leader of the Fourierists in the 1830s and 1840s. In 1843, he published *Manifeste de la Démocratie pacifique* (an introduction to the Fourierist newspaper of the same name) and reissued it in 1847 as *Principes du Socialisme, Manifeste de la Démocratie au xixème Siècle*. A number of French writers, going back to Georges Sorel at the beginning of the twentieth century, have argued that *The Communist Manifesto* drew heavily on Considerant's earlier *Manifesto* or even that he 'plagiarized' it. It is true that there are close similarities between the contemporary socio-economic analysis offered by Considerant – centring around the polarization of society into two great classes and the immiseration of the wage worker – and the treatment of similar themes in the first two sections of *The Communist Manifesto*. But by the 1840s many of these arguments formed part of the shared outlook of socialists and would no longer have been regarded as propositions 'plagiarized' from a particular source. The issue is discussed in R. V. Davidson, 'Reform versus Revolution: Victor Considerant and *The Communist Manifesto*', in F. L. Bender (ed.), *The Communist Manifesto*, Colorado, 1988, pp. 94–103.

In 1848 Considerant served in the National Assembly and on the Luxembourg Commission. He was exiled from France in 1849 and participated in the foundation of a Fourierist Community near Dallas, Texas. When Napoleon III allowed him to return he settled in the Latin Quarter, where he lived until his death in 1893.

155. Ludwig Feuerbach (1804–72) was the son of a famous jurist and follower of Kant. At first a supporter of romantic rationalism, he became a Hegelian and finally a student of Hegel in Berlin from 1824. Even at that time he expressed doubts about Hegel's reconciliation between philosophy and religion, which he expressed in his first anonymous publication in 1830, *Thoughts on Death and Immortality*, published in vol. 11 of *Sämtliche Werke*, ed. M. Sass, 13 vols., Stuttgart, 1964. In the 1830s, he worked as a Privatdozent at the University of Erlangen in Bavaria, but the strongly fundamentalist, Pietist tone of the university made permanent employment unlikely. Eventually marriage to a woman of independent means in 1837 made it possible for him to withdraw from university employment and write as a freelance scholar.

basic principle of the theory'.[156] Liberation must encompass not just mind, as the Hegelians promised, but the whole man; and man was first of all 'sensuous'. It was also from Feuerbach that Marx adopted the notion that Hegelian idealism needed only be 'reversed' or 'inverted' to become true: a metaphor to which he again reverted when discussing Hegel in the preface to his major work, *Capital*, in 1873.[157]

Feuerbach, another ex-pupil of Hegel, was the celebrated author of *The Essence of Christianity* (1841), translated into English soon after publication by Marion Evans, better known as the future novelist George Eliot. Marx, however, was more excited by an essay of 1842, 'Preliminary Theses on the Reform of Philosophy'. There Feuerbach enlarged his criticism of Christianity to include Hegel and gestured towards a connection between the Young Hegelian criticism of religion and the French socialist attack upon 'egoism'.[158]

The Essence of Christianity argued that religion was an alienated form of human emotion. Man had been enabled to make his emotions the object of thought through an imaginative identification with the divine. The emotions were projected onto an external being freed from the limitations of individual existence. In effect, Man imbued God with what was his own essence as a species. God was the perfected idea of the species viewed as an individual. The relation between subject and object was therefore reversed; henceforth, it no longer appeared that Man created God, but that God created Man.

Through this alienation of what Feuerbach called Man's 'species being', the essentially 'communal' character of the human species was transformed by Christianity into the particular union of each individual with a personal external being. Religion was, therefore,

156. K. Marx, 'Economic and Philosophical Manuscripts of 1844', *MECW*, vol. 3, p. 328.

157. 'With him it is standing on its head. It must be inverted, in order to discover the rational kernel within the mystical shell.' K. Marx, *Capital*, vol. 1, Harmondsworth, 1976, p. 103.

158. L. Feuerbach, 'Preliminary Theses on the Reform of Philosophy', in Z. Hanfi (ed.), *The Fiery Brook, Selected Writings of Ludwig Feuerbach*, New York, 1972, pp. 153–75. George Eliot's translation can be found in L. Feuerbach, *The Essence of Christianity*, tr. George Eliot (1854), New York, 1957.

responsible for the individualism of modern society. Between the individual and the universality of the species, there had been interposed an external mediator. In place of the primordial species unity of 'I and Thou', the role of 'Thou' had been usurped by Christ.

In the 'Preliminary Theses on the Reform of Philosophy', this criticism was extended to Hegel. The incarnation of 'absolute spirit' in history presupposed an extra-human perspective that had no natural basis. Hegelian philosophy was therefore simply an extension of Christian theology. It shared with Christian theology what Feuerbach called the method of 'abstraction'. Just as Christianity had originally alienated Man from his emotions, so Hegel had alienated Man from his thought.

To abstract means to posit the *essence* of nature *outside nature*, the *essence* of Man *outside Man*, the *essence* of thought *outside the act of thinking*. The Hegelian philosophy has alienated Man *from himself* in so far as its whole system is based on these acts of abstraction.[159]

In place of 'absolute spirit', Feuerbach's starting point was man-in-nature. Man still embodied reason and freedom, but only because he/she was first of all a 'sensuous being'. Just as thought had its genesis in 'real being', so 'suffering precedes thinking'. This meant that 'Man' could not be identical with the purely active and self-sufficient role assigned to 'spirit' by Hegel. Man-in-nature was both active and passive. As a natural being he stood in need of means of life that existed outside himself, above all of the elementary species-relationship, love. 'The first object of Man', wrote Feuerbach, 'is Man.' It was because Man was a natural being, a creature of need, that he was 'a communal being'. Man came to consciousness of his humanity, of his 'species being' through the agency of other men. 'The essence of Man is contained only in the community, in the unity of Man with Man.'[160]

According to Feuerbach, the task of 'true philosophy' was 'to posit

159. Hanfi (ed.), *Fiery Brook*, p. 157.
160. L. Feuerbach, 'Principles of the Philosophy of the Future', in Hanfi (ed.), *Fiery Brook*, p. 244.

the infinite in the finite'. In this way, Man's access to the universal and the infinite remained unaffected by the replacement of God or 'absolute spirit' by 'Man'. Feuerbach believed that anything that was an object of Man's consciousness was an expression of his being. Since the universal and the infinite were objects of Man's thought (in religion, for example), the being of Man as a species was likewise universal and infinite. Religion was, therefore, not false, but misdirected. The true infinite was not an external God, but 'Man' as 'species being'. The 'absolute' did not disappear, but was relocated within 'Man'. Once Man became conscious of his human 'essence', the limitations of individual finitude would be overcome.

Marx used Feuerbach's religious criticism to attack Hegel's claim that the modern state was a political community. In Christianity and in Hegel's thought, according to Feuerbach, Man's attributes, whether his emotions or his reason, were first removed from Man and ascribed to an alien or non-existent being, God or 'absolute spirit'. Subsequently, they were again restored to Man, but only at the end of a long process or in an imperfect form. In Feuerbach's words, 'although it again identifies what it separates, it does so only in a separate and mediated way'.[161]

This notion of *mediation* was crucial to Hegel's claim in the *Philosophy of Right* that the modern state was the embodiment of 'ethical life', meaning that it was the equivalent to the life which Plato and Aristotle had attributed to the ancient *polis*. The only difference was that the identity between the individual and the general will in the modern state was no longer 'immediate'. 'In the states of antiquity', Hegel wrote, 'the subjective end was entirely identical with the will of the state; in modern times, however, we expect to have our own views, our own volition and our own conscience.'[162] In other words, since antiquity, when (in Aristotle's phrase) the *polis* preceded the individual, there had been the rise of what Hegel called 'subjective particularity'. The *immediate* unity of the universal and the individual

161. L. Feuerbach, 'Preliminary Theses on the Reform of Philosophy', in Hanfi (ed.), *Fiery Brook*, p. 157.
162. *Elements of the Philosophy of Right*, para. 260, p. 283.

in the ancient *polis* had been dissolved. In its place there had emerged, both in the Christian conception of the soul and in the legal conception of a person, the notion of an individual whose subjectivity was not encompassed by the state. The *Philosophy of Right* was intended to demonstrate that the modern state was a higher form of political community that could encompass this feature of modernity.

The development of a modern exchange economy had also been crucial to Hegel's distinction between ancient and modern state. Aristotle's *Politics* had been based upon the contrast between *polis* and *oikos*, politics and household. Economic activity had either been conducted from within the household or performed by slaves. But this two-fold division was now insufficient. In modern times, most occupations had developed within a sphere that was no longer that of the family, a sphere whose dynamic had been described by Adam Smith and other writers on political economy. It was to take explicit account of this new sphere that Hegel introduced his novel conception of 'civil society'.[163]

But economic development was not the only reason for this change in terminology. It was also intended to underline Hegel's contention that the modern state was the equivalent of the ancient political community and not just, as modern theorists of a social contract believed, a means towards individual ends. Within 'civil society' Hegel included justice and the protection of property and person: in effect, what most seventeenth- and eighteenth-century writers had meant by the state. From Hobbes to Kant these writers – what Hegel called 'the modern school of natural law' – had started from the supposed interests of the individual as the basis of a contract by which to establish the state. This had meant that the state had become a 'provisional' entity, a mere means to individual ends. In Hegel's alternative, the modern state as the embodiment of reason and freedom represented an end in itself. It could both function as political community and fully incorporate the claims of modern subjectivity, whether these derived from the freedom of individual judgement championed by Protestant Christianity or the free-

163. See *Elements of the Philosophy of Right*, paras. 189–256, pp. 226–74.

dom to pursue particular ends contained in commercial society.[164]

In place of the immediacy of the ancient state, the 'higher principle of the modern era' was a concept of 'self' in which individuality and universality were mediated. In *The Philosophy of Right* Hegel assigned this task of mediation to a number of institutions, principally the corporations, representative assembly and bureaucracy. By means of these mediating institutions, the particular concerns of civil society were encompassed within the universal concerns of the state.

Inspired by Feuerbach, Marx objected both to the authenticity of these mediating institutions and to the idea of mediation itself. Hegel's mediations did not work. His state was not 'a totality', but a 'dualism'. Civil society and the political state were like two hostile armies; 'the citizen of the state and the citizen as member of civil society must effect a fundamental division within himself.' In antiquity, the *respublica* had been 'the true and only content of the life and will of the citizens', but now 'property, contract, marriage, civil society' had developed as 'particular modes of existence' of the private individual 'alongside the *political* state'. The modern state was 'a compromise between the political and the unpolitical state'.[165]

To explain this conflict between the 'political' and 'unpolitical' state, Marx drew upon Proudhon's analysis in *What is Property?* Proudhon had argued that the fundamental role ascribed to private property in France's new post-revolutionary legal code, the Code Napoléon, could not be reconciled with the goals of liberty, equality and fraternity proclaimed by the French Revolution.[166] Seen from a Feuerbachian perspective, private property was responsible for the predominance of individual over general interests in 'the social relationship of man to man'. This was the 'social truth' that Marx hoped would emerge from the battles over representative government and manhood suffrage currently surrounding 'the *political state* in all its modern forms'. 'For this question only expresses in a

164. See *Elements of the Philosophy of Right*, paras. 258, 260, pp. 276–7, 282.
165. K. Marx, 'Contribution to the Critique of Hegel's *Philosophy of Law*', *MECW*, vol. 3, pp. 31, 32, 50, 69, 77.
166. Proudhon, *What is Property?*, pp. 38–42.

political way the difference between rule by Man and rule by private property.'[167]

It was private property that undermined Hegel's claims for the modern state. Even in 1842, when reporting the proceedings of the Rhenish provincial assembly, Marx had been scathing about the inability of the deputies to rise above their petty private concerns. At that point his target had been 'the Prussian Christian state'. Now he saw something more universal and systematic. The modern state as such was the creature of private property and this made hollow all Hegel's claims about mediation. Private property was not simply a pillar of the constitution, but the constitution itself. Citizenship was an attribute of private property. Through the principle of primogeniture, which governed monarch and aristocracy, private property violated the principle of the family at the 'highest point' of the constitution. The state as 'the spiritual essence of society' had become the private property of the bureaucracy 'over against other private aims'. The members of the estates assembly provided no synthesis between state and civil society since, as the spokesmen of private interests, they were 'the posited contradiction of state and civil society within the state'. In short therefore, the modern state was not, as Hegel claimed, the highest actuality of social being, but a compromise between the rights of the citizen and the rights of private man.[168]

Bifurcation between state and civil society took the same form as that found in Feuerbach's depiction of Christianity. If religion registered 'the theoretical struggles of mankind', the 'political state' registered its 'practical struggles'. Just as Christ was 'the intermediary to whom Man transfers the burdens of all his divinity', so the state was 'the intermediary between Man and Man's freedom'. In the same way in which the Christian heaven had developed alongside 'Man's separation from community' on earth, there had been an 'abstraction' of the state. The political constitution had acquired 'an

167. K. Marx, 'Letters from the *Deutsch-Französische Jahrbücher*', *MECW*, vol. 3, p. 144.
168. K. Marx, 'Proceedings from the Sixth Rhine Province Assembly' (3 articles), *MECW*, vol. 1, pp. 132–82, 224–64; K. Marx, 'Contribution to the Critique of Hegel's *Philosophy of Law*', *MECW*, vol. 3, pp. 48, 67, 98, 108, 111.

unreal universality'. It had now come to function as 'the religion of national life', the 'idealism of the state' to accompany the 'material-ism of civil society'.[169]

The origins of this division could be traced back to the French Revolution, when the political revolution had destroyed 'all estates, corporations, guilds and privileges' and thereby 'abolished the politi-cal character of civil society'. The 'political spirit' had been freed from its admixture with civil life and established as 'the sphere of the community' . . . 'ideally independent' of 'particular elements of civil life'. By the same token, however, all the bonds that had 'restrained the egoistic spirit of civil society' had been removed.[170] Marx adopted this reading of modern French history, either directly from the writings of Louis Blanc or indirectly via the reports from Paris of Moses Hess. From the fall of the Jacobins, Blanc argued, the French had modelled their new society in the image of 'the bourgeoisie'. They had followed England in building a society based upon egoism and competition, upon 'the war of all against all'.[171] Marx's version of this interpretation centred around the celebrated *Declaration of the Rights of Man and the Citizen* proclaimed at the beginning of the French Revolution. This declaration was based, 'not on the association of Man with Man, but on the separation of Man from Man'. 'Political Community' was reduced to 'a mere *means* for maintaining these so-called rights of Man'. In effect, 'the *citoyen*' was 'declared to be the servant of egoistic *homme*'. Similarly, 'the practical application of Man's right to liberty' was 'Man's right to private property'. It was not, therefore, 'Man as *citoyen*, but Man as *bourgeois* who is considered to be the *essential* and *true* Man'.[172]

Like Feuerbach, Marx's aim was wholly to remove Hegel's mediations and return to immediacy. According to Feuerbach, the great defect of Hegel's philosophy was that it lacked 'immediate

169. K. Marx, 'On the Jewish Question', *MECW*, vol. 3, pp. 152, 154.
170. Ibid., pp. 166–7.
171. See Blanc, *Organisation*, p. 10 and *passim*; see also D. Gregory, 'Karl Marx's and Friedrich Engels' Knowledge of French Socialism in 1842–43', *Historical Reflections*, 10 (1983), pp. 169–73.
172. K. Marx, 'On the Jewish Question', *MECW*, vol. 3, pp. 162–4.

unity, immediate certainty, immediate truth'. In place of Hegel's process of bifurcation, mediation and reunion, what was needed was a philosophy of Man as an immediate whole.

This idea also lay behind Marx's alternative to Hegel's state, 'democracy', 'the solved riddle of all constitutions'. 'Democracy' did not mean a modern representative republic based upon universal suffrage. That would only have been another version of the discredited 'political state', whereas 'in true democracy the political state is annihilated'. This idea had originally been associated with the followers of Saint-Simon, who claimed that in the future organic order the government of men would be replaced by the administration of things. Marx added a Feuerbachian gloss. It would be a society in which the distinction between state and civil society would have been abolished. With the removal of mediating institutions, the constitution would be brought back to 'its actual basis, the actual human being, the actual people'. The distinction between political and unpolitical Man would be overcome.[173]

The return of 'Man' to himself would resolve the otherwise insoluble problems of modern representative states. If universality were a natural and individual possession, questions about the relationship between individual will and general will would cease to exist. The question whether 'civil society should participate in the legislative power either by entering it through delegates or by all individually sharing directly' was dismissed as a question that only arose 'within the abstract political state'. The problem was not whether one, many, or all individualities should participate; it was 'individuality' itself. Once the division between civil society and the political state came to an end, the problem of individuality would disappear. In democracy, 'universality' would be 'the essential, spiritual, actual quality of the individual'. The essence of a particular personality would be his or her 'social quality'. 'State functions' would be 'nothing but modes of being and modes of action of the social qualities of men'. The legislative power would only mean

173. K. Marx, 'Contribution to the Critique of Hegel's *Philosophy of Law*', *MECW*, vol. 3, pp. 29, 30.

... representation ... in the sense in which *every* function is representative
... in which every particular social activity as a species activity merely
represents the species, i.e. an attribute of my own nature, and in which
every person is the representative of every other.[174]

Marx left his commentary on Hegel unfinished, but in the two essays
he published at the beginning of 1844 in the first and only number
of the *Deutsch-Französische Jahrbücher* (German–French Annals) he
spelled out the political implications of his new approach. In particular he was concerned to demonstrate how it differed from 'criticism',
the position identified with his old mentor, Bruno Bauer.

The first essay, a response to Bauer on 'The Jewish Problem', gave
Marx the opportunity to criticize the assumptions that had informed
the battle between 'criticism' and 'The Christian State'. Bauer, like
Hegel, had distinguished between Judaism and Christianity as two
successive stages in the development of religious consciousness. He
therefore concluded that for Jews, unlike Christians, emancipation
required two steps: first to renounce Judaism, and second to renounce
Christianity, the higher religious form.[175]

174. K. Marx, 'Contribution to the Critique of Hegel's *Philosophy of Law*', *MECW*, vol.
3, pp. 21–2, 117, 119.
175. Bauer did not actually express the argument that Marx attributed to him. His
argument was rather that while advocates of emancipation were happy to force
Christianity to succumb to 'criticism', no such demand was made of Judaism in return
for its political emancipation. The general tenor of his essay was that the Jews should
not be congratulated for sticking to their beliefs, but should take responsibility for
wilfully retaining their separate identity. This was attributed by Bauer to the inability
of 'the Jewish national spirit' to 'develop with history', the result of its 'oriental nature'
and the fact that 'such stationary nations exist in the Orient'. See B. Bauer, 'The
Jewish Problem', in Stepelevich (ed.), *The Young Hegelians*, pp. 187–98.
  If traditional Christianity blamed the Jews for crucifying Christ and refusing to
acknowledge the divinity of the Messiah, the Enlightenment, for the most part
unintentionally, introduced a different line of reproach. The problem originated in
the new need towards the end of the seventeenth century to explain to an Enlightened
public the moral deficiencies and anomalies of the Old Testament. Particularly
influential was the solution suggested by John Locke in *The Reasonableness of Christianity*
(1695). This was to suggest that revelation was not a once and for all set of events
handed down from the Bible, but a continuous process developing through history.
The rider to the argument was that the form in which God revealed himself was
appropriate to the moral and cultural stage which humanity had reached. This

In place of Bauer's 'theological' approach, Marx proposed a 'social' distinction between Christianity and Judaism, much of which he took from an unpublished essay of Moses Hess. Hess's essay, 'On the Essence of Money', an attempt to combine Feuerbach's humanism with French socialism, was intended as a contribution for the journal. It was decisive in prompting Marx, for the first time, to address questions about economic life. Hess argued that at present humanity inhabited an 'upside down world'. Christianity provided 'the theory and logic' of this world, while money defined its 'practice'. Both Christianity and the 1789 Declaration of the Rights of Man treated the essence of Man as that of an isolated individual. The activity of the species was not ascribed to the individuals who composed it. Rather, God as species-essence was conceived to exist outside these individuals. In practical life, money was the equivalent of this inverted God, a materialized Christian God, who stripped Man of his social ties. In 'the modern Christian shopkeeper world' money represented the setting of species life outside the individual. In antiquity a similar part had been played by Judaism and slavery. Money had become the alienated wealth of Man, the bartering away of Man's life activity, the product of mutually estranged men who exchanged freedom in return for the satisfaction of their individual needs.[176]

---

argument was further elaborated in 1777 by Lessing in his *Education of the Human Race*, whose first proposition was that 'what education is to the individual man, revelation is to the whole human race'. The consequence of this position, which became an essential component of Hegelian idealism, was that Judaism belonged to a primitive stage of the development of Spirit. In Hegel's *Philosophy of History*, the religion of Judaea was considered alongside those of Persia and Egypt as part of 'The Oriental World'. But Hegel's discussion of Judaism had no bearing upon his support for Jewish emancipation. Bauer's position, which implied that Jewish emancipation depended upon whether the Jews deserved to be emancipated, had no precedent in Lessing or Hegel. Bauer's argument was also inconsistent. He both attacked the Jews for their supposedly obstinate resistance to historical development, and at the same time considered them incapable of historical development because 'in the Orient, Man does not yet know he is free and gifted with reason . . . He sees his highest task in the performance of mindless baseless ceremonies.'

176. Moses Hess, 'Über das Geldwesen', in Mönke (ed.), *Moses Hess*, pp. 331–45.

In Marx's extension of Hess's argument Judaism was equated with 'practical need', 'egoism' and civil society. The God of 'practical need' was money, which like 'the jealous God of Israel' destroyed all other Gods. It robbed the world and Man's work of all 'specific value'. 'Money' was 'the estranged essence of Man's work and Man's existence' . . . 'The God of the Jews has become secularized.' But Judaism was not enough to enable civil society to reach its 'highest point'. This could only be achieved by Christianity, which made 'all national, natural, moral and theoretical conditions extrinsic to Man' and dissolved 'the human world into a world of atomistic individuals who are inimically opposed to one another'. For Marx, therefore, solving 'the Jewish question' meant eliminating the *social* element that made it possible. Only, an emancipation from 'huckstering' and money would make the Jew – as a category apart from the community – 'impossible'.[177]

In his other contribution to the journal, an 'introduction' to his

177. K. Marx, 'On the Jewish Question', *MECW*, vol. 3, pp. 172–4. The hostility towards Jews that was common among socialists in the 1840s drew upon a number of different sources. First, among those, like Bauer, who regarded existing religions as the main obstacle to a republic or to social harmony, Judaism was attacked as a static, archaic or particularistic creed (an image derived especially from Leviticus). Second, there were the age-old associations, real or imagined, between the Jews and usury. These came once again to the fore in the economic dislocation, insecurity of employment and speculative crises of the 1815–48 period. But they were exacerbated by the suspicion, voiced in France by both Fourier and Proudhon, that the extent of indebtedness and pauperism had been made worse by the emancipation of the Jews at the time of the French Revolution. Frequent complaint was made about the financial power of the Jews despite the incompleteness of their emancipation. Both Bauer and Marx focused upon the supposed incongruity between the power of the Jew as capitalist and his subordination as citizen.

Although the breach between Marx and Bauer is usually considered to date from disagreement over the Jewish question, this did not bring their relationship wholly to an end. During the winter of 1855–6, Bruno stayed in Highgate with his brother, Edgar, and seems to have been in regular contact with Marx. Despite their political differences, especially over Russia (Marx later thought he was in the pay of the Russians), Marx's attitude to his old teacher appears to have been uncharacteristically indulgent: he saw him as absurdly vain, 'but in other respects a pleasant old gentleman'. See Marx to Engels, 18 January 1856, *MECW*, vol. 40, p. 4, and also Marx to Engels, 12 February 1856, ibid., pp. 11–12.

critique of Hegel's *Philosophy of Right*, Marx declared that the criticism of religion was now complete. If one started not with consciousness but with Feuerbach's relationship between man and man as the basis of society, then it could be seen that religion was not 'the cause, but only as the manifestation of secular narrowness'. What religion revealed was the existence of a 'defect' and this meant that the struggle against religion was a struggle against the world of which religion was 'the spiritual aroma'.[178]

Bauer was, therefore, wrong to imagine that religion would disappear with the removal of 'the Christian state' since 'the emancipation of the state from religion is not the emancipation of the real Man from religion'. Religion had become 'the spirit of civil society, of the sphere of egoism, of *bellum contra omnes*'. 'Political emancipation' bifurcated Man. He became on the one hand an egoistic independent individual, on the other a citizen or juridical person. But the citizen was the servant of the egoistic individual. Political community became 'a mere means for maintaining these so-called rights of Man'. The example of the United States, where religion flourished despite the separation of Church and State, proved that religious freedom was by no means the same thing as freedom from religion. What was required was not 'political emancipation', but 'human emancipation', a condition in which

the real individual Man reabsorbs in himself the abstract citizen, and as an individual human being has become a species being in his everyday life, in his particular work and in his particular situation.[179]

In his 'introduction', Marx also addressed the question of how change would come about in Germany. The assumption that 'criticism' would of itself lead to a transformation of the state had been proved false. As Marx put it, 'the weapon of criticism cannot replace the criticism of weapons. Material force must be overthrown by material force.' Nor was a merely 'political revolution' to be

178. K. Marx, 'Contribution to the Critique of Hegel's *Philosophy of Law*. Introduction', *MECW*, vol. 3, p. 175; K. Marx, 'On the Jewish Question', *MECW*, vol. 3, p. 174.
179. K. Marx, 'On the Jewish Question', *MECW*, vol. 3, pp. 155, 168.

expected. There was no class in Germany capable of acting like the French third estate in 1789. In Germany, therefore, 'universal emancipation' was 'the sine qua non of partial emancipation', and this could not be achieved politically.[180]

The writings of the French socialists reinforced Marx's disenchantment with the German middle classes. Neither Proudhon nor Blanc believed that political democracy could remedy the situation of the worker. Only a social revolution could restore Man to his true social nature. Marx was also impressed by the writings of the ex-Saint-Simonian, Pierre Leroux. Leroux had been the editor of the *Globe* and was a close companion of the novelist George Sand. Like Blanc, Leroux emphasized the egoism and avarice of middle-class rule and proclaimed the coming age to be that of the emancipation of 'the proletariat'. Even those who, like the Fourierist leader Victor Considerant, emphasized a peaceful and harmonious resolution of the social question warned that the new industrial order was another form of serfdom and that unless mechanization, overproduction and the growth of unemployment were halted, workers would be driven towards a violent revolution.[181]

What was now required in Germany was not political change, but a 'human' transformation carried through by a class outside and beneath existing society, a class with 'only a human title'. 'To be radical is to grasp the root of the matter. But for man the root is man himself.' The term radical came from the Latin word *radix*, root – what was therefore needed was 'a class with radical chains' . . . 'a sphere that cannot emancipate itself without emancipating all other spheres of society'. This was the proletariat, a class arising from '*industrial* development' and from 'the *drastic dissolution* of society'. It was 'the complete loss of Man' and 'the dissolution of the hitherto existing world order'.[182] Marx maintained

180. K. Marx, 'Contribution to the Critique of Hegel's *Philosophy of Law*. Introduction', *MECW*, vol. 3, pp. 182, 184–6.

181. For Marx's reading of French socialists in 1842–3 see D. Gregory, 'Karl Marx and Friedrich Engels' 'Knowledge of French Socialism in 1842–1843', *Historical Reflections*, 10 (1983), pp. 143–93.

182. K. Marx, 'Contribution to the Critique of Hegel's *Philosophy of Law*. Introduction', *MECW*, vol. 3, pp. 182, 186–7.

By demanding the negation of private property . . . the proletariat merely raises to the rank of a principle what society has made the principle of the proletariat.

From his reading, both of Lorenz von Stein and of the French socialists, Marx appears simply to have assumed that the outlook of the proletariat was that of a crude form of communism descending from Babeuf's 'conspiracy of the equals'. But evidence of their present outlook was immaterial. It was not 'a question what this or that proletarian, or even the whole proletariat, at the moment *regards* as its aim'. As Marx later explained, it was a question 'of *what the proletariat is* and what, in accordance with this being, it will historically be compelled to do'.[183]

Initially, however, Marx did not believe that the proletariat could act alone. The spark had to be lit by philosophy. Germany's revolutionary past was theoretical – the Reformation – and Feuerbach was the new Luther. 'As the revolution then began in the brain of the *monk*, so now it begins in the brain of the *philosopher*.' Feuerbach had set out the terms of the alliance in the 'Preliminary Theses'.

The true philosopher who is identical with life and Man must be of Franco-German parentage . . . we must make the mother French and the father German. The *heart* – the feminine principle, the *sense* of the finite and the seat of materialism – is of *French disposition*; the *head* – the masculine principle and the seat of idealism – of German.[184]

This had been the original inspiration of the plan to found the *Deutsch-Französische Jahrbücher*, back in May 1843. In his published correspondence with Ruge Marx had stated that the consistuency of the journal would consist of 'people who think' and 'people who suffer'. By the beginning of 1844, the role of suffering and of the heart had been assigned to the proletariat. Revolutions, it was said,

183. K. Marx and F. Engels, 'The Holy Family, or Critique of Critical Criticism', *MECW*, vol. 4, p. 37.
184. K. Marx, 'Contribution to the Critique of Hegel's *Philosophy of Law*. Introduction', *MECW*, vol. 3, p. 182; L. Feuerbach, 'Preliminary Theses on the Reform of Philosophy', Hanfi (ed.), *Fiery Brook*, p. 165.

required a '*passive* element, a *material* basis'. 'As philosophy finds its *material* weapons in the proletariat, so the proletariat finds its *spiritual* weapons in philosophy.' Once therefore

the lightning of thought has squarely struck this ingenuous soil of the people, the emancipation of the *Germans* into *human beings* will take place . . . The *head* of this emancipation is *philosophy*, its *heart* is the *proletariat*.[185]

185. K. Marx, 'Letters from the *Deutsch-Französische Jahrbücher*, Marx to Ruge, May 1843', *MECW*, vol. 3, p. 141; K. Marx, 'Contribution to the Critique of Hegel's *Philosophy of Law*. Introduction', *MECW*, vol. 3, p. 187. It is unclear whether it was to be the French or the German proletariat which would play this role. The last sentence of Marx's introduction reads: 'the day of German resurrection will be proclaimed by the ringing call of the Gallic cock'.

9. *Political Economy and 'The True Natural History of Man'*

In Paris from the beginning of 1844, Marx embarked upon what was to turn out to be his lifelong preoccupation, the critique of political economy. In three unpublished and unfinished manuscripts, now usually referred to as the Economic and Philosophical Manuscripts or Paris Manuscripts, he set out the first version of this critique. 'A Critique of Political Economy' was also the subtitle of his major work, *Capital*, published in 1867.

What caused Marx to shift his attention to political economy? In 1859 in the Preface to his book containing the first instalment of this critique, *Contribution to the Critique of Political Economy*, Marx provided a brief account of how he first became engaged in this project. His original interest had been in jurisprudence, which he had pursued as 'a subject subordinated to law and philosophy'. His attention had first been drawn to the problem of 'material interests' in 1842–3, while serving as editor of the *Rheinische Zeitung*. His uncertainty and 'embarrassment' about how to think about 'economic questions' had ranged from free trade to the condition of the Moselle peasantry. For similar reasons, he had been unwilling to participate in discussions in the German press about the relative merits of the different theories of socialism or communism at that time coming out of France. Soon after, because of his unwillingness to alter the stance of the paper to avoid its closure, Marx had resigned as editor and this had given him the opportunity to examine these questions more systematically. He had therefore embarked upon a critical re-examination of Hegel's *Philosophy of Right*.

From this critical scrutiny he had come to the conclusion that 'neither legal relations nor political forms' could be understood 'by themselves'; nor could they be understood as different expressions 'of a so-called general development of the human mind'. Instead, their origin was to be found 'in the material conditions of life, the totality of which Hegel, following the example of English and French thinkers of the eighteenth century' embraced within the term 'civil society'. Political economy had, therefore, become the centre of enquiry since within it was to be found 'the anatomy of this civil society'.[186]

With the invention of 'Marxism' in the last decades of the nineteenth century, this autobiographical retrospect and the accompanying summary of his theoretical approach acquired canonical status as the founding statement of the science of 'historical materialism'.[187] But while this account was true as far as it went, its terseness and guarded mode of expression suggest that it should not be taken entirely at face value. Intended for publication in Prussia at a time of continuing political repression and written in a form which might deflect the attentions of the censor, Marx presented his work as a form of disinterested scientific inquiry and his life as that of a scholar who had 'eagerly grasped the opportunity to withdraw from the public stage to my study'.[188]

What was omitted was at least as important as what was said. There was no direct reference to the political framework within which these ideas had developed, and no mention of the connection between political economy and Marx's theory of communism.[189] But

186. K. Marx, 'Preface' to 'A Contribution to the Critique of Political Economy' (January 1859), *MECW*, vol. 29, pp. 261–2.
187. See for instance the important work of G. A. Cohen, *Karl Marx's Theory of History A Defence*, Oxford, 1978, p. x, where the book begins with a long citation from the 1859 Preface and the author declares his intention to defend 'an old-fashioned historical materialism' . . . 'whose "most pregnant" statement', he agrees with Eric Hobsbawm, 'is the Preface to *The Critique of Political Economy*'.
188. K. Marx, 'Preface' to 'A Contribution to the Critique of Political Economy', *MECW*, vol. 29, p. 262.
189. The emphasis upon science and the down-playing of politics was clearly a deliberate stratagem. In a letter to Joseph Weydemeyer outlining the contents of the book, he wrote, 'you will understand the *political* motives that led me to hold back the third chapter on "Capital" until I have again become established' . . . 'I hope to win

when he first arrived in Paris around the beginning of 1844, it had not been the ambition to construct a science of history that had led him to 'his studies in the domain of political economy', but the promise of revealing the hidden foundations of communism. His assumption that these foundations might be uncovered through a 'critique of political economy' is largely to be explained by the impact made upon him by two of the essays that he had assembled for *Deutsch-Französische Jahrbücher*, those by Hess and Engels.

The shift towards a preoccupation with production started with Hess. Feuerbach's endorsement of Man's communal nature conveyed little beyond an unspecific notion of social union and an ethos of friendship or sexual love. Hess's essay on money offered a more tangible and practical focus. It defined life as 'the exchange of productive life activity' through 'the cooperative working together of different individuals'. Through this 'species activity', individuals achieved 'completion'. If at present cooperation did not define the relations between men, this was because they were living in an 'inverted' or 'upside-down' world ('*eine verkehrte Welt*'). Throughout creation, it was proof of the superiority of 'love' over 'egoism' that the instinct to propagate the species outweighed that of individual self-preservation. It was therefore a 'reversal' of human and natural life 'when the individual was raised to an end and the species degraded to a means'. In this 'inverted world', 'egoistic' Man employed his species-powers to satisfy his private needs.

But humanity was now nearly at the end of the last phase of a natural history of Man that had been dominated by the brutal struggle of isolated individuals. Natural forces were no longer so

---

a scientific victory for our party'. K. Marx to J. Weydemeyer, 1 Feb. 1859; Engels had evidently been somewhat disappointed when he read the first part of the manuscript. 'The study of your ABSTRACT of the first half-instalment has greatly exercised me; IT IS VERY ABSTRACT INDEED.' He hoped that 'the abstract dialectical tone' of the synopsis would 'disappear in the development'. F. Engels to K. Marx, 9 April 1858; Marx's justification of the manuscript later in the year was that 'since the whole thing has an EXCEEDINGLY serious and scientific air, the canaille will later on be compelled to take my views on capital RATHER SERIOUSLY.' K. Marx to F. Engels, 13–15 Jan. 1859, *MECW*, vol. 40, pp. 376, 377, 304, 368 (citation order).

hostile. Man now knew how to harness them to human ends. The current economic misery was also a striking portent of a new epoch. For as the example of England demonstrated, misery was no longer a product of dearth but of a superfluity of goods.[190]

Hess was a pioneer in the attempt to combine German humanism and French socialism. His essay built a bridge between the two by shifting attention from consciousness to practice. Marx adopted 'productive life activity', or what he called 'conscious life activity', as his new starting point. This definition of 'the life of the species' as 'the productive life' made possible the idea of 'alienated labour' as the foundation of estrangement. 'Religious estrangement', wrote Marx, 'occurs only in the realm of *consciousness*, of Man's inner life, but economic estrangement is that of *real life*; its transcendence therefore embraces both aspects.'[191]

Engels' essay 'Outlines of a Critique of Political Economy' was equally important. It pinpointed political economy as the pre-eminent theoretical expression of this estranged world. The essay's main point was that political economy presupposed private property, while never questioning its existence. Political economy as 'the science of enrichment born of the merchant's mutual envy and greed' was largely 'the elaboration of the laws of private property'. Yet, just as in politics 'no one dreamt of examining the premises of the state as such', so in economics it did not occur to anyone 'to question the *validity of private property*'. Engels directed at political economy some of the criticisms he had encountered among the Owenites in Manchester. His approach enabled Marx to consider, not just money, but trade, value, rent and 'the unnatural separation' of labour and 'stored up' labour or capital. Its consequence was that 'the product of labour' confronted 'labour as wages' in an 'ever more acute . . . division of mankind into capitalists and workers'.[192]

In Marx's portrayal, political economy mistook a world in which

190. M. Hess, 'Über das Geldwesen', Mönke (ed.), *Moses Hess*, pp. 330–34.
191. K. Marx, 'Economic and Philosophical Manuscripts of 1844', *MECW*, vol. 3, p. 297.
192. F. Engels, 'Outlines of a Critique of Political Economy', *MECW*, vol. 3, pp. 418, 419, 430, 431.

Man had alienated his essential human attributes for the true world of Man. In civil society, where every individual appeared as 'a totality of needs' and in which 'each becomes a means for the other', these attributes only appeared in alien guise. The patterns of behaviour observed and turned into laws by political economists were patterns produced by estrangement. Marx made no objection to the accuracy of these observations and, therefore, no specific economic criticism. The defects of political economy were not occasional, but fundamental. From the beginning, political economy treated the relation of Man to Man as a relationship between property owner and property owner. It proceeded as if private property were a natural attribute of Man or a simple consequence of 'the propensity to truck, barter and exchange' described by Adam Smith. As a result, political economy was unable to distinguish 'the productive life' of Man from the 'whole estrangement connected with the money system'. The task of the critic was to uncover the essential reality of species-man buried beneath this inverted world and to translate the estranged discourse of political economy into a truly *human* language.[193]

Marx's procedure bore some resemblance to Fourier's critique of 'civilization', in which authentic human passions found expression, but only in a distorted and anti-social form. Thus, for Marx the meaning of private property outside estrangement was 'the *existence of essential objects* for Man'. Exchange or barter was defined as 'the social act, the species act . . . within *private ownership*' and therefore 'the *alienated* species act', 'the opposite of the *social* relationship'. The division of labour became 'the economic expression of the social character of labour within . . . estrangement'. Money was 'the alienated *ability of mankind*'. In a 'human' world, by contrast, the general confounding and confusing of all natural and human qualities expressed by money and exchange value would be impossible. There, you could

exchange love only for love . . . Every one of your relations to Man and to

193. K. Marx, 'Economic and Philosophical Manuscripts of 1844', *MECW*, vol. 3, pp. 317, 276, 307; K. Marx, 'Comments on James Mill, *Eléments d'économie politique*', *MECW*, vol. 3, p. 217.

nature must be a *specific expression*, corresponding to the object of your will, of your *real individual* life.[194]

Underpinning this process was the estrangement of Man's most essential attribute, his capacity to produce. 'Conscious life activity', the fact that Man made his activity 'the object of his will and of his consciousness', was what distinguished Man from animal. Man produced 'universally'. He produced even when he was 'free from physical need'. He was able 'to produce in accordance with the standard of every species' and knew 'how to apply everywhere the inherent standard to the object'. He therefore formed objects 'in accordance with the laws of beauty'. This production was Man's 'active species life'.[195]

'Estranged labour' reversed 'this relationship'. The greater the development of private property and the division of labour, the more the labour of the producer fell 'into the category of *labour* to earn a living, until it only has this significance'. In contrast to the cynicism of political economists, who paid no attention to the worker's estrangement, Marx proceeded from 'an *actual* economic fact: the worker becomes poorer the more wealth he produces'. This 'fact', Marx claimed, meant that 'the worker is related to the *product of his labour* as to an *alien* object'.[196]

Estrangement related not only to the product of labour, but also to the activity of labour itself. The activity of the worker was 'an alien activity not belonging to him', a 'self-estrangement'. Man's '*essential being*' became 'a mere means to his *existence*'. 'The *life of the species*' became 'a means of individual life'. Labour was no longer the satisfaction of a need, but 'merely a *means* to satisfy needs external to it' – animal needs to maintain individual physical existence. Thus

194. K. Marx, 'Economic and Philosophical Manuscripts of 1844', *MECW*, vol. 3, pp. 322, 317, 325, 326; K. Marx, 'Comments on James Mill', *MECW*, vol. 3, p. 219. For Fourier's critique of 'civilization', see C. Fourier, *The Theory of the Four Movements*, ed. G. Stedman Jones, Cambridge, 1996.

195. K. Marx, 'Economic and Philosophical Manuscripts of 1844', *MECW*, vol. 3, pp. 276–7.

196. K. Marx, 'Comments on James Mill', *MECW*, vol. 3, p. 220; K. Marx, 'Economic and Philosophical Manuscripts of 1844', *MECW*, vol. 3, pp. 271, 172.

Man only felt himself 'freely active in his animal functions'. What was animal became human and what was human became animal.

Finally, estranged labour meant not only the estrangement of Man from his species-nature, but also the estrangement of Man from Man. 'The *alien* being, to whom labour and the product of labour belongs . . . can only be some *other man than the worker*.' Every self-estrangement of Man appeared in his relation to other men. His labour belonged to another and was therefore unfree. It was the labour 'of a man alien to labour and standing outside it', or the relation to it of 'a capitalist'.[197]

In the three or four decades after the rediscovery and republication of these manuscripts in 1932, this extension of the notion of alienation was to be acclaimed a masterpiece by a whole array of philosophically inclined socialists, humanists and radical Christians. Published at a time when the future was believed to be epitomized by the Ford Model T, the assembly line and Charlie Chaplin's *Modern Times*, these manuscripts were thought to have uncovered a profound existential truth about the nature of work under modern capitalism. In countries such as France, where communism was becoming the dominant force on the political left, they also acquired a more immediate political importance. Except for a small minority, Marxism had come to be identified with communism and unswerving support for the Soviet Union. Marx had been placed next to Lenin as the foremost icon in the surreal union of panglossian optimism and breathtaking brutality called Stalinism. It was not therefore surprising that critics in Western socialist parties seized upon these manuscripts as long-buried evidence of another Marx capable of voicing a more nuanced, humane or even tragic sense of Man.

This association of the 'young' Marx with a series of radically decontextualized twentieth-century preoccupations largely obscured what Marx himself was attempting to achieve in these manuscripts. But it is not difficult to reconstruct. The ambition was to

197. K. Marx, 'Economic and Philosophical Manuscripts of 1844', *MECW*, vol. 3, pp. 275, 276, 278.

elaborate a coherent theory of communism, of a 'human' world beyond the state, private property and religion, a theory that attempted to combine Feuerbach's humanism with the French socialist attack on private property. Seen from this angle, however, Marx's enlargement of the scope of alienation posed as many problems as it solved.

The difficulty surfaced as soon as it was asked why Man had become alienated and how this alienation would be overcome. If alienated labour were simply ascribed to private property, then the translation of economic into human categories would lose its point, and the mental deformation represented by alienation would amount to no more than another variant of the effects of force and fraud. Marx's approach would then become indistinguishable from that of those French communists like the followers of Babeuf or Cabet who proposed 'the positive community system', or those socialists like Proudhon who advocated the equality of wages.

This, Marx was determined to avoid. His goal was

the *positive* transcendence of *private property* as *human self-estrangement* and therefore . . . the real *appropriation* of the *human* essence by and for Man.

This 'return of Man' to 'his human, i.e. social, existence' would mean that need or enjoyment would lose 'its egotistical nature', that nature would lose its 'mere utility' and that the present 'sheer estrangement' of '*all* physical and mental senses' in 'the sense of *having*' would give way to 'the complete *emancipation* of all human senses and qualities'.[198]

Clearly, superseding private property as a form of 'human self-estrangement' was an attempt to model 'alienated labour' upon a Feuerbachian notion and followed from Marx's claim that 'the criticism of religion' was 'the premise of all criticism'. What this implied was that private property was not the cause, but the consequence of alienated labour. The situation was akin to that of religion, where the gods had not originally been the cause but the effect

198. K. Marx, 'Economic and Philosophical Manuscripts of 1844', *MECW*, vol. 3, pp. 296, 299–300.

of Man's intellectual confusion. Alienated labour, then, was produced by 'the external relation of the worker to nature and to himself'.[199]

But as the argument developed, Marx appears to have realized that alienated labour could not be presented in strictly Feuerbachian terms. Feuerbach's interest was in a psychological process. Religious consciousness was argued to be the result of a mental deformation containing a sequence of bifurcation, estrangement and recuperation, not unlike the psychic mechanisms later uncovered by Freud. The mediation offered by the Christ figure, though real in its effects, was of a purely imaginary kind. The concerns that informed Feuerbach's remedy were also located within the psyche. According to his 'transformative method':

we need only turn the predicate into the subject ... that is only reverse speculative philosophy [to have] the unconcealed, pure and untarnished truth.

Such a procedure only made sense if religion were a psychological malady. For then emancipation from religious consciousness would be equivalent to emancipation from religion itself.[200]

But alienated labour and private property were not simply forms of consciousness. They had also formed the basis of a developing historical and institutional reality, in which, unlike God or Christ, there was nothing imaginary about the mediation provided by the employer or master of labour. Feuerbach had nothing to say about these 'real life' institutional forms of mediation, and he expressed no interest in the question of private property. His attack on mediation formed part of his attack upon the psychological processes at work within Christianity and Hegelian philosophy. Similarly, his demand for the removal of this artificial sequence of splitting, estrangement and mediated reunion derived from a defence of the original

199. K. Marx, 'Contribution to the Critique of Hegel's *Philosophy of Law*. Introduction', *MECW*, vol. 3, p. 175; K. Marx, 'Economic and Philosophical Manuscripts of 1844', *MECW*, vol. 3, p. 279.

200. L. Feuerbach, 'Preliminary Theses on the Reform of Philosophy', Hanfi (ed.), *Fiery Brook*, p. 154.

wholeness and immediacy of Man and a call for the restoration of his lost attributes. Once this position was made the starting point of a historical argument, it became clear that this insistence upon the immediacy of Man's social attributes went together with a drastically anti-historical notion of an untutored natural Man, endowed from the start with all the qualities that German idealism attributed to a complex process of experience, culture or history. In short, the role assigned to mediation in Feuerbach's purely psychological narrative could not be simply replicated in the history of 'activity' or 'real life' without short-circuiting most of the founding presuppositions of the Young Hegelian movement.

This problem had not arisen in 1843. Marx had applied Feuerbach's 'transformative method' and had not been displeased with the result. By demanding the abolition of the state–civil society division and the elimination of all Hegel's mediating institutions, he had expressed his total rejection of representative government and modern politics. But a rejection of the modern economy could not be so unqualified. From the outset, Marx had been emphatic in his condemnation of 'the crude' levelling communism, 'which has not only failed to go beyond private property, but has not even reached it'. His goal was not merely 'the complete return of Man to himself', but 'a return . . . embracing the entire wealth of previous development'. He could not therefore ignore Adam Smith's view that exchange and the division of labour had been the motor of economic progress.

But this meant that, even if 'human life' now required 'the supersession of private property', in the past it had 'required *private property* for its realization'. In other words, estrangement was not a wholly negative phenomenon, but was somehow 'rooted in the nature of human development'.

Such assumptions could only lead Marx once more back to Hegel himself. For Hegel's first major work, his *Phenomenology of the Spirit* of 1807, appeared to offer precisely what was needed: a transhistorical combination of history and psychology in which a form of alienation was accorded a positive and necessary role. The 'outstanding achievement' of the book, wrote Marx, was that it conceived the self-creation of Man as a process . . . [and] . . . objectification as loss of the object, as alienation and as transcendence of this alienation.[201]

The German word for alienation in this passage was *Entäusserung* derived from the verb *entäussern*, to make outer, to make external. One of the main sources of Hegel's idea went back to Fichte's 'absolute ego' who produced the phenomenal world through a process of self-externalization – *Entäusserung*.[202] In Hegel's overall conception, spirit externalized itself into nature and then, through human history, once more came to recognize itself in its other. In charting this voyage of spirit through human experience, Marx argued that the *Phenomenology* had grasped the essence of labour: the creation of Man as 'the outcome of Man's *own labour*'.

Starting from Hess's conception of the cooperative engagement

201. G. W. F. Hegel, *Phenomenology of Spirit* (1807), tr. A. V. Miller, Oxford, 1977; K. Marx, 'Economic and Philosophical Manuscripts of 1844', *MECW*, vol. 3, pp. 281, 295, 296, 321, 332–3.

202. J. G. Fichte (1762–1814) was one of Kant's most radical followers. His idea of an 'absolute ego' was developed in his *Science of Knowledge*, 1794. It was devised in part to overcome a problem in the theory of knowledge that had arisen as a consequence of Kant's philosophy. Kant had destroyed traditional metaphysics by denying that there could be knowledge of objects beyond possible experience. But his own conception of empirical knowledge hypothesized an interaction between the faculty of sensibility (the senses), located within the world of experience, and that of the understanding (that which organized and classified the phenomena received by the senses), located outside it. The problem then was: if the concepts of understanding were outside and prior to the world of experience, how could it be known that they applied to experience? In the *Science of Knowledge*, Fichte argued that the only way to overcome the gulf between the understanding and sensibility, between knowing subject and known object was to start from a notion of 'self-knowledge' or 'subject–object identity'. The only being for whom all knowledge could be self-knowledge would be a so-called 'absolute ego', a God-like construct who created its objects in the act of knowing them. The status of this 'absolute ego' was that of a 'regulative idea', a rational norm to which human practice should be made to approximate. The 'absolute ego' represented not only an ideal of knowledge, but also a goal of moral striving. For it was the personification of the moral autonomy – action according to the laws of reason – enjoined by Kant's moral law. On Fichte's 'absolute ego', see F. C. Beiser, *Enlightenment, Revolution and Romanticism. The Genesis of Modern German Political Thought, 1790–1800*, Cambridge (Mass.), 1992, pp. 57–84; on the relevance of Fichte to Marx's notion of alienation, see N. Lobkowicz, *Theory and Practice: History of a Concept from Aristotle to Marx*, Notre Dame, 1967, pp. 300–304.

of humanity in 'productive life activity', Marx attempted to rework Hegel's developmental schemas in terms appropriate to the trajectory of Man as 'a sensuous being'. Following Feuerbach, he once again emphasized that Man was a natural being, 'a suffering, limited and conditioned creature'. This meant that 'the objects of his instinct exist outside him as objects independent of him'. The defect of Hegel's 'spirit', as Marx reiterated, was that 'a being which does not have its nature outside itself is not a *natural* being, and plays no part in the system of nature'.[203]

But Marx was not content simply to turn Man into a creature of his environment. For, as he noted in *The Holy Family* – yet another polemic against Bruno Bauer later that year – such a position would be indistinguishable from Owenite socialism and a whole Anglo-French 'materialist' tradition going back to Locke. Instead, he was determined not only to retain, but even to go beyond the transformative power ascribed to Man as the bearer of spirit in Hegel's speculative system. Marx insisted

Man is not merely a natural being . . . he is a *human* natural being . . . i.e. a being for himself. Therefore he is a species being and has to conform and manifest himself as such both in his being and in his knowing.[204]

Man's point of origin as '*human* natural being' was history. Like God, Man as *human* being created himself. History was 'a conscious self-transcending act of origin', 'the true natural history of Man'. History was the process of the humanization of nature through Man's 'conscious life activity'. It was 'in creating a *world of objects* by his practical activity, in his *work upon* inorganic nature', that Man proved himself 'a conscious species being'. By this means, Man was able to treat himself as 'a universal and therefore a free being' and this appeared in 'the universality which makes all nature his inorganic body'. Through this production, nature appeared as '*his*

203. K. Marx, 'Economic and Philosophical Manuscripts of 1844', *MECW*, vol. 3, pp. 333, 336, 337.
204. K. Marx and F. Engels, 'The Holy Family or Critique of Critical Criticism against Bruno Bauer and Company', *MECW*, vol. 4, pp. 124–34; K. Marx, 'Economic and Philosophical Manuscripts of 1844', *MECW*, vol. 3, p. 337.

work', industry as 'the open book of Man's essential powers', and the object of labour as 'the *objectification of Man's species-life*'. Man would therefore be able to see himself 'in a world that he has created'.[205]

Equally, history was the process of the humanization of Man himself through the enlargement and transformation of his needs.

All history is the history of preparing and developing 'Man' to become the object of sensuous consciousness and turning the requirements of 'Man' as 'Man' into his needs.

Thus 'the forming of the five senses' had been 'the labour of the entire world down to the present'. For this reason, '*human* objects' were not 'natural objects as they immediately present themselves'. History was the process of Man becoming species being. Thus, 'history itself is a *real* part of *natural history* – of nature developing into Man'.[206] Like Montesquieu and Fourier, Marx treated the condition of women as the best measure of humanization. The relationship between man and woman showed 'the extent to which Man's need has become a *human* need'.[207]

But if history was driven by Man's inherent species-sociality (Man's destiny as a social being), its goal could only be reached after first passing through the vale of estrangement. 'The *real, active* orientation of Man to himself as a species being ... is only possible if he brings out all his *species powers* – something which in turn is only possible through the co-operative action of all of mankind, only as

205. K. Marx, 'Economic and Philosophical Manuscripts of 1844', *MECW*, vol. 3, pp. 337, 304–5, 276, 302.
206. K. Marx, 'Economic and Philosophical Manuscripts of 1844', *MECW*, vol. 3, pp. 302–4.
207. From the time of Aristotle's *Politics*, it was customary to consider civil and domestic society in parallel. In the eighteenth century, it became common to regard the condition of women in terms of a historical transition from slavery to liberty, both in society and in the household, and to judge the contemporary world's states by these criteria. It was within this framework that Montesquieu argued, in *The Spirit of the Laws*, 'Everything is closely related: the despotism of the prince is naturally conjoined to the servitude of women.' Montesquieu, *The Spirit of the Laws*, Cambridge, 1989, Bk 19, ch. 15, p. 315, and see also pp. 104, 270. See also S. Tomaselli, 'The Enlightenment Debate on Women', *History Workshop*, 20 (1985), pp. 101–25. On Fourier's position, see Fourier, *The Theory of the Four Movements*, pp. xiii–xiv.

the result of history – and treats these powers as objects: and this, to begin with, is . . . only possible in the form of estrangement.'[208]

Following Engels, Marx had started from the relationship between political economy and private property. If capital was 'private property in the products of other men's labour' and the laws of political economy arose from 'the very nature of private property', this meant that the movement of private property 'is the *perceptible* revelation of the movement of all production until now'. It was also 'easy to see' that

the entire revolutionary movement necessarily finds its empirical and its theoretical basis in the movement of *private property* – more precisely, in that of the economy.

The determinant role of private property was attested by the fact that 'religion, family, state, law, morality, science, art, etc. are only *particular* modes of production and fall under its general law.'[209]

But private property was not the root of the problem. An examination of the 'movement of private property' in political economy had revealed that it was 'the material perceptible expression of *estranged human life*', 'the product of alienated labour', the means by which labour alienated itself. It was for this reason that

the emancipation of society from private property etc., from servitude, is expressed in the *political* form of the *emancipation of the workers* . . . because the emancipation of the workers contains universal human emancipation . . . because the whole of human servitude is involved in the relation of the worker to production.[210]

This 'secret' (that private property was the product of alienated labour) was only revealed at 'the culmination of the development of private property'. It could only be uncovered when private

208. K. Marx, 'Economic and Philosophical Manuscripts of 1844', *MECW*, vol. 3, p. 333.
209. K. Marx, 'Economic and Philosophical Manuscripts of 1844', *MECW*, vol. 3, pp. 246, 271, 297.
210. K. Marx, 'Economic and Philosophical Manuscripts of 1844', *MECW*, vol. 3, pp. 297, 279, 280.

property had completed its dominion over Man and became 'a world historical power', when all wealth had become industrial wealth and the factory system 'the perfected essence of industry'. 'All human activity hitherto' had been 'labour – that is, industry – activity estranged from itself'. But no 'developed state of contradiction', no 'dynamic relationship driving towards resolution' had developed until the antithesis between property and lack of property became the antithesis between labour and capital.[211]

Once private property became a 'world-historical power', every new product meant 'a new potentiality of mutual swindling and mutual plundering'. The need for money became the only need produced by the economic system and neediness grew as the power of money increased. Everything was reduced to 'quantitative being'. 'Excess and intemperance' came to be 'its true norm'. Private property did not know 'how to change crude need into *human* need'. Its extension of products and needs therefore became 'a *contriving* and *ever-calculating* subservience to inhuman, sophisticated, unnatural and *imaginary* appetites'. Estrangement had produced sophistication of needs on the one hand and 'bestial barbarization' on the other. Even the need for fresh air ceased to be a need for the worker. 'Man returns to a cave dwelling, which is now, however, contaminated with the pestilential breath of civilization.' The crudest methods of production, like the treadmill of Roman slaves, were returning. The Irishman no longer knew any need except the need to eat 'scabby potatoes' and 'in each of their industrial towns England and France have already a *little* Ireland'. Political economy, a reflection of the needs of 'empirical businessmen' in the form of a 'scientific creed', validated this process 'by reducing the worker's need to the barest and most miserable level and by reducing his activity to the most abstract mechanical movement'.[212]

But in reducing 'the greater part of mankind to abstract labour' in producing the proletariat, private property had produced a class

211. K. Marx, 'Economic and Philosophical Manuscripts of 1844', *MECW*, vol. 3, pp. 303, 293–4.
212. K. Marx, 'Economic and Philosophical Manuscripts of 1844', *MECW*, vol. 3, pp. 306–7, 308.

driven by the contradiction between its human *nature* and its condition of life, which is the outright, resolute and comprehensive negation of that nature ... The proletariat ... is compelled as proletariat to abolish itself and thereby its opposite private property ... [Thus,] private property drives itself in its economic movement towards its own dissolution ... through a development which does not depend on it [and] which is unconscious ... [For] the proletariat executes the sentence that private property pronounces on itself by producing the proletariat.[213]

But although it was 'the necessary form and dynamic principle of the immediate future', communism was not as such 'the goal of human development'. Communism was the abolition of private property, 'the negation of the negation', just as atheism was 'the negation of God'. 'The riddle of history solved' was 'Socialism' or what Marx elsewhere confusingly called communism as 'humanism' or 'naturalism', 'Man's *positive self-consciousness*, no longer mediated through the abolition of religion' or 'the *positive* transcendence of private property and therefore ... the real appropriation of the *human* essence by and for Man'.[214]

At the beginning of the manuscripts, Marx chided 'criticism' (Bauer and his followers) for not settling accounts with 'its point of origin – the Hegelian dialectic and German philosophy as a whole'. In the third manuscript, therefore, he attempted his own assessment by confronting the *Phenomenology*. He attacked Hegel for treating entities such as wealth and state power purely as 'thought entities' and for treating *human* activity – 'the nature created by history' – as if it were the product of an 'abstract mind'. Lastly, Hegel was also accused of treating 'the reappropriation of the objective essence of Man' as the annulment of 'objectivity' as such.[215]

Such criticism, however, only demonstrated the extent of the

---

213. K. Marx, 'Economic and Philosophical Manuscripts of 1844', *MECW*, vol. 3, p. 241; K. Marx and F. Engels, 'The Holy Family', *MECW*, vol. 4, p. 36.
214. K. Marx, 'Economic and Philosophical Manuscripts of 1844', *MECW*, vol. 3, pp. 296–7, 306.
215. K. Marx, 'Economic and Philosophical Manuscripts of 1844', *MECW*, vol. 3, pp. 233, 331–3, 338.

imaginative gulf that had opened up between Hegel's philosophy and the strange hybrid form resulting from the marriage between socialism and Young Hegelianism. Hegel had written about different forms of consciousness and the way in which the defects of one form led on to another in 'the rise of knowledge'. Knowledge was considered an interpersonal rather than an individual creation and was not sharply distinguished from different forms of practical activity. It therefore made little sense for Marx to accuse Hegel of treating different forms of activity as 'entities estranged from the human being' or the rise of knowledge as the product of 'abstract mind'.[216]

More obviously vulnerable as a metaphysical assumption was the teleological process that guided spirit to the threshold of absolute knowledge. But the process evoked in Marx's alternative was no less purposive than that found in Hegel, and in its particular conception of narrative sequence scarcely less indebted to its ancestry in Protestant thought. For by employing the notion of alienation in the form of *Entäusserung* (making outer) as a framework in which members of the proletariat – standing for humanity as a whole – are driven to the most inhuman extreme of degradation and yet at the same time bear within them the promise of ultimate emancipation, Marx, no doubt unwittingly, recaptured much of the drama attached to the original Lutheran reading of Christ. The theological significance of the term *entäussern*, derived from Luther's translation of St Paul's Epistle to the Philippians (2:6–9), in which Jesus

though he was in the form of God, did not count equality with God a thing to be grasped, but emptied himself (*sich geäussert*), taking the form of a servant, being born in the likeness of Man. And being found in human form he humbled himself and became obedient unto death, even death on the cross.

Marx developed a variant of the same idea when he wrote of the sheer estrangement of 'all physical and mental senses' in 'the sense

216. K. Marx, 'Economic and Philosophical Manuscripts of 1844', *MECW*, vol. 3, pp. 332–3.

of having'. 'The human being had to be reduced to this absolute poverty in order that he might yield his inner wealth to the outside world.'[217]

The real gulf was not between Marx's 'true materialism' and Hegel's 'non-objective beings'. What these disagreements obscured was a profound difference of purpose. However novel the role of 'absolute spirit' and however sublime Man's role as its bearer, the aim of Hegel's philosophy belonged to a tradition going back to Aristotle, which sought to understand Man's place in the world, and through that understanding make Man feel at home within it. Man's access to the absolute was through knowledge, and it was only insofar as he had access to absolute knowledge that he could participate in the infinite. The end of 'objectivity', about which Marx made such heavy weather, made sense once it was made clear that the relationship of identity between subject and object at the end of the *Phenomenology* was to be understood within the framework of absolute knowledge. It meant the realization that persons and things all formed part of a single substance-become-subject, of whom Man, insofar as he participated in absolute knowledge, was the articulate voice. Hegel's absolute was from the beginning a single infinite substance, of which Man, at first the unconscious bearer of its subjectivity, was always a part. 'The rise of knowledge' was a journey through different shapes and figures of thought towards ultimate awareness of this fact.

Marx's alternative was an attempt to validate Feuerbach's more unlikely claim that the infinite could be derived from the finite in the form of a historical transformation from Man as natural being to Man as natural *human* being. He pushed the argument even further by extending its scope from thought to action. It was because Hegel considered that Man's capacities as actor in the world were not infinite, that the accidents of individual fortune could not be anticipated and that the contingencies of economic life might be

---

217. K. Marx, 'Economic and Philosophical Manuscripts of 1844', *MECW*, vol. 3, p. 300; for the Lutheran background to the notion of *Entäusserung*, see G. M. M. Cottier, *L'Athéisme du Jeune Marx*, Paris, 1969.

contained but not removed, that his notion of political community did not attempt wholly to encompass the everyday life of civil society.

Marx, on the other hand, placed no such limits upon the destiny of Man. Marx's first objection to political economy had been that 'the true law of political economy is *chance*, from whose movement we, the scientific men, isolate certain factors in the form of laws.' In his conception, the abolition of private property would be followed by 'the complete emancipation of all human senses and qualities'. In the higher stage of communism all objects would be recognized as objectifications of Man. All Man's organs or senses would be directly social in form. For 'social Man', nature possessed a 'human aspect'; 'for only then does nature exist for him as a *bond* with *Man*'. Emancipation would not only be a matter of 'knowing', but also of 'being'. For 'Man appropriates his comprehensive essence in a comprehensive manner, that is to say, as a whole Man.'[218]

In these manuscripts, together with *The Holy Family*, written shortly afterwards, many of the basic elements in Marx's theory received their first formulation. In the juxtaposition of 'the true natural history of Man' with the effects of private property or alienated labour it is not difficult to see an inchoate version of what in 1859 Marx would depict as the more scientific and economic-sounding relationship between the forces and relations of production.[219] In the 1844 manuscripts the instigating role of the philosopher had already virtually disappeared. The revolt of the proletariat was shown as a consequence of the self-destructive trajectory of private property in its last phase. Thereafter the association between communism and the revolutionary abolition of private property by the proletariat remained constant, as did the depiction of political economy as the scientific creed of the capitalist. The two stages of communism or socialism, the first as the abolition of private property, the second as 'the complete return of Man to himself', also looked forward to an

218. K. Marx, 'Comments on James Mill', *MECW*, vol. 3, p. 211; K. Marx, 'Economic and Philosophical Manuscripts of 1844', *MECW*, vol. 3, pp. 299–300.
219. K. Marx, 'A Contribution to the Critique of Political Economy. Preface', *MECW*, vol. 29, pp. 263–4.

analogous distinction in *The Critique of the Gotha Programme* in 1873.[220] The list could go on. . . .

Was this, then, the theory of history and conception of political action found in the *Manifesto*? Not quite. For those features later considered most distinctive of Marxism or 'the materialist conception of history' only came to the fore after one further shuffle in the Young Hegelian pack, this time occasioned by the publication of Max Stirner's *The Ego and Its Own* in late 1844.

220. K. Marx, 'Critique of the Gotha Programme', *MECW*, vol. 24, p. 87.

10. *The Impact of Stirner*

Max Stirner was a teacher at a Berlin girls' school. Between 1841 and 1843 he had been one of the *Freien* (the 'Free'). This was a loose Bohemian coterie of radical atheist Young Hegelians, who had irritated Marx by sending anti-religious diatribes to the *Rheinische Zeitung* when he was editor of the newspaper in 1842. Stirner's presence at meetings of the Free is attested by a sketch by the young Frederick Engels, at that time also a member. By 1844, however, Stirner had developed a position of his own, quite distinct from both Bauer and Feuerbach.

The main target of Stirner's book was the new 'humanism' of Feuerbach. In particular, he contested Feuerbach's claim to have completed the criticism of religion. For Feuerbach, the essence of religion had consisted in the separation of human attributes ('predicates') from human individuals ('subjects') and the removal of these predicates to another world where they were reassembled to form a fictive 'subject', God or 'spirit'. By reclaiming these alienated attributes for Man, or reversing 'subject' and 'predicate', Feuerbach claimed that the process of religious alienation would come to an end. But, as Stirner noted, this did nothing to dislodge the underlying structure of religious consciousness. For attributes ascribed to the divine were not restored to human individuals, but to another ideal construct, the 'essence of Man', the (human) 'species', 'species being' or 'Man with a capital M'.[221] God as human 'essence' was equally set

221. Max Stirner, *The Ego and Its Own*, ed. D. Leopold, Cambridge, 1995, p. 55.

above mere men as their judge and goal, as their 'vocation'. Thus Feuerbach's 'Man' was one more extension of the Protestant God, whose power had derived from 'the tearing apart of Man into natural impulse and conscience'.[222]

Marx was not only implicated in this assault upon the Feuerbachian approach, but at one point explicitly identified with the demand that 'I become a real generic being'.[223] Commenting on this demand, Stirner wrote,

the *human* religion is only the last metamorphosis of the Christian religion . . . it separates my essence from me and sets it above me . . . it exalts 'Man' to the same extent as any other religion does its God or idol . . . it makes what is mine into something other worldly . . . in short . . . it sets me beneath Man, and thereby creates for me a vocation.

Marx was directly threatened by this attack in two ways. First, there was the embarrassment of being associated with the religiosity of Feuerbach. This embarrassment was compounded by Feuerbach's own admission that he had derived his notion of 'species' from Strauss, who had introduced the term as a dynamic substitute for the place of Christ in traditional Christianity. But, more fundamentally, Stirner challenged the whole normative basis of Young Hegelian politics. The Young Hegelians had presupposed the intolerable character of the present, had assumed that they stood at a turning point in history and had therefore looked forward to the prospect of imminent redemption. Marx had clearly spelt out their position in 1843.

The criticism of religion ends with the teaching that *Man is the highest being for Man* hence with the *categorical imperative to overthrow all relations* in which Man is a debased, enslaved, forsaken, despicable being.[224]

Stirner's juxtaposition, not of Man to God, but of the individual to Man, and his exposure of the quasi-religious basis of such an

222. Ibid., p. 82.
223. Ibid., p. 158.
224. K. Marx, 'Contribution to the Critique of Hegel's *Philosophy of Law*. Introduction', *MECW*, vol. 3, p. 182.

imperative, effectively punctured this rhetoric. From Stirner's argument, it became clear that once an escape were made from the neo-Christian ethics of humanism, the sense of crisis invoked by Young Hegelianism largely evaporated. As Stirner concluded:

to the Christian the world's history is the higher thing, because it is the history of Christ or 'Man', to the egoist only *his* history has value, because he wants to develop only *himself*, not the mankind-idea, not God's plan, not the purpose of Providence, not liberty, and the like. He does not look upon himself as a tool of the idea or a vessel of God, he recognises no calling, he does not fancy that he exists for the further development of mankind and that he must contribute his mite to it, but he lives himself out, careless of how well or ill humanity may fare thereby.[225]

Faced with Stirner's challenge, Marx drastically changed his stance. As late as the beginning of 1845, in a set of notes entitled 'ad. Feuerbach' (later known as 'Theses on Feuerbach'), Marx's main objection to Feuerbach's 'contemplative materialism' was its lack of a notion of 'sensuousness' as 'practical human-sensuous activity', and he had rounded off his objections with the injunction: 'the philosophers have only *interpreted* the world in various ways; the point is to *change* it'.[226] Thereafter, however, not only does this normative and voluntarist theme disappear, but any sense in which ideas might play an innovatory or independent role in history was abruptly abandoned. In 'The German Ideology', written between 1845 and 1847, Marx and Engels declared:

Communism is not for us a *state of affairs* which is to be established, an *ideal* to which reality (will) have to adjust itself. We call Communism the *real* movement which abolishes the present state of things.[227]

225. Stirner, *The Ego and Its Own*, p. 323.
226. K. Marx, '[Theses on Feuerbach]', *MECW*, vol. 5, pp. 4–5.
227. K. Marx and F. Engels, 'The German Ideology. The Critique of Modern German Philosophy according to its Representatives Feuerbach, B. Bauer and Stirner, and of German Socialism According to its Various Prophets', *MECW*, vol. 5, p, 49.
  But in this respect as well, the position of Marx appears to have differed from that of Engels. After the reply to Stirner Marx made every effort to avoid having to write anything further of significance, either about religion in general or Christianity in

In the *Manifesto*, communists were defined as those who understood 'the line of march' of the 'proletarian movement'. 'They merely express, in general terms, actual relations springing from an existing class struggle.' More generally, 'The German Ideology' declared:

morality, religion, metaphysics and all the rest of ideology as well as the forms of consciousness corresponding to these ... no longer retain the semblance of independence. They have no history, no development.[228]

If, therefore, Marx warded off Stirner's challenge, it was by recourse to a thermo-nuclear response; and the collateral damage was commensurate. Since Marx could not escape association with a moralizing and quasi-religious form of humanism by rejecting the validity of a humanist or socialist goal as such, his solution was to divest *all* ideas of any autonomous role whatsoever. In this way, a goal that had begun as a 'categorical imperative', or as the conclusion to 'the criticism of religion', could be preserved, and yet at the same time any association between socialism and ethics could be brutally

---

particular. But not Engels, who in a late letter to Kautsky (28 July 1894), stated that he had continued to be interested in the debate about the origins of Christianity since 1841. In this debate, Engels was dismissive of the position of Strauss and considered the success of Ernest Renan's *Life of Jesus* (1863) that of a plagiarist. He remained a not uncritical but generally enthusiastic admirer of Bauer. After Bauer's death in 1882, Engels wrote an appreciative obituary, in which he stated that Bauer had proved the chronological order of the Gospels and demonstrated the importance of the ideas of Philo and Seneca in the constitution of Christianity, even if he had not found a convincing historical explanation of how and when such ideas were introduced. In 1883 he wrote an interpretation of the Book of Revelation as the oldest part of the New Testament, a position going back to the lectures of Ferdinand Benary which Engels had attended in Berlin in 1841. Finally, in 1894 he wrote a substantial essay 'On the History of Early Christianity', in which he once again gave the main credit to Bauer. The essay began 'the history of early Christianity has notable points of resemblance with the modern working-class movement', a point of comparison which Marx had studiously avoided. See F. Engels, 'Bruno Bauer and early Christianity' (1882), *MECW*, vol. 24, pp. 427–35; F. Engels, 'The Book of Revelation' (1883), *MECW*, vol. 26, pp. 112–17; F. Engels, 'On the History of Early Christianity' (1894), *MECW*, vol. 27, pp. 447–69.

228. K. Marx and F. Engels, 'The German Ideology . . .', *MECW*, vol. 5, p. 36.

denied.[229] As an answer it was ingenious but disingenuous. In later years, both Marx and Engels made attempts to retreat from its more inconvenient implications,[230] while their followers were saddled with the self-defeating task of explaining the place of a voluntarist movement in an economically determined historical process.

229. 'The criticism of religion ends with the teaching that *Man is the highest being for Man*, hence with the *categorical imperative to overthrow all relations* in which Man is a debased, enslaved, forsaken, despicable being . . .' K. Marx, 'Contribution to the Critique of Hegel's *Philosophy of Law*. Introduction', *MECW*, vol. 3, p. 182.

230. See, for example, the attempt to qualify the position adopted around the time of 'The German Ideology' in a letter written by Engels in the 1890s. 'According to the materialist conception of history, the *ultimately* determining element in history is the production and reproduction of real life. More than this neither Marx nor I have ever asserted' . . . 'Marx and I are ourselves partly to blame for the fact that the younger people sometimes lay more stress on the economic side than is due to it. We had to emphasize the main principle vis-à-vis our adversaries, who denied it, and we had not always the time, the place or the opportunity to give their due to the other elements involved in the interaction.' F. Engels to J. Bloch, 21–2 Sept. 1890, K. Marx and F. Engels, *Selected Works*, 3 vols., Moscow, 1973, vol. 3, pp. 487–8.

11. *Communism*

If Marx did not feel too devastated by Stirner's attack, it was because in the course of 1844 he had already begun to elaborate an alternative route to communism. As will become apparent, this new theory was scarcely less speculative and certainly more reductive than the position he had outlined in the 1844 manuscripts. But its great attraction was that it provided an escape from dependence upon the psychological pieties of Feuerbachian anthropology, and more generally from any visible association with the neo-Christian moralism characteristic of most French and German socialism at the time. The new position was outlined in the unpublished 'German Ideology', which Marx composed together with Engels in Brussels between 1845 and 1847. This new theory was built out of three overlapping preoccupations that had emerged from Marx's abandonment of a Hegelian form of political rationalism in 1843. These were political economy, the history of law and property and the debate about communism.

(i) The Contribution of Adam Smith

First, as a result of his reading of *The Wealth of Nations*, Marx replaced the still somewhat abstract opposition between 'alienated labour' and Man's 'species being' by Adam Smith's conception of the development of the division of labour.

Smith began with a description of 'the eighteen distinct operations' performed by ten men in the making of a pin. Smith estimated that through this subdivision of tasks, the ten men were able to produce 48,000 pins per day or 4,800 each. Had every pin been individually produced, Smith thought it unlikely that as many as twenty pins could be produced, 'perhaps not one pin in a day'. Building upon this example, Smith argued that

the division of labour ... so far as it can be introduced ... occasions, in every art, a proportionable increase in the productive powers of labour ... [that] ... the separation of different trades and employments from one another seems to have taken place, in consequence of this advantage ... [and that] ... this separation ... is generally carried furthest in those countries which enjoy the highest degree of industry and improvement.

The division of labour, in Smith's account, began not as the result of human wisdom or foresight, but rather as

the necessary, though very slow and gradual consequence of a certain propensity in human nature ... the propensity to truck, barter, and exchange one thing for another.

What motivated this propensity to exchange was not benevolence, but self-love. 'It is not from the benevolence of the butcher, the brewer, or the baker, that we expect our dinner, but from their regard to their own interest.' Lastly, since the division of labour was a result of 'the power of exchanging', it followed that the extent of the division of labour was always limited by 'the extent of the market'. In other words, human material progress had proceeded in parallel with the growth of the market.[231]

231. The argument is to be found in A. Smith (1723–90), *An Enquiry into the Nature and Causes of the Wealth of Nations*, 1776, Bk 1, chs. 1–3. See A. Smith, *An Inquiry into the Nature and Causes of the Wealth of Nations*, ed. E. Cannan, Chicago, 1976, pp. 8–9, 17–18, 21. For an account of how Adam Smith was read in Germany, see E. Rothschild, '*Smithianismus* and Enlightenment in nineteenth-century Europe', paper presented at the Leverhulme-Thyssen Conference on 19th century Historical Political Economy (Oct. 1998), Centre for History and Economics, King's College, Cambridge, and more generally E. Rothschild, *Economic Sentiments: Adam Smith, Condorcet and the Enlightenment*, Harvard, 2001.

Unlike the somewhat static idea of alienated labour, division of labour could be turned into the dynamic core of a theory of social and historical development capable of operating in antagonistic conjunction with what in 1844 Marx had called 'the true natural history of Man'. In 'The German Ideology' this 'true natural history' was re-described as the development of Man's 'productive forces'. The 'level' of the division of labour was now made dependent upon 'the development of the productive power at any particular time'. 'Each new productive force . . . causes a further development of the division of labour.'[232]

It was the growth of productive forces that had been responsible for the introduction of the division of labour into human history: a consequence of increased productivity, the development of needs and the growth of population.[233] Originally an extension of 'the natural division of labour in the family and the separation of society into individual families opposed to one another', the division of labour presupposed the 'unequal distribution, both quantitative and qualitative, of labour and its products, hence property'. Similarly, as a result

232. K. Marx and F. Engels, 'The German Ideology', *MECW*, vol. 5, pp. 93, 32.
233. The connection between the development of needs and the development of different forms of production or modes of subsistence was not an innovation of Marx or even of Smith. It had originally been the product of seventeenth-century natural-law theories of property, beginning with *Of the Law of War and Peace* of Hugo Grotius in 1625. In the writings of Samuel Pufendorf, especially *On the Duty of Man* (1673), this approach was refined into what was later to be known as the 'Four-Stages Theory' of history, in which the development of human society proceeded from hunting and gathering, through pasture and agriculture to a final commercial stage. The theory reached Scotland through an English translation of the fourth edition of this work, edited by Jean Barbeyrac, and was developed by Smith in his *Lectures on Jurisprudence*. Initially at least Smith thought of his work as an elaboration of the theory of natural law. See D. Forbes, 'Natural Law and the Scottish Enlightenment', in R. H. Campbell and A. S. Skinner (eds.), *The Origins and Nature of the Scottish Enlightenment*, Edinburgh, 1982, pp. 186–204; J. Moore and M. Silverthorne, 'Gershom Carmichael and the natural jurisprudence tradition in eighteenth-century Scotland', in I. Hont and M. Ignatieff (eds.), *Wealth and Virtue: The Shaping of Political Economy in the Scottish Enlightenment*, Cambridge, 1983, pp. 73–88; I. Hont, 'The Language of Sociability and Commerce: Samuel Pufendorf and the Theoretical Foundations of the "Four-Stages Theory"', in A. Pagden (ed.), *The Languages of Political Theory in Early Modern Europe*, Cambridge, 1987, pp. 253–76.

of the consequent need to regulate 'the contradiction between the particular and the common interests', 'the common interest' assumed 'an independent form as *the state*' . . . 'an illusory community'. The essence of the division of labour, like alienated labour, was that it was not voluntary.

As long as Man remains in naturally evolved society . . . as long . . . as activity is not voluntarily, but naturally divided, Man's own deed becomes an alien power opposed to him, which enslaves him instead of being controlled by him.

Indeed, the division of labour encapsulated on a global historical scale what Marx had first found objectionable in Hegel's portrayal of civil society: the abandonment of the everyday social life of modern Man to chance. Because of the division of labour, Marx wrote,

the relation of supply and demand . . . hovers over the earth like the fate of the ancients, and with invisible hand allots fortune and misfortune to men, sets up empires and wrecks empires, causes nations to rise and disappear . . .

But with the abolition of private property, the communistic regulation of production and the abolition of 'the alien attitude of men to their own product', the power of supply and demand would be 'dissolved into nothing' and men would 'once more gain control of exchange, production and the way they behave to one another'.[234]

(ii) The History of Law and Property

But however helpful Smith's picture of the division of labour in illuminating the contradictory character of the increase in wealth and productivity in human history, there was nothing in *The Wealth of Nations* to suggest a future stage beyond commercial society, let alone an end to private property or the supersession of the division of labour. At this point Marx was able to turn to a second body of literature with which in some sense he had already been familiar

234. K. Marx and F. Engels, 'The German Ideology', *MECW*, vol. 5, pp. 46–7, 48.

from his first years as a law student. This was the nineteenth-century European debate on the nature and history of property.

Ever since the famous abolition of feudal rights in France on the night of 4 August 1789, the question of property had been central to the debate about the legitimacy and significance of the revolution. The 'Declaration of the Rights of Man and of the Citizen' had listed property, alongside liberty, security and resistance to oppression as one of the 'natural and imprescriptible rights of Man'; it was 'an inviolable and sacred right'.[235] But already by 1790, the attempt to render property 'inviolable' had begun to be countered by those pressing for a more equal division of the soil. The radical case appealed to the classical precedent of 'the agrarian law', a series of legislative measures dating from the Roman Republic and particularly associated with the Gracchus brothers. It was for that reason that the generally acknowledged forefather of modern revolutionary communism, François Noel Babeuf, assumed the name Gracchus in May 1793. Under the supposed terms of these *leges agrariae*, the ancient state had laid down the maximum acreage of land to be owned by individual citizens and had redistributed the surplus to those without. Support for such measures had a weighty and respectable lineage. A long line of republican thinkers, starting from Machiavelli and including Harrington, Montesquieu and Mably, had praised the practice as a symbol of the preparedness of a republic to limit private property and, if necessary, transfer land from rich to poor as a means of strengthening the state. So sensitive did the issue become that on 18 March 1793 the Convention decreed the death penalty for anyone proposing the 'agrarian law'.[236]

With the defeat of the radicals and the stabilization of the state, private property as the foundation of the new order acquired permanent legal and institutional form. In another appeal to classical precedent, this time to empire rather than republic, Napoleon

235. D. Van Kley (ed.), *The French Idea of Freedom: The Old Regime and the Declaration of Rights of 1789*, Stanford, 1994, pp. 2, 4.
236. See Rose, *Gracchus Babeuf*, pp. 131–8. On the babouvist understanding of the agrarian law as a precipitant of the German transformation of the understanding of Roman history, see below.

assumed the mantle of the modern 'Justinian' and issued a new legal code embodying the new rights of Man, the Code Napoléon of 1804.[237] To ensure permanence, Napoleon even forbade commentaries on the new code. But in much of its content, and especially in its treatment of property, the code only reiterated the precepts of Roman Law. Provided 'laws and regulations' were not contravened, property was 'the right to enjoy and dispose of things in the most absolute manner'. This was more or less a transcription of the Roman *ius utendi et abutendi*, the right to use or abuse a thing within the limits of the law.

Around this conception of property as a 'natural right' French jurists constructed a stylized history in which 'property' was made the foundation of civilization and 'possession' its prelude. Property began with the principle of first occupancy, might also additionally be justified by labour and was then given theoretical recognition in the law. Such a view of history could also, without too much difficulty, accommodate the conceptions of eighteenth-century conjectural historians – Smith, Turgot and others – in which the history of society proceeded through four stages – hunting, pasture, agriculture and commerce. In one of the most authoritative commentaries on the code that appeared after Napoleon's fall, by Charles Toullier, the natural right of first occupancy became permanent with the progress of agriculture and gradually evolved into 'full property'. It became standard in many legal commentaries in the period to suggest that history was the transition from possession as 'fact' to property as 'law'.[238]

237. Justinian was Roman emperor of the East (Byzantium) between AD 527 and 565. During his long reign, Roman law was codified (the *Codex vetus* and the Fifty Decisions). At the same time, an authoritative summary was made of the extensive literature of juristic commentary of the late classical period (the *Digest* or *Pandects*). Finally, an introductory student textbook was compiled (the *Institutes*), which also received the force of law. The Roman law, which came to form the foundation of the legal codes of Western Europe, was that codified by Justinian.

238. C. B. M. Toullier (and J. B. Duvergier), *Le Droit Civil Français suivant L'Ordre du Code*, 6th edn, Paris, n.d., vol. 3, paras. 64–71, pp. 26–8; D. R. Kelley, *Historians and the Law in Postrevolutionary France*, Princeton, 1984, pp. 132–3; and see also D. R. Kelley and B. G. Smith, 'What was property? Legal dimensions of the social question in France (1789–1848)', *Proceedings of the American Philosophical Society*, 128:3 (1984), pp. 200–230.

In the years following the battle of Waterloo these were not simply academic matters. With the return of the Bourbons questions about the status of land acquired during the revolution, clamour by returning émigrés for the restitution of their possessions and demands from colonial planters for new supplies of slaves were among the most pressing political questions in the years leading up to the 1830 revolution.[239] This was why the strongest endorsements of the new view of 'absolute property' tended to come from liberal supporters of the gains of 1789. Private property along with civil equality and constitutional government as the basis of modern civilization formed the mainstay of the case made by defenders of the July monarchy between 1830 and 1848. In a similar spirit, in the *Philosophy of Right* Hegel had also put forward an emphatic philosophical case for private property as the imposition of the subjective will upon nature, and hence the foundation of individuality.[240]

Set beside the continuing existence of unfree labour on the land in large parts of central and eastern Europe, and the jumble of particular tenures and special privileges associated with the feudal world before 1789, the case for 'absolute' property looked strong. The debate also had more global dimensions. In the wake of the emancipation of colonial slaves by revolutionary France, followed by the outlawing of the slave trade by Britain, controversy over slavery intensified in the United States and Britain as well as France in the decades following the Napoleonic wars. In Britain, the radical followers of Thomas Spence questioned the aristocratic ownership of the land. At the same time Thomas Hodgskin, in an early controversy about the claims of labour, distinguished between a 'natural' right to property arising from labour and an 'artificial' right resulting from the law-making privileges of a landed class, which owed its position to conquest and usurpation. In Russia as well, with the beginnings of an opposition movement in the 1820s,

---

239. On the politics of restoration France, see G. de Bertier de Sauvigny, *La Restauration*, Paris, 1955; on the question of slavery in France and its colonies, see R. Blackburn, *The Overthrow of Colonial Slavery 1776–1848*, London, 1988, ch. xii.
240. *Elements of the Philosophy of Right*, paras. 44–6.

the question of serfdom moved to the centre of the reform agenda.[241]

It is therefore not surprising that until the 1830s the main opposition to this new world of absolute property and to the promulgation of 'enlightened' and uniform legal codes enshrining civil equality and 'absolute' private property came from conservatives. Starting from Burke's association of the revolution with the excesses of disembodied reason, drawing upon Herder's emphasis upon language, custom and culture and employing quite new standards of archival research, the most intellectually formidable form of this conservative reaction came from the so-called German Historical School of Law. The school became famous throughout Europe at the end of the Napoleonic wars, when its case against rational codification and, in particular, against the elaboration of a uniform legal code in the Germanic Confederation, was powerfully voiced by Karl von Savigny.[242] Members of the German Historical School were close to

241. In France, the attempt was made to discriminate between property legitimately acquired through labour and that, like serfdom or slavery, which had been the product of force or fraud. On these grounds, the Roman Law basis of the Code Napoléon was condemned since it condoned slavery. See Charles Comte, *Traité de la Propriété*, 2 vols., Paris, 1834; on Hodgskin and Spence, see G. Stedman Jones, 'Rethinking Chartism', in *Languages of Class*, Cambridge, 1983, pp. 134–57; on the beginnings of the Russian debate on serfdom, see F. Venturi, *The Roots of Revolution: A History of the Populist and Socialist Movements in Nineteenth-Century Russia*, London, 1960, chs. 1–3.

242. Frederick Karl von Savigny (1779–1861) was the acknowledged leader of the Historical School of Law. His magnum opus was a six-volume *History of Roman Law in the Middle Ages*, which appeared in 1815. From an aristocratic family, Savigny took the unusual step of entering the academy and became a professor at the new University of Berlin. Savigny remained prominent in conservative and government circles throughout the first half of the nineteenth century and between 1842 and 1848 served as the Prussian Minister of Justice.

His most famous work, *On the Vocation of Our Age for Legislation and Jurisprudence*, was a manifesto directed against an abstract liberal individualism presented as characteristic of the late-eighteenth-century enlightenment. In Savigny's alternative picture, every individual was necessarily a member of a family, a people, a state, just as each age of a nation was the continuation and development of all past ages. Thus history was not just a source of example, but the only path that leads to the 'true knowledge of our own condition'. See F. K. von Savigny, *On the Vocation of Our Age for Legislation and Jurisprudence*, tr. A. Hayward, London, 1831.

Compare Savigny's criticism of liberal rationalist jurisprudence in 1814 with that directed at revolutionary France by Joseph de Maistre in 1797. 'The Constitution of

'the Romantic School', with its idealization of the late medieval and pre-absolutist German Empire. They believed in the possibility of a gradual, peaceful and non-political path to peasant emancipation from feudalism opened up by the scholarship of professors armed with a 'learned knowledge of the law'. Savigny's manifesto was a response to the liberal reforming Heidelberg jurist, A. F. J. Thibaut, who had proposed the drafting of a general German legal code and had objected to the entrusting of the wellbeing of the German people to scholars. But Savigny had been equally important in undermining the credentials of private property as a transhistorical natural right.[243]

The intellectual origins of the Historical School predated the Revolution. The school emerged in Göttingen, the intellectual centre of the English-inclining Electorate of Hanover, in the 1780s, starting as a reaction against the stylized type of quasi-history used as illustration in the teaching of Roman Law. Indeed the standard manual used, that of Heineccius (1719), was also the one still relied upon in France at the time of the construction of the Napoleonic code. The founder of the school, Gustav Hugo, began with a translation and a commentary on the chapter on the history of Roman Law in Gibbon's recently published *Decline and Fall of the Roman Empire*. In place of the unchanging corpus of law assumed by Heineccius and other standard commentators, Gibbon showed how the law had adapted itself to changes in Roman society, and how conflicting arguments could be discerned behind its apparently apodictic legal formulations.[244]

1795, like its predecessors, was made for Man. But there is no such thing as Man in the world. In my lifetime I have seen Frenchmen, Italians, Russians etc; thanks to Montesquieu, I even know that *one can be Persian*. But as for *Man*. I declare that I have never in my life met him; if he exists, he is unknown to me.' J. de Maistre, *Considerations on France*, Cambridge, 1994, p. 53.

243. See J. Q. Whitman, *The Legacy of Roman Law in the German Romantic Era: Historical Vision and Legal Change*, Princeton, 1990, ch. 4.
244. E. Gibbon, *The History of the Decline and Fall of the Roman Empire*, 6 vols., 1776–88, ch. 44; on the history of the German Historical School of Law, see P. Stein, *Legal Evolution, The Story of an Idea*, Cambridge, 1980, ch. 3; Whitman, *The Legacy of Roman Law*, chs. 2 and 3; and see also H. Kantorowicz, 'Savigny and the Historical School of Law', *Law Quarterly Review*, July 1937, pp. 326–43.

The precocious publication in 1803 of Savigny's first work, *The Right of Possession*, had greatest relevance to the subsequent debate about property. This work, based on a detailed and historically informed study of Roman Law, argued that 'possession' was not a prior form of property, but a distinct legal form with its own quite separate history.[245] Savigny's findings were in turn greatly strengthened by the path-breaking writings of his friend in Berlin, Barthold Niebuhr, whose studies of the history of the Roman Republic were first made public in 1810–11. Of especial importance was Niebuhr's pioneering work on the *ager publicus*, the 'public land' captured from conquered people. During most of the history of the Roman Republic, Niebuhr revealed, this land was not private property. Legally, it was owned by the state and held in common for the use of all Roman citizens, each to hold no more than a certain acreage. This meant that the aim of the Gracchus brothers, in attempting to enforce the 'agrarian law', had not been 'to make a tyrannical onslaught upon the property of others', but to reclaim public land that had been taken over by patricians in violation of the Licinian law.[246]

245. There was an English translation of Savigny's book. See *Von Savigny's Treatise on Possession or the Ius Possessionis of the Civil Law*, tr. E. Perry, 6th edn, London, 1848. In the last twenty years of the eighteenth century, and especially after the outbreak of the French Revolution, there was growing legal controversy about the status of feudal obligations in the countryside. Customary obligations were increasingly challenged in court. Thibaut argued in 1802 that the Roman Law of possession did not support the claims of feudal lords that their demesnes were held by right of 'acquisitive prescription'. Such rights could be lost through prescription (i. e. disuse over a certain period of time), but not acquired, since feudal rights were not known to the Romans. Savigny's book was written as a reply to Thibaut. He agreed with Thibaut that feudal rights could be lost through prescription, but argued that the fundamental principle of the Roman Law of possession, when applied to German conditions, did establish a legal and constitutional basis, both for property rights and constitutional powers, which had been seized by feudal lords. See Whitman, *The Legacy of Roman Law*, pp. 181–4; M. H. Hoffheimer, *Eduard Gans and the Hegelian Philosophy of Law*, Dordrecht, 1995, p. 45.

246. See B. G. Niebuhr, *Lectures on Roman History*, tr. H. L. Chepmell and F. C. F. Demmler, 3 vols., London, 1855, vol. 1, pp. 249–72; vol. 2, pp. 269–81. The English translation is of lectures delivered at the University of Bonn in the winter of 1828–9.

B. G. Niebuhr (1776–1831), a civil servant and diplomat as well as historian, moved to Berlin in 1806 where he was involved in the 1807 emancipation of the serfs by royal

Not only did this research demonstrate that there was no straight-forward progression from first occupancy through possession to private property, but it also buttressed Savigny's point that possession was both fact and law and had nothing to do with private property either legally or historically. In his subsequent *Lectures on Roman History*, Niebuhr showed how the earliest political organization in Rome was based on 'gentes' – tribes or clans – and that property had been owned communally on a tribal basis. Later, with the consolidation of the city, tribal ownership changed into state ownership of the land. Citizenship was a condition for participating in ownership.[247]

At the same time, the work of Hugo and Pfister on early Germanic societies highlighted the contrast between antiquity, where citizenship and access to land had been centred on the city, and the new forms of political and social organization that emerged after the Germanic invasions, in which law and property were understood in terms of associations of people scattered over large territorial areas.

---

edict. Originally drawn into Roman agrarian history through a desire to refute Babeuf's notion of 'the agrarian law', Niebuhr aimed to show that the Romans had never used agrarian laws to undermine private ownership of the land. His interpretation of the *ager publicus* was also inspired by an East India Company expert on taxation, James Grant, an acquaintance of his during his stay in Scotland in 1798. In India, it was believed, the state owned the land, while peasants held the land in hereditary concessions for which they paid a fixed sum. This sum was collected by a state official, the *Zamindar*. In Bengal and elsewhere, however, the English found that the *Zamindar* de facto had come to be considered the owners of village land. Niebuhr believed that Roman patricians like the *Zamindar* had taken advantage of their control over public land to transform it into permanent and hereditary ownership.

In his *Right of Possession* Savigny had established the legal distinction between property and possession, but was unable to account for its origin. Niebuhr was initially unable to understand the difference in Roman Law between ownership of private land and permanent and hereditary occupation of public land. Putting their insights together in Berlin in 1810, they argued not only that the law of possession provided the best explanation for the hereditary control of the *ager publicus*, but also that this hereditary control of *ager publicus* provided the earliest instance and probably the model of the law of possession. See A. Momigliano, 'Niebuhr and the Agrarian Problems of Rome', in A. Momigliano (ed.), 'New Paths of Classicism in the Nineteenth Century', *History and Theory*, 21:4, Beiheft 21, 1982, pp. 3–15.

247. Niebuhr, *Lectures on Roman History*, vol. 1, pp. 159–83.

But in these Germanic societies as well, the right to land use remained dependent upon membership of the community and the preparedness to bear arms.[248]

In Niebuhr's *Lectures on Roman History* and his more general and comparative *Lectures on Ancient History*, also delivered in Bonn in the winter of 1829–30, the historical existence of three different forms of property ownership prior to modern commercial society – the oriental, the tribal and the classical – were discussed in some detail, and the fourth – the feudal – used as a frequent point of comparison.

In his discussion of the 'oriental' Niebuhr followed earlier discussions of oriental despotism, stressing that the sovereign was the real owner of the soil and the cultivator a mere tenant-at-will, who paid a certain proportion of the produce of the land he cultivated to the sovereign. However, he also released this theory from its narrowly 'asiatic' perspective. He wrote 'this arrangement, which bears a great resemblance to the possession of *ager publicus* among the Romans, is found in India, Persia, among the Carthaginians and therefore also in Phoenicia.'[249]

On the 'tribal', Niebuhr stressed its political centrality in early Roman history, but once again highlighted its similarity to other early forms of political organization.[250] He wrote:

I assume it as a certain fact that among the Romans the division of the

248. G. Hugo, *Lehrbuch eines civilistischen Cursus*, 5 vols., Berlin, 1832; J. C. Pfister, *Geschichte der Teutschen*, Hamburg, 1829. Marx's use of these sources has been documented in N. Levine, 'The German Historical School of Law and the Origins of Historical Materialism', *Journal of the History of Ideas*, July–Sept. 1987, pp. 431–51.

249. B. G. Niehbuhr, *Lectures on Ancient History from the earliest times to the taking of Alexandria by Octavianus*, tr. L. Schmitz, 3 vols., 1852, pp. 98–9.

250. In early Rome, 'the state was divided into a certain number of associations, each of which consisted of several families. These associations had among themselves their assemblies, their rights of inheritance etc., and especially their sanctuaries. Whoever belonged to them bequeathed these to his children; and wherever he might live, within or without the state, he was always deemed to belong to that association. Whoever, on the contrary, did not belong to it by right of birth, could only come in as an exception, if that association acknowledged him ... such an association is a clan, and by no means what we call a family, which implies an origin from a common root.' Niebuhr, *Lectures on Roman History*, vol. 1, pp. 157–8.

nation was into *gentes*, which were analogous to the gene (γενοσ) of the Greeks, and to the *Geschlechter* of our German forefathers.[251]

Even writing on the peculiarities of the Roman so-called 'agrarian law' Niebuhr placed the institution within a broader comparative perspective. He wrote:

The general notion of the Italian nations was this, that there is an indissoluble bond between the land and the right of citizenship; that every kind of ownership is derived from the state alone. The soil is merely the substratum on which the preconceived idea of the civil organization rests ... The political forms of the Romans have almost always an analogy in the Greek constitutions, and so has often the civil law; but with regard to the *ius agrarium* (the agrarian law) the Romans stand alone. The Greek state made conquests and founded colonies, but the *possessio agri publici* (the possession of public land) is unknown to that people.[252]

In place, therefore, of private property as a natural right or of a world naturally inhabited from the beginning by would-be 'absolute' proprietors, the German Historical School had uncovered a new past, during most of which the great bulk of mankind had lived in societies in which possession of the land was communal and conditional.

It should now be clear why Marx's early legal training mattered. As a law student in 1836–7, Marx had attended Savigny's lectures on the *Pandects*, and it is clear from a letter to his father in 1837 that he had read Savigny's *Right of Possession*.[253] It also seems certain that he would have been familiar with the controversy, which became public in 1839, between Savigny and the Hegelian law professor Eduard

251. Ibid., and see also Niebuhr, *Lectures on Ancient History*, vol. 1, pp. 221–2.

252. Niebuhr, *Lectures on Roman History*, vol. 1, pp. 252–3; On 'the feudal system', Niebuhr made only scattered remarks. He argued for example that in the Italian conception – that every kind of ownership of the soil was derived from the state alone – there was to be found 'great similarity' ... 'to the feudal system'. 'According to strict feudal law, there is no land whatever, but what has a liege lord. All fiefs derive from the prince as the lord paramount, and then follow the mesne tenures.' Ibid., p. 252.

253. K. Marx, 'Letter from Marx to his father in Trier', 10–11 November 1837', *MECW*, vol. 1, p. 15.

Gans precisely over the relationship between possession and right. Hostility between Gans and Savigny was deep, but muffled. Just as in France after 1815, censorship displaced political debate into ostensibly academic contention over rival views of national history, so in Germany debate over points of legal history came to substitute for the direct expression of political views. Thus fundamental political antagonisms were channelled into arguments about codification, possession and the character of Roman Law.

Gans, following Thibaut, considered that the study of law derived its validity from its coherence as a system of relations and obligations. The appeal of Roman law was of a body of substantive legal doctrine whose universality had emerged through time and across cultures, independently from local quirks of political power. His unfinished major work on the law of succession was designed to bring a systematic and universal order into a chaos of local jurisdictions, which arbitrarily favoured existing powers. Codification would reinforce the law's universality and marginalize the discretionary role played by a conservative professorial elite.

In his last work, 'On the basis of Possession' (1838), which was a direct attack on Savigny, Gans likened the Historical School's discovery of the roots of German law in unarticulated custom or tradition or in the particularities of late medieval practice to the minutiae of rabbinical scholarship. Gans particularly attacked Savigny's claim that the law of possession developed out of 'the fact' of possession. This, in Gans's view, was a confusion of natural and legal fact. 'Possession is no mere factum, and it does not arise *as law* by the circuitous path of *injustice*.' The legal rights of possession did not evolve out of actual possession, because legal rights could not derive from relationships that were purely natural. Legally, a right (possession) could not be based upon a wrong (wrongful dispossession). In other words, possession presupposed property rights and was not a mere exercise of domination over a thing.[254]

254. Eduard Gans (1798–1839), from an affluent Berlin Jewish family, was a student and disciple of Thibaut at Heidelberg and subsequently professorial colleague, follower and friend of Hegel in Berlin. Gans's career was intimately intertwined with the chequered course of Jewish emancipation in Prussia before 1848. In 1812, a

During these years it is not surprising that a young man anxious about 'the opposition between what is and what ought to be', and keen to identify law with universality and reason, should not have been attracted to Savigny's conservative brand of historicism. In an 1842 article on the Historical School of Law for the *Rheinische Zeitung*, Marx accused Hugo of 'a debauched frivolity', dwelling upon his qualified admission of slavery and his insistence upon the 'animal nature' of Man as his 'sole juristic distinguishing feature'. Equally, in 1843 he repeated his condemnation of 'a school that legitimates the baseness of today by the baseness of yesterday'.[255]

Hugo had argued from the beginning that law was part of history and not a branch of applied ethics. But it was only from the beginning of the 1840s that this criticism, which had so long been associated with the right, began to be echoed on the left. After 1830, particularly in the France of the July Monarchy, but also in England when seen through the eyes of Thomas Carlyle or Charles Dickens, a visible gap had begun to open up between society as it was defined by jurists and the material realities of social life as it was perceived to be experienced by the majority of the population.

---

government edict had opened academic positions to Jews. Thereafter, the status of the Jews became a major issue in the conflict between conservative-romantic and liberal-rational conceptions of the nation. Already forced to defend his family against anti-Semitic attack as a law student in Göttingen (a stronghold of the Historical School), Gans moved to Heidelberg, where Thibaut (and later Hegel) publicly defended Jews. In response to the increasingly conservative turn after the Carlsbad decrees in 1819, Gans and others founded the Union for the Culture and Science of Jews, whose aim was to reconcile Judaism with a universal conception of science and culture.

In 1822 he applied for the professorship of law in Berlin University. In response the king declared that Jews were no longer eligible. In 1825, he converted to Christianity, was appointed in Berlin in 1826 and became Hegel's closest companion. Savigny, who was also a professor in the Law Faculty, pushed to secure the reversal of Jewish emancipation throughout the 1820s and made vigorous efforts to prevent Gans's appointment. See Hoffheimer, *Eduard Gans*, pp. 41–6 and passim.

255. K. Marx, 'Letter from Marx to his father in Trier', *MECW*, vol. 1, p. 12; K. Marx, 'The Philosophical Manifesto of the Historical School of Law', *MECW*, vol. 1, p. 206; K. Marx, 'Contribution to the Critique of Hegel's *Philosophy of Law*. Introduction', *MECW*, vol. 3, p. 177.

Proudhon's shocking pronouncement that property was theft followed from his discovery that property was 'impossible' because it claimed to create something from nothing. In other words, it confirmed the claim of Savigny and his followers that, historically, right had derived from fact. Similarly, Marx's close scrutiny of the *Philosophy of Right* revealed that even Hegel had been prepared to descend to a crude positivism extolling the 'physical' (i.e. birth) in preference to 'reason', if that were required for a defence of monarchy and primogeniture.[256]

Once, therefore, he became to believe that 'law has just as little an independent history as religion', Marx could begin to appreciate the importance of the researches of the Historical School as one of the starting points of his own attempt to construct a theory of a society beyond private property and the division of labour. The historical record, which this school had revealed, did not suggest that there was any reason to assume that the history of forms of property would necessarily come to an end with commercial society or the establishment of private property as a universal natural right. What Marx referred to in 1859 as 'the modern bourgeois' form of property was only the last in a succession of forms of property that had accompanied the historical development of the productive forces.[257]

In 'The German Ideology' Marx followed very closely what Niebuhr had written about 'tribal property' and 'ancient communal and state property'. Similarly, he drew directly upon Hugo and Pfister in his account of 'feudal or estate property' and in his contrast between antiquity and the German military constitution of the middle ages.[258] But unlike Niebuhr or Hugo, who regarded these different types of property primarily as forms of political or military

256. Proudhon, *What is Property?*, p. 122; K. Marx, 'Contribution to the Critique of Hegel's *Philosophy of Law*', *MECW*, vol. 3, p. 33. Marx was criticizing Hegel's *Philosophy of Right*, para. 280.
257. K. Marx and F. Engels, 'The German Ideology', *MECW*, vol. 5, p. 91; K. Marx, 'A Contribution to the Critique of Political Economy. Preface', *MECW*, vol. 29, p. 263.
258. K. Marx and F. Engels, 'The German Ideology', *MECW*, vol. 5, pp. 32–5.

organization, Marx connected them with progressive stages in the development of the division of labour. Or, as he was to continue to maintain fourteen years later in his famous 1859 Preface to the *Critique of Political Economy*, as 'progressive epochs in the economic formation of society'.[259]

259. K. Marx, 'A Contribution to the Critique of Political Economy. Preface', *MECW*, vol. 29, p. 263. In the 'Preface', the forms listed were slightly different. Marx listed the 'asiatic, ancient, feudal and modern bourgeois modes of production'.

Marx's continuing interest in ancient and precapitalist forms of property was first highlighted in a collection of passages taken mainly from the Economic Manuscripts of 1857–8 (the so-called *Grundrisse*), edited and introduced by Eric Hobsbawm. See Karl Marx, *Precapitalist Economic Formations*, ed. E. J. Hobsbawm, London, 1964. The evidence that Hobsbawm assembled is now available in the complete works. See K. Marx, 'Forms preceding Capitalist Production' in 'Outlines of the Critique of Political Economy', *MECW*, vol. 28, pp. 399–439. And see also Marx's letter to Engels, 25 March 1868.

In the Marxist tradition little attempt was made to connect Marx's interest in precapitalist societies with his theory of communism. Instead, these manuscripts were treated as evidence of the rigorous and scholarly procedures attending Marx's elaboration of a materialist science of history. It was also considered important, doctrinally, to minimize Marx's commitment to the politically unacceptable 'asiatic mode of production'.

Once decoupled from his theory of communism, however, the persistence of Marx's interest in this area makes little sense. A clue from Marx himself is provided in a letter to Engels. Writing in 1868 about the development of interest in precapitalist forms after 1789, Marx noted that after the first romantic and medievalist reaction to the Revolution, the second reaction had been 'to look beyond the Middle Ages into the primitive age of every people – and this corresponds to the socialist tendency, though these learned men have no idea they are connected with it.' See Marx to Engels, 25 March 1868, *MECW*, vol. 42, p. 557.

The extent to which Marx and Engels considered that their approach to the history of property had been vindicated by subsequent research, particularly that of Maurer and Morgan, is indicated by Engels' second note to the English 1888 edition of the *Manifesto*, see p. 219; and see also his essay, 'The Origin of the Family, Private Property and the State. In the light of the Researches of Lewis H. Morgan' (1884), *MECW*, vol. 26, pp. 129–277.

(iii) The Contemporary Discussion of Communism

The third body of literature drawn upon by Marx in putting together his new theory was of course the contemporary discussion about communism itself, or more accurately in France at least, 'community'. But before considering the issues involved here, it is first necessary to dispose of the pretend-debate described in the third section of the *Manifesto*, 'Socialist and Communist Literature'.

The method of approach adopted in this section set the tone for countless polemics in the later Marxist tradition. The naming and shaming of opponents by affixing to them sandwich-boards proclaiming their social identity proved particularly contagious. Henceforth, battles were increasingly waged not between individuals or even ideas, but between classes or social fractions and their standard-bearers – 'orthodox Marxists', 'anarchists', 'reformists', 'possibilists' and 'revisionists'; or, in the twentieth century, in still shriller terms, 'renegades', 'lackeys' and 'running dogs'. From the very beginning, these designations were wilful and mutable. In this communist revival of the medieval morality play, Proudhon changed costume three times in three years. In act one, he appeared as the author of 'the scientific manifesto of the French proletariat'; in act two, as champion of 'the petty bourgeois ideal'; and in the final act, as archetypal spokesman of 'conservative or bourgeois socialism'. The transformation was all the more remarkable given that the lines voiced in the last two acts were exactly the same.[260]

Equally lasting and scarcely less misleading was the impact made by this polemic upon the subsequent understanding of the intellectual development of socialism. Through its alchemy, the minutiae of sectarian difference were rearranged into a broad historical narrative, in which the views of former mentors or allies – Owenites, Fourierists, Saint-Simonians, Sismondi, Considerant, Proudhon,

---

260. K. Marx and F. Engels, 'The Holy Family', *MECW*, vol. 4, p. 41; K. Marx, 'The Poverty of Philosophy', *MECW*, vol. 6, p. 190; K. Marx and F. Engels, *The Communist Manifesto*; both the last two designations refer to Proudhon's *Philosophie de la Misère* (The Philosophy of Poverty).

Feuerbach and Hess – reappeared as the bearers of superseded positions from the past; their views of necessity discarded in the forward march of the newly invented subject of the drama, 'the proletariat'. But 'the proletariat' was only the ostensible subject of the story. What it provided was a fairly thick smokescreen, behind which was to be found a somewhat muffled and selective form of intellectual and political autobiography.

The real questions involved in the mid 1840s debate over communism received little mention in the *Manifesto*. In particular, it would be quite impossible to detect the crucial role played by Proudhon in initiating the search for a modern social form that combined liberty and community. Perhaps one reason for the shiftiness and irritation, which always seemed to accompany Marx's references to Proudhon after 1845–6, was an uneasy awareness of how much he had actually owed to him, both in his abandonment of a rationalist conception of law after 1842 and in the formation of his initial view of communism.

In *What is Property?* Proudhon had condemned not only property, but also 'community' for 'the iron yoke it fastens on the will, the moral torture it inflicts on the conscience, the pious and stupid uniformity it enforces'. He had also attributed the defects of community to the continuing dominion of private property. Referring to the Jesuits of Paraguay and to the babouvists, he wrote, 'the deliberate negation of property is conceived under the direct influence of the prejudice of property' and concluded that 'it is property that is to be found at the root of all communistic theories'. His remedy was a 'third social form', 'the synthesis of community and property, we shall call liberty'. In this form would be combined the freedom associated with property and the harmony associated with community.[261]

261. Proudhon, *What is Property?*, pp. 196, 212. Misleadingly, both the Benjamin Tucker translation (1890) and that of Kelley and Smith (1994) translate 'communauté' as 'communism'. This loses some of the sense of Proudhon's term, which refers as much to the classical, Christian or early modern notion of 'community of goods' (*communio bonorum* or *Gütergemeinschaft*) as to contemporary movements. Proudhon in his first *Mémoire* never uses any term other than 'communauté'. I have therefore amended it to 'community'. Marx, probably following Von Stein, uses the term *Kommunismus* from the beginning. See 'Ein Briefwechsel von 1843' (Marx to Ruge, Sept. 1843), *Deutsch-Französische Jahrbücher*, Paris, 1844 (repr. Leipzig, 1973), p. 126.

The immediate impact made upon Marx by Proudhon was evident even in his contributions to the *Rheinische Zeitung*. In 1842, Marx echoed Proudhon in questioning the singling out of peasants for the 'theft' of dead wood: 'if every violation of property without distinction, without a more exact definition is termed theft, will not all private property be theft?' At the beginning of 1843, he appeared to endorse Proudhon's call for the equality of wages. Later in that year, it was his reading of *What is Property?* that enabled him to insist that communism and the abolition of private property were not the same thing. In 1844 his dismissal of existing forms of communism again closely followed Proudhon's text. Marx like Proudhon considered that a communism based upon 'envy' and 'levelling down', since it negated 'the personality of Man in every sphere', was 'but the logical expression of private property'. It was also Proudhon's argument that set Marx unequivocally against any notion of communism as the positive community of goods. This 'crude communism . . . which wants to set itself up as the positive community system' was only another 'manifestation of the vileness of private property'.[262]

But if Marx rejected communism as 'positive community', what other sort of communism could there be? Here again Proudhon may unwittingly have inspired Marx to investigate the possibilities of a different idea of communism. For in *What is Property?*, Proudhon makes reference several times to the notion of communism as 'negative community'. This 'association in a simple mode' was 'the necessary goal and the original aspiration of sociability'. For Man, it was 'the first phase of civilization'.

In this state of society which the jurists have called negative community,

---

262. K. Marx, 'Debates on the Law on Thefts of Wood', (*Rheinische Zeitung*, 25 Oct. 1842), *MECW*, vol. 1, p. 228; K. Marx, '*Red. Notiz über Proudhon zu einer Korrespondenz aus Berlin über Steuern*' (Editorial Note on Proudhon relating to a report from Berlin on taxes), *Rheinische Zeitung*, 7 Jan. 1843 and reprinted in *Marx–Engels Gesamt-Ausgabe*, 1,1 (2), pp. 141–2; and see Gregory, 'Marx's and Engels' Knowledge of French Socialism', pp. 162–3; 'Letters from *Deutsch-Französische Jahrbücher*' (Marx to Ruge, Sept. 1843), *MECW*, vol. 3, p. 143; K. Marx, 'Economic and Philosophical Manuscripts of 1844', *MECW*, vol. 3, pp. 295–6.

Man draws near to Man and shares with him the fruits of the field and the milk and flesh of animals.

Proudhon associated the idea with the seventeenth-century founder of modern natural law, Hugo Grotius.

Originally, all things were common and undivided; they were the property of all ... Grotius tells us how this original community ended in ambition and cupidity, how the age of gold was followed by the age of iron, etc., so that property was based first on war and conquest, then on treaties and contracts.[263]

Proudhon himself, however, set no store by this idea. 'What kind of reasoning is it', he reproached Grotius, 'to seek the origin of a right, said to be natural, anywhere but in nature?' Proudhon questioned

how the equality of conditions, having once existed in nature, could afterwards occupy a state outside nature. What was the cause of such degeneration?

263. Proudhon, *What is Property?*, pp. 195, 45. Grotius himself did not employ the term 'negative community'. It was introduced forty years later by his follower, Samuel Pufendorf, as an elaboration and formalization of Grotius's account.

The idea of connecting the seventeenth-century natural-law conception of 'negative community' with nineteenth-century notions of 'community' or 'communism' owes much to the compelling argument put forward by Istvan Hont. See I. Hont, 'Negative Community: the Natural Law Heritage from Pufendorf to Marx', Workshop in the John M. Olin Program in the History of Political Culture, University of Chicago, 1989. Particularly valuable is the clear distinction he makes between a discourse based upon need and a discourse based upon rights. It will be argued here that although the similarities in the structure of argument are very suggestive, the linkages are likely to have been indirect. See also Hont, 'The Language of Sociability and Commerce', in Pagden (ed.), *The Languages of Political Theory*, pp. 253–76; O. Gierke, *Natural Law and the Theory of Society 1500–1800*, ed. and tr. E. Barker, Cambridge, 1934.

Grotius's account of this first human epoch is found in H. Grotius, *De Jure Belli ac Pacis* (Of the Law of War and Peace), 1625, Bk 2, ch. 2, paras. 1–11; Pufendorf's definition of 'negative community' is to be found in S. Pufendorf, *De Jure naturae et gentium* (On the Law of Nature and Nations), 1672, Bk 4, ch. 4, para 2. No modern English edition of Grotius exists. But see the 1738 edition, *The Rights of War and Peace*, ed. Jean Barbeyrac. For Pufendorf, see S. Pufendorf, *On the Law of Nature and Nations*, 2 vols., vol. 2, tr. C. H. and W. A. Oldfather, Oxford, 1934.

Proudhon was sceptical of 'community, whether positive or negative it matters little'. He associated 'negative community' with a 'spontaneous' and 'instinctual' stage of mankind before Man began to 'produce'. At that stage, negative community gave way to positive community and reasoning taught men that if equality was a necessary condition of society, community was the first kind of slavery.

Unlike the jurists, who believed that property and political authority began together, Proudhon thought that 'royalty dates from the creation of Man; it existed in the age of negative community'. His picture, insofar as it was historical at all, was closer to that of radical *philosophes* such as Condorcet or to the *idéologues* than to political economists and Scottish conjectural historians.

Man has but one nature, constant and unalterable: he follows it through instinct, breaks with it through reflection, and returns to it through judgement.

If historical development contained a principle of hope, it was to be found not in the succession of modes of subsistence elaborated by natural lawyers and conjectural historians, but in the growth of knowledge and science that could finally deliver mankind from the oppression of property and political authority.

According to his German admirer, Karl Grün, in a rough and unscientific way occupation of the land had originally presupposed a principle of equality and even inheritance had been justified as a means to safeguard the entitlements of warriors whose defence of cultivators had precluded them from personal cultivation of the soil. But jurists, instead of adjusting the law to social need, had simply proceeded from 'the brute facts' of land holding as they had found them among uncivilized nations and turned them into forms of property. The French Revolution had not changed this situation, since it had been based upon the sovereignty of the people rather than the sovereignty of law and reason. The people had continued to follow the practice of the old regime and Roman Law, hence the division between wealth and misery in the present. But politics would become a science and 'the function of the legislator' would be reduced to 'the methodical search for truth'. Proudhon hoped that interaction between 'community' and 'property' might produce 'liberty', the 'third social form', but he certainly did not associate this synthesis with a vision of 'negative community'.[264]

'Negative community' had originally been devised to answer a question about the origin of private property and rights. Seventeenth-century arguments about the origins of property proceeded from Genesis and the scholastic tradition, according to which God had given the earth to mankind for use in common. The aim of Grotius and his successors had been to find a way between two reiterated seventeenth-century positions: on the one hand, those who like the Levellers argued that this gift meant that the land should remain in common use for ever and therefore that private property was illegitimate; on the other, those who, like the royalist political theorist Sir Robert Filmer, argued that God had given the earth to Adam – one man and his legitimate heirs – and therefore that there had been private property from the beginning.

In contrast to these two immutable and incompatible versions of the natural law, Grotius, Pufendorf and (in a different way) Locke constructed developmental schemas, capable of explaining the

264. Proudhon, *What is Property?*, pp. 45, 57, 205, 204, 208, 211–14; K. Grün, *Die soziale Bewegung in Frankreich und Belgien, Briefe und Studien* (The Social Movement in France and Belgium, Letters and Studies), Darmstadt, 1845, pp. 416–23. Proudhon was wary of any association with the word community. In a letter he wrote to Marx on 17 May 1846, he argued that rather than turning the theory of property against property in order to engender community like the Germans, he would for the moment confine himself to an appeal to liberty and equality. See groupe Fresnes-Antony de la Fédération anarchiste (ed.), *P.J. Proudhon, Philosophie de la Misère, K. Marx Misère de la Philosophie, Textes Intégraux*, Les Imprimeurs Libres, Paris, vol. 3, p. 327. Proudhon's notebooks show that he read and annotated part of Grotius's *De jure belli ac pacis* in January 1840. He himself estimated that he had not read more than one sixth of Grotius's treatise, the rest being too remote from his topic. See P. Hauptmann, *Pierre-Joseph Proudhon, Sa Vie et Sa Pensée (1809–1849)*, Paris, 1982, p. 249. There is no record of him reading Pufendorf. In *What is Property?*, Proudhon refers to 'the state of society which the jurists have called negative community' (p. 195), and several of the texts that he did consult contained résumés of the idea. See for example, Toullier, *Le Droit Civil Français*, vol. 2, para. 64, p. 26; or see criticism of the idea in Comte, *Traité de la Propriété*, pp. 356–9.

change that had occurred between God's original gift of the earth in common and the predominance of private property in the present.[265] God's gift did not mean that the first men practised 'positive community', nor did it mean that they possessed the rights of proprietors in a later age. What Pufendorf was to call 'negative community' better described this first age of mankind, in which Man roamed over the earth as he still now roamed over the sea, innocent of *any* notion of property, whether private or communal.[266]

In this primeval age of the history of mankind, according to the natural law theory, the concern of Man was the direct and individual satisfaction of need. The predominant relation was that between person and thing; relations between person and person were relatively unimportant. Generally, the satisfaction of need – archetypally, the picking of acorns and other fruit in the great primeval forest – did not involve others, and there was no correlative duty on the part of others to aid in the satisfaction of individual need. There were thus no rights and no property. For rights and property concerned relations between persons. Rights implied correlative duties on the part of others not to infringe them and property implied an agreement on the part of others that such property be respected. In the first age of mankind, both were unnecessary. Man lived by hunting and gathering, by keeping flocks or by engaging in rudimentary forms of agriculture. Social interaction was slight, social cooperation occasional and, most important of all, there was an abundance of resources relative to Man's needs.

Rights only became necessary when needs increased and popu-

265. The extent to which Locke can be included in a 'negative community' conception of the first ages of Man is far less clear. See James Tully, *A Discourse on Property: John Locke and his Adversaries*, Cambridge, 1980.

266. Grotius's theory of primitive communism/negative community was originally the offshoot of an attempt to establish the right of the Dutch to the free navigation of the sea together with the right to hunt or gather its products (*Mare Liberum*, 1609). Grotius likened this right to the original ability of mankind to roam the earth to gather its fruits, to hunt wild animals or pasture flocks, before growing population and encroaching scarcity of resources led to the division of the land, first between nations and then between families. R. Tuck, *Natural Rights Theories: Their Origins and Development*, Cambridge, 1979, ch. 3.

lation grew. At that stage, the satisfaction of need began to require cooperation and the beginnings of a division of labour. Forms of scarcity appeared and, as needs grew more diverse, more objects of consumption began to be socially produced. This meant that each contributor to the production process had to be apportioned an appropriate share of the product, necessitating the formation of a state as the institutional guardian of the rights of those involved and as an agency capable of limiting greed and violations of property and person.[267]

Whatever the precise combination of elements that inspired Marx's theory, what is striking is the extent to which his picture of communism, laconic and schematic though it was, reproduced the characteristic emphases of this natural-law approach: its juxtaposition between needs and rights, its conjunction of communism with the man 'rich in needs', its identification of rights with the allocation of potentially contested resources in an environment of scarcity and its association of rights and justice with the political state. Marx consistently rejected all theories of communism based upon rights. Rights, justice and the state went together. Communism, on the other hand, would not be about 'the government of men', but about 'the administration of things'. Communism or socialism concerned a society in which the 'self-activity' of individuals would be directed towards the satisfaction of need. That Marx stuck to this vision is clear from his 'Critique of the Gotha Programme' written in 1875. There he evoked again 'a higher phase of communist society'.

Only then can the narrow horizon of bourgeois right be crossed in its entirety and society inscribe on its banners: from each according to his ability, to each according to his needs.[268]

Whether Marx made conscious use of the natural-law conception

267. On the importance of the so-called 'correlativity thesis' in separating out a new and more strictly defined conceptual vocabulary of rights from a more basic and aboriginal vocabulary of need, see Hont, 'Negative Community', pp. 24–9; Tuck, *Natural Rights*, pp. 159–60.
268. K. Marx, 'Critique of the Gotha Programme', *MECW*, vol. 24, p. 87.

of primitive communism is not known. Apart from Proudhon, there were many other channels through which Marx could have become aware of such an account.[269] The writings of jurists offer one possibility. The eighteenth-century juristic tradition in Germany ceased to build upon the conjectural history sketched by seventeenth-century natural lawyers.[270] But knowledge of that tradition did not disappear; it remained preserved in frozen form. Both Heineccius and the German rationalist philosopher, Christian Wolff, for example, made reference to the 'negative community' theory.[271]

Another obvious thread connecting nineteenth-century theories

---

269. Although a large number of Marx's notebooks survive from the period 1840–48, they cannot be used as a comprehensive record of what he read. To give some examples, it is clear from the 1844 manuscripts that Marx had read or at least consulted the work of the French Christian Socialist Constantin Pecqueur, yet there is no record in his notebooks. Similarly, a number of his writings suggest that he was familiar with the works of the Saint-Simonians and of Fourier. But again, there is no trace of this in the notebooks. He also showed some awareness of the writings of Charles Comte, whose *Traité de la Propriété* explicitly refers to the idea of negative community. But whether he read him or simply read about him is unclear, and again the notebooks offer no help. Similarly, in his criticism of Karl Grün Marx referred to the work of the French jurist and enthusiast for Savigny Eugène Lerminier, but no record of reading exists. The archive catalogue of the International Institute for Social History in Amsterdam lists 39 notebooks covering the period 1840–48. For Marx's references to Pecqueur, see K. Marx, 'Economic and Philosophical Manuscripts of 1844', *MECW*, vol. 3, pp. 243, 254. For Marx's discussions of the Saint-Simonians and Fourier, see K. Marx, 'Draft of an Article on Friedrich List's Book *Das nationale System der politischen Oekonomie*', *MECW*, vol. 4, pp. 282–3; K. Marx, 'Karl Grün: *Die Soziale Bewegung in Frankreich und Belgien*, or the Philosophy of True Socialism', ch. 4 of 'The German Ideology', *MECW*, vol. 5, pp. 493–519; for the reference to Lerminier, ibid., p. 489. For Marx's references to Charles Comte, see in particular K. Marx and F. Engels, 'The Holy Family', *MECW*, vol. 4, pp. 44–6.

270. See Stein, *Legal Evolution*, p. 51. The apparent absence of a historical dimension in the teaching of Roman law condemned by the German historical school, or the inconsequentiality and abstraction of natural right defences of private property exposed by Proudhon in France, were specifically the result of eighteenth-century developments. In particular these were the concentration upon a-priori legal and political reasoning, encouraged for different reasons both by Thommasius and Wolff in Germany, and the deliberately anti-historical reading of rights and law in revolutionary France.

271. C. Wolff, *Jus naturae methodo scientifica pertractatum*, Frankfurt, 1764, part 2, para. 104; J. G. Heineccius, *De Jure Naturae*, bk 1, para. 233.

of historical development with seventeenth-century debates on natural law was the eighteenth-century Scottish Enlightenment. An extraordinary galaxy of writers and thinkers, including David Hume, Adam Smith, Adam Ferguson, Henry Home (Lord Kames), William Robertson and John Millar, had contributed towards the elaboration of the 'Four-Stages Theory' of the development of society. These characteristic and shared preoccupations appear to have dated back to the beginning of the eighteenth century, when an edition of Pufendorf had become the standard textbook in moral philosophy in Scottish universities.[272] But attempts to establish a direct link between the young Marx and the conjectural histories of the Scots have so far failed. Evidence of Adam Smith's interest in the 'Four-Stages Theory' of history and his interest in natural law were most visible in his unpublished 'Lectures on Jurisprudence'. *The Wealth of Nations*, which Marx studied in some detail, did not make direct reference to these questions. There was also one reference to Adam Ferguson's *Essay on the History of Civil Society*, but this occurred in 1847, by which time the shape of Marx's theory was already set.[273]

It is of course possible that this quest for a connecting link is misguided, that it is an attempt to resolve a non-existent problem. The names of Grotius and Pufendorf are now fairly obscure. But in the 1840s they were well known across educated Europe, particularly to anyone with the slightest acquaintance with jurisprudence. Could Marx not therefore simply have read these authorities for himself? The possibility cannot be ruled out. But even if he did in the course of his legal studies, it seems unlikely that they directly could have provided the inspiration for his theory. By the 1830s and 1840s, the theories of seventeenth-century jurists were well over a century old,

272. This was the 1718 edition by Gershom Carmichael of Pufendorf's *De Officio Hominis et Civis juxta Legem Naturalem*. A modern translation of this text exists. See S. Pufendorf, *On the Duty of Man and Citizen*, ed. J. Tully, Cambridge, 1991. On the importance of Carmichael's edition in eighteenth-century Scotland, see Moore and Silverthorne, 'Gershom Carmichael' in Hont and Ignatieff (eds.), *Wealth and Virtue*, pp. 73–88.

273. K. Marx, 'The Poverty of Philosophy', *MECW*, vol. 6, p. 181.

and appeal to such authorities had largely become rhetorical or ornamental.[274] It is improbable that Marx would have paid such close attention to what by then had become an academic and old-fashioned tradition of legal learning, let alone put it to such startling use. More likely, Marx's recuperation of the characteristic emphases of this tradition was indirect. In other words, propositions derived originally from natural law reached him, not in pristine form, but as different and disconnected strands of an inheritance dispersed in an array of social and political debates occasioned by the French Revolution and its aftermath.

The employment of a dynamic and historically developmental conception of need within political economy was one clear example of the indirect inheritance of a natural-law conception. In this case, even without direct contact with the jurists or the Scots Marx would certainly have absorbed the underlying conception of the development of human needs that underpinned conjectural history through his close reading of Hegel's section on 'the system of needs' in the *Philosophy of Right*.[275] Here also lay one of the fundamental differences between Proudhon and Marx. Proudhon had read Grotius and other jurists, and he had begun to engage with the political economists. Yet the most obvious practical proposal associated with his 'third social form' – the equalization of wages – was the result of his preoccupation with the demands of justice rather than the satisfaction of need. From Marx's perspective, Proudhon abolished

274. See for example the Chartist leader, Bronterre O'Brien, 'Read Paine, Locke, Puffendorf, and a host of others and they will tell you that labour is the only genuine property', *True Scotsman*, 6 July 1839; or Etienne Cabet, 'Listen to the *Baron* of Puffendorf, professor of natural law in Germany . . . who in his *Law of Nature and Nations* . . . proclaims *natural equality, fraternity*, the primitive *community of goods*; and who recognizes that *property* is a human institution; that it results from an agreed dividing up to assure to each and especially to workers, perpetual possession, undivided or divided; and that consequently, the present inequality of fortune is an injustice which only draws in other inequalities through *the insolence of the rich* and the *cowardice of the poor*.' Cabet, p. 486.

275. *Elements of the Philosophy of Right*, paras. 189–208. This first section of the concept of 'civil society' relied heavily upon Hegel's detailed reading of Smith's *Wealth of Nations* and Sir James Steuart's *Inquiry into the Principles of Political Oeconomy* (1767) in Frankfurt at the end of the 1790s.

'economic estrangement *within* economic estrangement'.[276] The aspect of the theory most crucial to Marx was absent from Proudhon's argument. Because he associated the end of political authority with intellectual rather than economic progress, he showed no interest in abundance or its relationship to the satisfaction of each according to his need.

The use of a historical conception of property and of the state was yet another example of the indirect impact of the natural-law approach. The first form of socialism to which Marx had originally been introduced in his teenage years by his future father-in-law, Ludwig Westphalen, was that of Saint-Simon.[277] From at least 1817, Saint-Simon and his followers worked with a historically relative conception of property. The later *Doctrine of Saint-Simon* summed up their view by stating that 'this great word "property" has represented something different at every epoch of history'. Furthermore, Saint-Simon himself never connected his ideas of social and political reorganization with notions of positive community, and he made no appeal to natural rights. His conception of modern society and economy was based in large part upon the political economist Jean-Baptiste Say, the main French follower of Adam Smith. Like others of his generation in the 1810s and 1820s, Saint-Simon built his social theory upon the contrast between the ancient dependence upon war, conquest and plunder, and modern independence produced by peace and the progress of industry.[278] Like the natural lawyers and the Scottish conjectural historians, Saint-Simon and his followers looked upon the state as a historical product. It had been designed for the warlike infancy of mankind. But in the peaceful and industrious world of associated producers, the need for the state

---

276. K. Marx and F. Engels, 'The Holy Family', *MECW*, vol. 4, p. 43.
277. W. Blumenberg, *Karl Marx: An Illustrated Biography*, London, 1972, p. 15.
278. Iggers (tr. and ed.), *The Doctrine of Saint-Simon*, pp. 116–17. On Saint-Simon's debt to Say, see in particular J. B. Say, 'De l'indépendance née chez les modernes des progrès de l'industrie', *Traité D'Economie politique*, 5th edn, Paris, 1826, vol. 2, pp. 295–301; followers of Say believed that the French Revolution had witnessed the overthrow of a state based upon 'force and fraud' (the privileged place accorded to the unproductive aristocracy and clergy during the *ancien régime*) and the emergence of a society based upon 'industry' or work.

would recede. The government of men would give way to the administration of things.[279]

What then of the conception of communism itself? In the original seventeenth-century conception of primitive communism, the absence of property, rights and the state had been treated as a consequence of a primeval state of abundance in relation to human needs. Here again, if there was a connection it was indirect. Marx was imaginatively seized by the idea of equating communism with abundance, not because of his acquaintance with the seventeenth-century debate, but because the question had reappeared after 1789. Inspired by the heady optimism of the early years of the Revolution, Godwin in England and Condorcet in France had raised the possibility of a society based on abundance; and it was in response to these radical speculations that Malthus had first introduced his principle of population in 1798.[280]

But the question of abundance did not go away. It became one of the starting points of the new 'sciences' of 'utopian Socialism' at the beginning of the nineteenth century. In England, not only was Owen a disciple of Godwin, but establishing the possibility of abundance remained a central preoccupation of Owenite socialism, especially from the time of Malthus's attack upon Robert Owen in the 1817 edition of *Essay on the Principle of Population*. In France, Fourier wrote

279. This was Engels' later gloss upon what Saint-Simon had written. 'The government of persons is replaced by the administration of things . . . The state is not "abolished". *It dies out*' (in the original German, '*stirbt ab*' or 'withers away', as older translations have it). F. Engels, 'Anti-Dühring. Herr Dühring's Revolution in Science', *MECW*, vol. 25, p. 268.

The original statement is to be found in 'Catéchisme des Industriels', a text Saint-Simon co-authored with Auguste Comte. 'The human race has been destined by its organization to live in society. It has been called first to live under the *governmental* regime. It has been destined to pass from the governmental or military regime to the administrative or industrial regime, once sufficient progress has been made in the positive sciences and in industry.' *Oeuvres de Claude-Henri de Saint-Simon*, Paris, 1966, vol. 4 (1er Cahier), p. 87.

280. See W. Godwin, *An Enquiry Concerning Political Justice*, ed. I. Kramnick, Harmondsworth, 1973; Marquis de Condorcet, *Sketch for a Historical Picture of the Progress of the Human Mind* (1794), London, 1955; T. R. Malthus, *An Essay on the Principle of Population*, London, 1798.

of a new kind of economic crisis, which he called '*crises pléthoriques*'. These 'plethoric crises' were the result not of scarcity but of overproduction. This theme was eloquently elaborated during the economic depression of 1842–3 in Thomas Carlyle's evocation in *Past and Present* of an England of 'gold walls and full barns', in which 'in the midst of plethoric plenty, the people perish'.[281]

This picture of misery in the midst of abundance was in turn reproduced in Engels' 1843 'Outlines of a Critique of Political Economy', an essay that relied heavily upon the criticisms of Malthus by the Owenite lecturer John Watts.[282] Soon after, Marx also learnt about the progress of modern industry in England when he met and began his collaboration with Frederick Engels in Paris in the summer of 1844. Thereafter, this vision of abundance could be placed at the centre of a theory of the imminent end of private property and the return of Man to himself.

Finally, it is important to remember that, even apart from the words of the book of Genesis, it was not necessary to have read the Jurists to have some conception of the association of primitive communism with abundance. Rather, both the jurists and Marx after them were reworking a theme that had been well known since the ancients and invoked afresh at the end of the Napoleonic Wars. In 1814, in a proposal for *The Reorganization of European Society*, Saint-Simon announced,

the imagination of the poets placed the Golden Age in the cradle of mankind, in the ignorance and brutality of early times. It is rather the iron age that should be relegated there. The Golden Age of the human species is not behind us, it is before us.[283]

For the educated classes of early nineteenth-century Europe, reference to 'the golden age' did not simply evoke a vague and unspecific notion of good times. It referred to particular works of ancient poetry, especially Hesiod, Vergil and Ovid. Most famous of all was

281. T. Carlyle, *Past and Present*, ed. R. Altick, New York, 1977, p. 7.
282. See Claeys, *Machinery, Money and the Millennium*, pp. 166–79.
283. C. H. de Saint-Simon (with Augustin Thierry 'his pupil'), '*De la Réorganisation de la Société Européenne*', *Oeuvres de Saint-Simon*, Paris, 1966, vol. 1, p. 248.

Book One of Ovid's *Metamorphoses*, for hundreds of years 'one of the most popular schoolbooks in Western Europe'.[284] The last word on the sources of Marx's communism should therefore be left to Ovid.

> The Golden Age was first; when Man yet new,
> No rule but uncorrupted Reason knew:
> And, with a Nature bent, did Good pursue
> Unforc'd by Punishment, unaw'd by Fear,
> His words were simple, and his Soul sincere:
> Needless was written Law, where none opprest:
> The Law of Man was written in his Breast:
> No suppliant Crowds before the Judge appear'd,
> No court erected yet, nor Cause was heard:
> But all was safe, for Conscience was their Guard.
>
> * * *
>
> No Walls were yet; nor Fence, nor Mote, nor Mound,
> Nor Drum was heard, nor Trumpet's angry sound:
> Nor Swords were forg'd; but void of Care and Crime,
> The soft Creation slept away their time.
> The teeming Earth, yet guiltless of the Plough,
> And unprovok'd, did fruitful stores allow:
> Content with Food, which Nature freely bred,
> On Wildings, and on Strawberries they fed;
> Cornels and Bramble-berries gave the rest,
> And falling Acorns furnish't out a Feast.
> The Flow'rs unsown, in Fields and Meadows reign'd:
> And Western Winds immortal Spring maintain'd
> In following Years, the bearded Corn ensu'd,
> From Veins of Vallies, Milk and Nectar broke;
> And Honey sweating through the pores of Oak.[285]

284. F. E. Manuel and F. P. Manuel, *Utopian Thought in the Western World*, Oxford, 1979, p. 74.
285. S. Garth (ed.) *Ovid's Metamorphoses in fifteen books translated by the most eminent hands*, London, 1717, bk I, p. 5. This translation was by John Dryden. For an alternative translation, see T Hughes, *Tales from Ovid*, London 1997, pp. 8–10.

12. *Conclusion*

It is now, therefore, possible to answer the question raised at the beginning of this introduction: why did the *Manifesto* devote so much space to a panegyric extolling the achievements of the bourgeoisie? It was because the bourgeoisie was driving the world to the threshold of a new epoch of relative abundance in which rights, justice, labour, private property and the political state could be left behind, and the world could again become open to every form of human activity as it once had been in primeval time. What Engels had written about England in 1844 was not, as Hess and Engels himself had first believed, a social crisis peculiar to England, as politics were peculiar to France and philosophy to Germany. It was rather a portent of the imminent transformation of the human race.

The prospect was sketched most fully in 'The German Ideology'. Communism would only be possible as 'the act of the dominant peoples "all at once" and simultaneously'. It would presuppose 'the universal development of productive forces and the world inter-course bound up with them'. These conditions were now being fulfilled. The growth of large-scale industry and machinery had 'called into existence the third period of private property since the Middle Ages'. It had produced 'world history' for the first time, made natural science subservient to capital, taken from the division of labour 'the last semblance of its natural character, resolved all natural relations into money relations'. It had created the modern large industrial cities, completed the victory of town over country and produced a mass of productive forces for which private property had become 'a fetter'. Large-scale industry based upon the 'automatic system' had 'created everywhere the same relations between the classes of society' and therefore destroyed 'the peculiar features between different nationalities'.[286]

There was no further need to worry about awakening the inherent sociality of Feuerbach's Man, for 'the existence of revolutionary ideas in a particular period' presupposed 'the existence of a revolutionary class'. Communism would mean 'the transformation of labour into self-activity'. It would replace the state as 'the illusory community', which always 'took on an independent existence' in relation to the individuals who composed it, with 'a real community' in which 'individuals obtain their freedom in and through their association'.[287]

Such, in short, were the components of Marx's conception of communism in the years leading up to the *Manifesto*: first, an apocalyptic reading of Smith's theory of the division of labour, in which the progress of commercial society had turned towards self-destruction; second, the assumption that the modern bourgeois form of private property, like the previous forms of property discussed by the Historical School, was ephemeral; and third, the assumption that modern industry and 'the automatic system' were creating a new epoch of abundance relative to human need and comparable to, though infinitely richer than, the first primeval age of human history.

In later years, what at first had seemed so coherent and logically compelling began to fall apart. Perhaps Marx never brought his major work, *Capital*, to a conclusion because the theory threatened to implode. In the first place, he had had to concede in the *Grundrisse* of 1857 that 'the self-activity' of 'associated producers' did not remove the need for 'necessary labour', that is, the unavoidable and involuntary labour that would have to be performed if the social economy were to reproduce itself. In 'The German Ideology' Marx had maintained that 'labour' (forced, unspontaneous or waged work) would be superseded by self-activity.[288] In a famous passage he evoked

286. K. Marx and F. Engels, 'The German Ideology', *MECW*, vol. 5, pp. 49, 72–3.
287. K. Marx and F. Engels, 'The German Ideology', *MECW*, vol. 5, pp. 60, 88, 78.
288. See K. Marx and F. Engels, 'The German Ideology', *MECW*, vol. 5, p. 88.

communist society, where nobody has one exclusive sphere of activity but each can become accomplished in any branch he wishes, society regulates the general production and thus makes it possible for me to do one thing today and another tomorrow, to hunt in the morning, fish in the afternoon, rear cattle in the evening, criticize after dinner, just as I have a mind, without ever becoming hunter, fisherman, shepherd or critic.[289]

By the mid 1850s, however, even allowing for the prospect that much menial work might be performed by machines, Marx had come to realize that some form of 'labour' of an unspontaneous and undesirable sort would remain necessary. In the *Grundrisse*, after ridiculing Fourier's 'childishly naive conception' and remarking 'how little Proudhon understands the matter', Marx wrote,

the labour time necessary for the satisfaction of absolute needs leaves *free* time (the amount differs in different stages of the development of productive forces) . . . The aim is to transcend the relation itself (the division of the product into necessary and surplus) . . . so that finally material production leaves every person surplus time for other activities.

Presumably the 'labour time necessary for the satisfaction of absolute needs' would have to be allocated and this would require the reintroduction of principles of right and 'the government of men'.[290] Such an admission sat uneasily with any prospect that the state might wither away; and that meant that all the problems of government, justice and right that Marx thought he had thrown out of the window in the mid 1840s appeared to be clamouring for readmittance at the back door.

In other areas too, closer observation of the relationship between the development of human needs and the possibility of an advanced non-market form of communism belied the simple assumptions of the years before 1848. Marx's identification of communism with the

289. Ibid., p. 47.
290. See K. Marx, 'Outlines of the Critique of Political Economy (Rough Draft of 1857–8)', *MECW*, vol. 28, pp. 530–31.

Incidentally, Marx was wrong to believe that Fourier had not considered the problem of 'necessary labour'. See M. Spencer, *Charles Fourier*, Boston, 1981, p. 68.

possibility of *immediate* relationships, whether between Man and Man or Man and thing, so evident at the time of his infatuation with Feuerbach, did not disappear. His formulation of the notion of use value in the 1850s represented a new version of this preoccupation. It was essential, if Marx's theory was to succeed, to show that capitalism was no more than an economic *form* and was only appropriate to a certain stage of development in 'the true natural history of Man'. In the published volume of *Capital* the concept of 'use value' was presented as a direct and authentic characterization of human need concealed beneath the trafficking of the market, the essential clue to the presence of that 'true natural history' and the demonstration of its ultimate power at times of economic crisis.

'Use value' also occupied a central place in Marx's theory of communism. In the society of the future, there would be no mediation through the market. Wealth would satisfy needs directly. It would be the restoration of the 'natural relationship between things and men'. Use value pointed to the useful character of objects in their natural particularity. It was a non-economic way of considering wealth without relation to the market, wealth as a sum of useful objects or human capacities and as a direct indication of human need. If a society based upon use value were to prevail, the market would have to be abolished. Socialism or communism would replace the market by a rational plan worked out between the associated producers. Needs would be satisfied directly and the qualitative differences between individuals would be restored, according the principle, from each according to their ability to each according to their need.

The market had to be abolished because it epitomized what Marx had first found most objectionable in his criticism of civil society – the subjection of modern man to chance. Through the generalization of market relations the economy had escaped social or political control. Modern bourgeois society had created an unleashed Frankenstein and, as a result, 'the process of production has the mastery over Man, instead of being controlled by him.' Within market relations, both production and the satisfaction of need had become atomized. The market paid no attention to the qualitative differences between individuals. All were measured by the same yardstick. Finally, and perhaps worst of all, the market appeared to mock purposive human action. Freed from the constraints imposed by custom or traditional authority, producers and traders had to calculate for themselves how the market might receive what they had to offer. But the market only corrected imbalances between production and the satisfaction of need *retrospectively* – or if need did not coincide with what the market recognized as effective demand, not at all.

A denunciation of the injustices of the market came easily to socialists, but for Marx it posed a problem. His communism had supposedly started from the dynamism of the modern exchange economy and its capacity to satisfy the needs of the all-round human personality. To remove the market as the means whereby needs were harmonized with resources was to remove the central dynamic feature of this economy; and on this question his theory of history was little help. For whether or not the succession of economic forms mentioned in 1859 really did represent successive stages in the development of human productive forces, the most striking fact remained the enormous difference between the capitalist mode of production and the rest.

The common characteristic of all pre-capitalist societies, as Marx's researches demonstrated, was that the harmonization of resources and needs was effected by forces other than the market: by customary norms, by time-hallowed traditions and by political or religious institutions. In such societies, the institutions that regulated and organized production also tended to be responsible for the organization of all other aspects of life. These institutions regulated production to meet a pre-given and traditional set of needs.

Capitalism was the first form to break free from this rigid and highly regulated framework. Only within a generalized system of commodity production and exchange, including the purchase and sale of the capacity to labour itself ('labour power'), was it possible for the 'economic' to become separated from other spheres of life. It was this generalized freedom from the many forms of pre-capitalist institutional restraint that explained the enormous superiority of capitalism in forwarding human productive advance. For only capitalism had a built-in interest in the continuous expansion and proliferation of new needs.

Not only did the resort to use value threaten the modernist stance from which Marx had first started out, but the terms in which he invoked its appeal undermined his original position still further. 'Use value', he insisted, expressed 'the natural relationship between things and men'. The use value of objects existed independently of the market or any other particular social form since it referred to 'natural needs'. In contrast to the limitless character of exchange values, the world of use values imposed a 'natural limit'.

Indeed, the language in which Marx extolled the return to use value in communist society was uncomfortably close to the language in which he recalled the merits of pre-capitalist societies. Marx wrote about 'the original unity between the worker and the conditions of production' within 'a naturally arisen spontaneous community'. Division of labour and methods of production were said to be 'natural'. 'Each individual' conducted himself 'only as a link, as member of this community' . . . 'under natural and divine presuppositions'. Unlike the modern economy, dominated by the pursuit of wealth, in these economies geared to the direct satisfaction of use value 'Man always appears . . . as the aim of production'.

It seems unlikely that Marx was unaware of the implications of a resort to a normative language of the natural. But whether this represented an intellectual defeat or the resurfacing of an ambiguity in his thinking from the beginning is hard to judge. Undoubtedly, however, something changed. In the writings of the 1840s, there was no pathos in the evocation of ancient societies. Nor was there such a strongly developed distinction between 'natural' and other needs. What distinguished Man from animal was his capacity to create *new* needs, and this capacity was most fully expressed within modern bourgeois society. By distinguishing between 'natural' and other needs, Marx was in danger of undermining what had been most novel and valuable about capitalism. It was difficult to conceive how the forces of production could carry on developing at the same pace once the market was removed. Pre-capitalist systems operated upon the unconscious assumption of the fixity of needs. If such a fixity was removed, the whole point of use value was put in doubt. Had he persisted through to the end with the concept of use value that he developed in the first and only completed volume of *Capital*, Marx would have been in danger of replacing Capitalism with a pre-market form.[291]

In the confident days of 1847, Marx had mocked Proudhon: 'you want the correct proportions of past centuries, with present day means of production, in which case you are both reactionary and utopian'.[292] But the evidence of the 1850s and 1860s suggests that Marx had stumbled into the same trap himself and had not been able to extricate himself. The consequences of that failure were far from academic, for it was from the mass of Marx papers, published and unpublished, that twentieth-century communists attempted to turn communism into reality – and with not wholly unpredictable results. As the famous socialist economist Michael Kalecki (who had returned enthusiastically to Poland as communist rule got established there) remarked in answer to a journalist's question about Poland's progress from capitalism to socialism, 'Yes, we have successfully abolished capitalism; all we have to do now is to abolish feudalism.'[293]

Perhaps it was this failure to produce a theory of modern communism that explains why Marx preferred to spend the last fifteen years of his life not in an attempt to complete *Capital*, but rather burying himself in the intensive study of ancient, communal and pre-capitalist forms from the prairies of North America to the villages of the Russian steppes. Perhaps he hoped that these villages and tribes

291. The theoretical difficulties entailed in Marx's attempt to construct a form of socialism beyond the market were most seriously examined by reforming or opposition groups in Eastern Europe between the 1960s and the 1980s. From Hungary, see in particular G. Bence, J. Kis, G. Markus, 'Is Critical Economics possible at all?', Samizdat circulation, 1971. The points contained in this argument in relation to Marx's attempt to construct a theory of use value in *Capital* were resumed and developed by Istvan Hont, 'The Antinomies of the Concept of Use Value in Marx's *Capital*', Working Papers in Political Economy and Society, King's College Research Centre, 1983.

292. K. Marx, 'The Poverty of Philosophy', *MECW*, vol. 6, p. 138.

293. Cited in Amartya Sen, *Development as Freedom*, Oxford, 1999, p. 114.

might contain the secret of another and more certain route to a post-capitalist future.[294]

At the time of the composition of the *Manifesto*, these were still unforeseen problems. In 1848 it was more simple. Once the 'gigantic means of production and exchange' conjured up by 'modern bourgeois society' had been brought under human control, there would arise 'an association, in which the free development of each' would be 'the condition for the free development of all'. Tragically, it was on the basis of this slimly secured and, as it turned out, uncashable cheque, all-but-forgotten beneath the torrent of words about 'building' socialism and 'the dictatorship of the proletariat', that twentieth-century communism proceeded so brutally and self-righteously on its imaginary path to the emancipation of mankind.

294. On Marx's change of position in the period after 1870, see H. Wada, 'Marx and Revolutionary Russia', in T. Shanin (ed.), *The Late Marx and the Russian Road*, London, 1983, pp. 40–75; D. R. Kelley, 'The Science of Anthropology: an Essay on the very old Marx', *Journal of the History of Ideas*, 45:2 (1984), pp. 245–62.

13. *A Guide to Further Reading*

Sources on particular topics have been indicated at appropriate points in the footnotes. Books mentioned here have been chosen first because they are written in English; second, because they are accessible to the general reader; and third, because they enlarge upon important questions relevant to the political and intellectual context within which the *Manifesto* was composed.

The best general discussion of German culture and politics in the first half of the nineteenth century is James J. Sheehan, *German History 1770–1866*, Oxford, 1989. Less extensive but also useful is David Blackbourn, *The Fontana History of Germany 1780–1918*, London, 1997. On the specific problems of the Rhineland in the years leading up to 1848, see Jonathan Sperber, *Rhineland Radicals: The Democratic Movement and the Revolution of 1848–1849*, Princeton, 1991. On the revolutions of 1848, see in addition Sperber, *The European Revolutions, 1848–1851*, Cambridge, 1994, and Jean Sigman, *1848: The Romantic and Democratic Revolutions in Europe*, London, 1973.

On the Young Hegelians, the best overall discussion is to be found in John E. Toews, *Hegelianism: The Path Toward Dialectical Humanism, 1805–1841*, Cambridge, 1980. But see also Karl Löwith, *From Hegel to Nietzsche: The Revolution in Nineteenth-century Thought*, New York, 1964; and (on the theological side) Albert Schweitzer, *The Quest of the Historical Jesus*, London, 2000. On Marx's relationship with the Young Hegelians, see D. McLellan, *The Young Hegelians and Karl Marx*, London, 1969, and N. Lobkowicz, *Theory and Practice: History of a Concept from Aristotle to Marx*, Notre Dame, 1967. There is a good collection of Young Hegelian writings in Lawrence S. Stepelevich (ed.), *The Young Hegelians: An Anthology*, Cambridge, 1983.

On so-called 'utopian socialism' the general literature is rather dated, but there are good individual studies. See especially, Jonathan Beecher, *Charles Fourier: The Visionary and His World*, Berkeley, 1986; Frank E. Manuel, *The New World of Henri de Saint-Simon*, South Bend, Indiana, 1963; Christopher H. Johnson, *Utopian Communism in France: Cabet and the Icarians, 1839–1851*, Ithaca, 1974; Gregory Claeys, *Machinery, Money and the Millennium From Moral Economy to Socialism 1815–1860*, Princeton, 1987 (on the Owenites). And for a large general study, Frank E. & Fritzie P. Manuel, *Utopian Thought in the Western World*, Oxford, 1979. The best study of the League of the Just and its relationship to Marx and Engels is Christina Lattek, *Revolutionary Refugees: German Socialism in Britain, 1840–1860*, London, 2002.

On Marx and Engels themselves, all will be grateful that the massive scholarly project, the *Karl Marx Frederick Engels Collected Works*, London, Lawrence and Wishart, 1975–2001, has now been completed in fifty volumes. This will make possible not only a consistent system of reference, but also a more scholarly and historically informed approach to their writings. But the existence of the *Collected Works* does not remove the need for intelligent selections of their writings. Compilations of excerpts arranged according to preselected themes are not as useful as those that reproduce integral texts. See in particular David Fernbach (ed.), *The Pelican Marx Library* (Penguin & New Left Review), Harmondsworth, 1973–; J. O'Malley (ed.), Marx, *Early Political Writings*, Cambridge, 1994; T. Carver (ed.), Marx, *Later Political Writings*, Cambridge, 1996.

The first major biography of Marx, by Franz Mehring, *Karl Marx the story of his life*, London, 1936, appeared in German in 1918 and is still worth reading. The standard modern biography is that by David McLellan, *Karl Marx – His Life and Thought*, London, 1980. There is also an excellent short illustrated biography, Werner Blumenberg, *Karl Marx: An Illustrated Biography*, London, 1972. On Marx's personal life, the compellingly readable biography by Francis Wheen, *Karl Marx*, London, 1999, is not to be missed.

On the relationship between Marx and Engels, see on the one hand Terrell Carver, *Marx and Engels: The Intellectual Relationship*, Brighton, 1983, and for an opposed position, J. D. Hunley, *The Life and Thought of Friedrich Engels*, New Haven, 1991.

There is a vast literature on Marxism, but comparatively little on the theoretical construction of *The Communist Manifesto* and very little on the character or antecedents of the notion of communism contained within it. For a recent collection of views on the significance of the *Manifesto*, see M. Cowling (ed.), *The Communist Manifesto: New Interpretations*, Edinburgh, 1998.

PART II

Karl Marx and Friedrich Engels

THE COMMUNIST
MANIFESTO

A Note on the Text

The text of the *Manifesto* reproduced here is Samuel Moore's translation of the second German edition of 1872 for the first English edition of 1888. Moore, a barrister and manufacturer, was an old Manchester friend of Engels and his legal adviser. The translation was checked by Engels, who added explanatory footnotes. The translation was in places quite free, and occasionally misleading. Significant departures from the German original have been noted in the endnotes. An alternative translation has recently been made by Terrell Carver, who has also written about the arguments for and against the Moore/Engels version.[1] Carver is right to point out that the spirit in which Moore and Engels approached the text in 1888 was quite different from that in which Marx had written the text forty years before. Nevertheless, no one has claimed that Moore produced a bad translation and it cannot be denied that Engels' authorization bestows an additional authority upon that version. In the end, however, the best argument for retaining Moore's translation is not that it is always the most faithful rendition of the German original, but that it was the form in which, for over a century, the *Manifesto* became familiar in the English-speaking world.

The punctuation and capitalization of the 1888 edition is preserved here.

1. See T. Carver (tr.), 'Manifesto of the Communist Party', in M. Cowling (ed.), *The Communist Manifesto: New Interpretations*, Edinburgh, 1998, pp. 14–41; and see also T. Carver, 'Re-translating the *Manifesto*: New Histories, New Ideas', ibid. pp. 51–63.

Preface to the German Edition of 1872[1]

The Communist League, an international association of workers, which could of course be only a secret one under the conditions obtaining at the time, commissioned the undersigned, at the Congress held in London in November, 1847, to draw up for publication a detailed theoretical and practical programme of the Party. Such was the origin of the following Manifesto, the manuscript of which travelled to London, to be printed, a few weeks before the February Revolution.[2] First published in German, it has been republished in that language in at least twelve different editions in Germany, England and America. It was published in English for the first time in 1850 in the *Red Republican*, London, translated by Miss Helen Macfarlane, and in 1871 in at least three different translations in America. A French version first appeared in Paris shortly before the June insurrection of 1848 and recently in *Le Socialiste* of New York.[3] A new translation is in the course of preparation. A Polish version appeared in London shortly after it was first published in German. A Russian translation was published in Geneva in the sixties. Into Danish, too, it was translated shortly after its first appearance.

However much the state of things may have altered during the last twenty-five years, the general principles laid down in this Manifesto are, on the whole, as correct today as ever. Here and there some detail might be improved. The practical application of the principles will depend, as the Manifesto itself states, every-where and at all times, on the historical conditions for the time being existing, and, for that reason, no special stress is laid on the revolutionary measures proposed at the end of Section II. That passage would, in many respects, be very differently worded today. In view of the gigantic strides of Modern Industry in the last twenty-five years, and of the accompanying improved and extended party organization of the working class, in view of the practical experience gained, first in the February Revolution, and then, still more, in the Paris Commune, where the proletariat for the first time held political power for two whole months, this programme has in some details become antiquated.[4] One thing especially was proved by the Commune, viz., that 'the working class cannot simply lay hold of the ready-made State machinery, and wield it for its own purposes'. (See *The Civil War in France; Address of the General Council of the International Working Men's Association*, London, Truelove, 1871, p. 15, where this point is further developed.) Further, it is self-evident that the criticism of Socialist literature is deficient in relation to the present time, because it comes down only to 1847; also that the remarks on the relation of the Communists to the various opposition parties (Section IV), although in principle still correct, yet in practice are antiquated, because the political situation has been entirely changed, and the progress of history has swept from off the earth the greater portion of the political parties there enumerated.

But, then, the Manifesto has become a historical document which we have no longer any right to alter. A subsequent edition may perhaps appear with an introduction bridging the gap from 1847 to the present day; this reprint was too unexpected to leave us time for that.

London, 24 June 1872

KARL MARX
FREDERICK ENGELS

Preface to the Russian Edition of 1882[5]

The first Russian edition of the *Manifesto of the Communist Party*, translated by Bakunin, was published early in the sixties by the printing office of the *Kolokol*.[6] Then the West could see in it (the *Russian* edition of the Manifesto) only a literary curiosity. Such a view would be impossible today.

What a limited field the proletarian movement still occupied at that time (December 1847) is most clearly shown by the last section of the Manifesto: the position of the Communists in relation to the various opposition parties in the various countries. Precisely Russia and the United States are missing here. It was the time when Russia constituted the last great reserve of all European reaction, when the United States absorbed the surplus proletarian forces of Europe through immigration. Both countries provided Europe with raw materials and were at the same time markets for the sale of its industrial products. At that time both were, therefore, in one way or another, pillars of the existing European order.

How very different today! Precisely European immigration fitted North America for a gigantic agricultural production, whose competition is shaking the very foundations of European landed property – large and small.[7] In addition it enabled the United States to exploit its tremendous industrial resources with an energy and on a scale that must shortly break the industrial monopoly of Western Europe, and especially of England, existing up to now. Both circumstances react in revolutionary manner upon America itself. Step by step the small and middle landowner-ship of the farmers, the basis of the whole political constitution, is succumbing to the competition of giant farms; simultaneously, a mass proletariat and a fabulous concentration of capitals are developing for the first time in the industrial regions.

And now Russia! During the Revolution of 1848–49 not only the European princes, but the European bourgeois as well, found their only salvation from the proletariat, just beginning to awaken, in Russian intervention. The tsar was proclaimed the chief of European reaction. Today he is a prisoner of war of the revolution, in Gatchina, and Russia forms the vanguard of revolutionary action in Europe.[8]

The Communist Manifesto had as its object the proclamation of the inevitably impending dissolution of modern bourgeois property. But in Russia we find, face to face with the rapidly developing capitalist swindle and bourgeois landed property, just beginning to develop, more than half the land owned in common by the peasants. Now the question is: can the Russian *obshchina*, though greatly undermined, yet a form of the primeval common ownership of land, pass directly to the higher form of communist common ownership?[9] Or on the contrary, must it first pass through the same process of dissolution as constitutes the historical evolution of the West?

The only answer to that possible today is this: If the Russian Revolution becomes the signal for a proletarian revolution in the West, so that both complement each other, the present Russian common ownership of land may serve as the starting point for a communist development.[10]

London, 21 January 1882

KARL MARX

FREDERICK ENGELS

Preface to the German Edition of 1883

The preface to the present edition I must, alas, sign alone.[11] Marx – the man to whom the whole working class of Europe and America owes more than to anyone else – rests at Highgate Cemetery and over his grave the first grass is already growing. Since his death, there can be even less thought of revising or supplementing the Manifesto. All the more do I consider it necessary again to state here the following expressly:

The basic thought running through the Manifesto – that economic production and the structure of society of every historical epoch necessarily arising therefrom constitute the foundation for the political and intellectual history of that epoch; that consequently (ever since the dissolution of the primeval communal ownership of land) all history has been a history of class struggles, of struggles between exploited and exploiting, between dominated and dominating classes at various stages of social development; that this struggle, however, has now reached a stage where the exploited and oppressed class (the proletariat) can no longer emancipate itself from the class which exploits and oppresses it (the bourgeoisie), without at the same time for ever freeing the whole of society from exploitation, oppression and class struggles – this basic thought belongs solely and exclusively to Marx.*

* 'This proposition,' I wrote in the preface to the English translation, 'which, in my opinion, is destined to do for history what Darwin's theory has done for biology, we,

I have already stated this many times; but precisely now it is necessary that it also stand in front of the Manifesto itself.

London, 28 June 1883   F. ENGELS

---

both of us, had been gradually approaching for some years before 1845. How far I had independently progressed towards it, is best shown by my *Condition of the Working Class in England*. But when I again met Marx at Brussels, in spring, 1845, he had it ready worked out, and put it before me, in terms almost as clear as those in which I have stated it here.' [*Note by Engels to the German edition of 1890.*]

Preface to the English Edition of 1888

The Manifesto was published as the platform of the 'Communist League', a working men's association, first exclusively German, later on international, and, under the political conditions of the Continent before 1848, unavoidably a secret society. At a Congress of the League, held in London in November, 1847, Marx and Engels were commissioned to prepare for publication a complete theoretical and practical party programme. Drawn up in German, in January, 1848, the manuscript was sent to the printer in London a few weeks before the French revolution of February 24th. A French translation was brought out in Paris, shortly before the insurrection of June, 1848. The first English translation, by Miss Helen Macfarlane, appeared in George Julian Harney's *Red Republican*, London, 1850. A Danish and a Polish edition had also been published.

The defeat of the Parisian insurrection of June, 1848 – the first great battle between Proletariat and Bourgeoisie – drove again into the background, for a time, the social and political aspirations of the European working class. Thenceforth, the struggle for supremacy was again, as it had been before the revolution of February, solely between different sections of the propertied class; the working class was reduced to a fight for political elbow-room, and to the position of extreme wing of the middle-class Radicals. Wherever independent proletarian movements continued to show signs of life, they were ruthlessly hunted down. Thus the Prussian police hunted out the Central Board of the Communist League, then located in Cologne. The members were arrested, and, after eighteen months' imprisonment, they were tried in October, 1852. This celebrated 'Cologne Communist trial' lasted from October 4th till November 12th; seven of the prisoners were sentenced to terms of imprisonment in a fortress, varying from three to six years. Immediately after the sentence, the League was formally dissolved by the remaining members. As to the Manifesto, it seemed thenceforth to be doomed to oblivion.

When the European working class had recovered sufficient strength for another attack on the ruling classes, the International Working Men's Association sprang up. But this association, formed with the express aim of welding into one body the whole militant proletariat of Europe and America, could not at once proclaim the principles laid down in the Manifesto. The International was bound to have a programme broad enough to be acceptable to the English Trades Unions, to the followers of Proudhon in France, Belgium, Italy, and Spain, and to the Lassalleans in Germany.[12]* Marx who drew up this programme to the satisfaction of all parties, entirely trusted to the intellectual development of the working class, which was sure to result from combined action and mutual discussion. The very events and vicissitudes of the struggle against Capital, the defeats even more than the victories, could not help bringing home to men's minds the insufficiency of their various favourite nostrums, and preparing the way for a more complete insight into the true conditions of working-class emancipation. And

* Lassalle personally, to us, always acknowledged himself to be a disciple of Marx, and, as such, stood on the ground of the Manifesto. But in his public agitation, 1862–4, he did not go beyond demanding cooperative workshops supported by state credit. [*Note by Engels.*]

Marx was right. The International, on its breaking up in 1874, left the workers quite different men from what it had found them in 1864.[13] Proudhonism in France, Lassalleanism in Germany were dying out, and even the conservative English Trades Unions, though most of them had long since severed their connexion with the International, were gradually advancing towards that point at which, last year at Swansea, their President could say in their name 'Continental Socialism has lost its terrors for us'. In fact: the principles of the Manifesto had made considerable headway among the working men of all countries.

The Manifesto itself thus came to the front again. The German text had been, since 1850, reprinted several times in Switzerland, England and America. In 1872, it was translated into English in New York, where the translation was published in *Woodhull and Claflin's Weekly*. From this English version, a French one was made in *Le Socialiste* of New York. Since then at least two more English translations, more or less mutilated, have been brought out in America, and one of them has been reprinted in England. The first Russian translation, made by Bakunin, was published at Herzen's *Kolokol* office in Geneva, about 1863; a second one, by the heroic Vera Zasulich, also in Geneva, 1882. A new Danish edition is to be found in *Socialde-mokratisk Bibliothek*, Copenhagen, 1885; a fresh French translation in *Le Socialiste*, Paris 1885. From this latter a Spanish version was prepared and published in Madrid, 1886. The German reprints are not to be counted, there have been twelve altogether at the least. An Armenian translation, which was to be published in Constantinople some months ago, did not see the light, I am told, because the publisher was afraid of bringing out a book with the name of Marx on it, while the translator declined to call it his own production. Of further translations into other languages I have heard, but have not seen them. Thus the history of the Manifesto reflects, to a great extent, the history of the modern working-class movement; at present it is undoubtedly the most widespread, the most international production of all Socialist literature, the common platform acknowledged by millions of working men from Siberia to California.

Yet, when it was written, we could not have called it a *Socialist* Manifesto. By Socialists, in 1847, were understood, on the one hand, the adherents of the various Utopian systems: Owenites in England, Fourierists in France, both of them already reduced to the position of mere sects, and gradually dying out; on the other hand, the most multifarious social quacks, who, by all manners of tinkering, professed to redress, without any danger to capital and profit, all sorts of social grievances; in both cases men outside the working-class movement, and looking rather to the 'educated' classes for support. Whatever portion of the working class had become convinced of the insufficiency of mere political revolutions, and had proclaimed the necessity of a total social change, that portion then called itself Communist. It was a crude, rough-hewn, purely instinctive sort of Communism; still, it touched the cardinal point and was powerful enough amongst the working class to produce the Utopian Communism, in France, of Cabet, and in Germany, of Weitling. Thus, Socialism was, in 1847, a middle-class movement, Communism, a working-class movement. Socialism was, on the Continent at least, 'respectable'; Communism was the very opposite. And as our notion, from the very beginning, was that 'the emancipation of the working class must be the act of the working class itself', there could be no doubt as to which of the two names we must take. Moreover, we have, ever since, been far from repudiating it.

The Manifesto being our joint production, I consider myself bound to state that the fundamental proposition, which forms its nucleus, belongs to Marx. That proposition is: that in every historical epoch, the prevailing mode of economic production and exchange, and the social organization necessarily following from it, form the basis upon which is built up, and from which alone can be explained, the political and intellectual history of that epoch; that consequently the whole history of mankind (since the dissolution of primitive tribal society, holding land in common ownership) has been a history of class struggles, contests between exploiting and exploited, ruling and oppressed classes; that the history of these class struggles forms a series of evolutions in which, nowadays, a stage has been reached where the exploited and oppressed class – the proletariat – cannot attain its emancipation from the sway of the exploiting and ruling class – the bourgeoisie – without, at the same time, and once and for all, emancipating society at large from all exploitation, oppression, class distinctions and class struggles.

This proposition which, in my opinion, is destined to do for history what Darwin's theory has done for biology, we, both of us, had been gradually approaching for some years before 1845.[14] How far I had independently progressed towards it, is best shown by my *Condition of the Working Class in England*.* But when I again met Marx at Brussels, in spring, 1845, he had it ready worked out, and put it before me, in terms almost as clear as those in which I have stated it here.

From our joint preface to the German edition of 1872, I quote the following:

'However much the state of things may have altered during the last twenty-five years, the general principles laid down in this Manifesto are, on the whole, as correct today as ever. Here and there some detail might be improved. The practical application of the principles will depend, as the Manifesto itself states, everywhere and at all times, on the historical conditions

* *The Condition of the Working Class in England in 1844*. By Frederick Engels. Translated by Florence K. Wischnewetzky, New York. Lovell – London. W. Reeves, 1888. [*Note by Engels.*]

for the time being existing, and, for that reason, no special stress is laid on the revolutionary measures proposed at the end of Section II. That passage would, in many respects, be very differently worded today. In view of the gigantic strides of Modern Industry since 1848, and of the accompanying improved and extended organization of the working class, in view of the practical experience gained, first in the February Revolution, and then, still more, in the Paris Commune, where the proletariat for the first time held political power for two whole months, this programme has in some details become antiquated. One thing especially was proved by the Commune, viz., that "the working class cannot simply lay hold of the ready-made State machinery, and wield it for its own purposes". (See *The Civil War in France; Address of the General Council of the International Working Men's Association*, London, Truelove, 1871, p. 15, where this point is further developed.) Further, it is self-evident that the criticism of Socialist literature is deficient in relation to the present time, because it comes down only to 1847; also, that the remarks on the relation of the Communists to the various opposition parties (Section IV), although in principle still correct, yet in practice are antiquated, because the political situation has been entirely changed, and the progress of history has swept from off the earth the greater portion of the political parties there enumerated.

'But then, the Manifesto has become a historical document which we have no longer any right to alter.'

The present translation is by Mr Samuel Moore, the translator of the greater portion of Marx's *Capital*. We have revised it in common, and I have added a few notes explanatory of historical allusions.

London, 30 January 1888   F. ENGELS

Preface to the German Edition of 1890

Since the above was written,* a new German edition of the Manifesto has again become necessary, and much has also happened to the Manifesto which should be recorded here.

A second Russian translation – by Vera Zasulich – appeared at Geneva in 1882; the preface to that edition was written by Marx and myself. Unfortunately, the original German manuscript has gone astray; I must therefore retranslate from the Russian, which will in no way improve the text. It reads:

'The first Russian edition of the *Manifesto of the Communist Party*, translated by Bakunin, was published early in the sixties by the printing office of the *Kolokol*. Then the West could see in it (the Russian edition of the Manifesto) only a literary curiosity. Such a view would be impossible today.

'What a limited field the proletarian movement still occupied at that time (December 1847) is most clearly shown by the last section of the Manifesto: the position of the Communists in relation to the various opposition parties in the various countries. Precisely Russia and the United States are missing here. It was the time when Russia constituted the last great reserve of all European reaction, when the United States absorbed the

* Engels is referring to his preface to the German edition of 1883, pp. 197–8.

surplus proletarian forces of Europe through immigration. Both countries provided Europe with raw materials and were at the same time markets for the sale of its industrial products. At that time both were, therefore, in one way or another, pillars of the existing European order.

'How very different today! Precisely European immigration fitted North America for a gigantic agricultural production, whose competition is shaking the very foundations of European landed property – large and small. In addition it enabled the United States to exploit its tremendous industrial resources with an energy and on a scale that must shortly break the industrial monopoly of Western Europe, and especially of England, existing up to now. Both circumstances react in revolutionary manner upon America itself. Step by step the small and middle landownership of the farmers, the basis of the whole political constitution, is succumbing to the competition of giant farms; simultaneously, a mass proletariat and a fabulous concentration of capitals are developing for the first time in the industrial regions.

'And now Russia! During the Revolution of 1848–49 not only the European princes, but the European bourgeois as well, found their only salvation from the proletariat, just beginning to awaken, in Russian intervention. The tsar was proclaimed the chief of European reaction. Today he is a prisoner of war of the revolution, in Gatchina, and Russia forms the vanguard of revolutionary action in Europe.

'The Communist Manifesto had as its object the proclamation of the inevitably impending dissolution of modern bourgeois property. But in Russia we find, face to face with the rapidly developing capitalist swindle and bourgeois landed property, just beginning to develop, more than half the land owned in common by the peasants. Now the question is: can the Russian *obshchina*, though greatly undermined, yet a form of the primeval common ownership of land, pass directly to the higher form of communist common ownership? Or on the contrary, must it first pass through the same process of dissolution as constitutes the historical evolution of the West?

'The only answer to that possible today is this: If the Russian Revolution becomes the signal for a proletarian revolution in the West, so that both complement each other, the present Russian common ownership of land may serve as the starting point for a communist development.

'London, 21 January 1882   KARL MARX
                                        FREDERICK ENGELS'

At about the same date, a new Polish version appeared in Geneva: *Manifest Komunistyczny.*

Furthermore, a new Danish translation has appeared in the *Social-demokratisk Bibliothek*, Copenhagen, 1885. Unfortunately it is not quite complete; certain essential passages, which seem to have presented difficulties to the translator, have been omitted, and in addition there are signs of carelessness here and there, which are all the more unpleasantly conspicuous since the translation indicates that had the translator taken a little more pains he would have done an excellent piece of work.

A new French version appeared in 1885 in *Le Socialiste* of Paris; it is the best published to date.

From this latter a Spanish version was published the same year, first in *El Socialista* of Madrid, and then reissued in pamphlet form: *Manifiesto del Partido Comunista* por Carlos Marx y F. Engels, Madrid, Administración de *El Socialista*, Hernán Cortés 8.

As a matter of curiosity I may also mention that in 1887

the manuscript of an Armenian translation was offered to a publisher in Constantinople. But the good man did not have the courage to publish something bearing the name of Marx and suggested that the translator set down his own name as author, which the latter, however, declined.

After one and then another of the more or less inaccurate American translations had been repeatedly reprinted in England, an authentic version at last appeared in 1888. This was by my friend Samuel Moore, and we went through it together once more before it was sent to press. It is entitled: *Manifesto of the Communist Party*, by Karl Marx and Frederick Engels. Authorized English Translation, edited and annotated by Frederick Engels, 1888. London, William Reeves, 185 Fleet st., E.C. I have added some of the notes of that edition to the present one.

The Manifesto has had a history of its own. Greeted with enthusiasm, at the time of its appearance, by the then still not at all numerous vanguard of scientific Socialism (as is proved by the translations mentioned in the first preface), it was soon forced into the background by the reaction that began with the defeat of the Paris workers in June 1848, and was finally excommunicated 'according to law' by the conviction of the Cologne Communists in November 1852. With the disappearance from the public scene of the workers' movement that had begun with the February Revolution, the Manifesto too passed into the background.

When the working class of Europe had again gathered sufficient strength for a new onslaught upon the power of the ruling classes, the International Working Men's Association came into being. Its aim was to weld together into *one* huge army the whole militant working class of Europe and America. Therefore it could not *set out* from the principles laid down in the Manifesto. It was bound to have a programme which would not shut the door on the English trade unions, the French,

Belgian, Italian and Spanish Proudhonists and the German Lassalleans.*

This programme – the preamble to the Rules of the International – was drawn up by Marx with a master hand acknowledged even by Bakunin and the Anarchists. For the ultimate triumph of the ideas set forth in the Manifesto Marx relied solely and exclusively upon the intellectual development of the working class, as it necessarily had to ensue from united action and discussion. The events and vicissitudes in the struggle against capital, the defeats even more than the successes, could not but demonstrate to the fighters the inadequacy hitherto of their universal panaceas and make their minds more receptive to a thorough understanding of the true conditions for the emancipation of the workers. And Marx was right. The working class of 1874, at the dissolution of the International, was altogether different from that of 1864, at its foundation. Proudhonism in the Latin countries and the specific Lassalleanism in Germany were dying out, and even the then arch-conservative English trade unions were gradually approaching the point where in 1887 the chairman of their Swansea Congress could say in their name 'Continental Socialism has lost its terrors for us'. Yet by 1887 Continental Socialism was almost exclusively the theory heralded in the Manifesto. Thus, to a certain extent, the history of the Manifesto reflects the history of the modern working-class movement since 1848. At present it is doubtless the most widely circulated, the most international product of all Socialist literature, the common programme of many millions of workers of all countries, from Siberia to California.

---

* Lassalle personally, to us, always acknowledged himself to be a 'disciple' of Marx, and, as such, stood, of course, on the ground of the Manifesto. Matters were quite different with regard to those of his followers who did not go beyond his demand for producers' cooperatives supported by state credits and who divided the whole working class into supporters of state assistance and supporters of self-assistance. [*Note by Engels.*]

Nevertheless, when it appeared we could not have called it a *Socialist* Manifesto. In 1847 two kinds of people were considered Socialists. On the one hand were the adherents of the various Utopian systems, notably the Owenites in England and the Fourierists in France, both of whom at that date had already dwindled to mere sects gradually dying out. On the other, the manifold types of social quacks who wanted to eliminate social abuses through their various universal panaceas and all kinds of patchwork, without hurting capital and profit in the least. In both cases, people who stood outside the labour movement and who looked for support rather to the 'educated' classes. The section of the working class, however, which demanded a radical reconstruction of society, convinced that mere political revolutions were not enough, then called itself *Communist*. It was still a rough-hewn, only instinctive, and frequently somewhat crude Communism. Yet it was powerful enough to bring into being two systems of Utopian Communism – in France the 'Icarian' Communism of Cabet, and in Germany that of Weitling. Socialism in 1847 signified a bourgeois movement, Communism, a working-class movement. Socialism was, on the Continent at least, quite respectable, whereas Communism was the very opposite. And since we were very decidedly of the opinion as early as then that 'the emancipation of the workers must be the act of the working class itself', we could have no hesitation as to which of the two names we should choose. Nor has it ever occurred to us since to repudiate it.

'Working men of all countries, unite!' But few voices responded when we proclaimed these words to the world forty-two years ago, on the eve of the first Paris Revolution in which the proletariat came out with demands of its own. On 28 September 1864, however, the proletarians of most of the Western European countries joined hands in the International Working Men's Association of glorious memory. True, the

International itself lived only nine years. But that the eternal union of the proletarians of all countries created by it is still alive and lives stronger than ever, there is no better witness than this day. Because today, as I write these lines, the European and American proletariat is reviewing its fighting forces, mobilized for the first time, mobilized as one army, under *one* flag, for one immediate aim: the standard eight-hour working day, to be established by legal enactment, as proclaimed by the Geneva Congress of the International in 1866, and again by the Paris Workers' Congress in 1889.[15] And today's spectacle will open the eyes of the capitalists and landlords of all countries to the fact that today the working men of all countries are united indeed.

If only Marx were still by my side to see this with his own eyes!

London, 1 May 1890   F. ENGELS

Preface to the Polish Edition of 1892*

The fact that a new Polish edition of the Communist Manifesto has become necessary gives rise to various thoughts.

First of all, it is noteworthy that of late the Manifesto has become an index, as it were, on the development of large-scale industry on the European continent. In proportion as large-scale industry expands in a given country, the demand grows among the workers of that country for enlightenment regarding their position as the working class in relation to the possessing classes, the socialist movement spreads among them and the demand for the Manifesto increases. Thus, not only the state of the labour movement but also the degree of development of large-scale industry can be measured with fair accuracy in every country by the number of copies of the Manifesto circulated in the language of that country.

Accordingly, the new Polish edition indicates a decided progress of Polish industry. And there can be no doubt whatever that this progress since the previous edition published ten years ago has actually taken place. Russian Poland, Congress Poland, has become the big industrial region of the Russian Empire. Whereas Russian large-scale industry is scattered sporadically

* The translation of the Preface to the Polish edition given here is from the German original.

– a part round the Gulf of Finland, another in the centre (Moscow and Vladimir), a third along the coasts of the Black and Azov seas, and still others elsewhere – Polish industry has been packed into a relatively small area and enjoys both the advantages and the disadvantages arising from such concentration. The competing Russian manufacturers acknowledged the advantages when they demanded protective tariffs against Poland, in spite of their ardent desire to transform the Poles into Russians. The disadvantages – for the Polish manufacturers and the Russian government – are manifest in the rapid spread of socialist ideas among the Polish workers and in the growing demand for the Manifesto.

But the rapid development of Polish industry, outstripping that of Russia, is in its turn a new proof of the inexhaustible vitality of the Polish people and a new guarantee of its impending national restoration. And the restoration of an independent strong Poland is a matter which concerns not only the Poles but all of us. A sincere international collaboration of the European nations is possible only if each of these nations is fully autonomous in its own house. The Revolution of 1848, which under the banner of the proletariat, after all, merely let the proletarian fighters do the work of the bourgeoisie, also secured the independence of Italy, Germany, and Hungary through its testamentary executors, Louis Bonaparte and Bismarck; but Poland, which since 1792 had done more for the Revolution than all these three together, was left to its own resources when it succumbed in 1863 to a tenfold greater Russian force.[16] The nobility could neither maintain nor regain Polish independence; today, to the bourgeoisie, this independence is, to say the least, immaterial. Nevertheless, it is a necessity for the harmonious collaboration of the European nations. It can be gained only by the young Polish proletariat, and in its hands it is secure. For the workers of all the rest of Europe need the independence of Poland just as much as the Polish workers themselves.

London, 10 February 1892   F. ENGELS

Preface to the Italian Edition of 1893

Publication of the *Manifesto of the Communist Party* coincided, one may say, with 18 March 1848, the day of the revolutions in Milan and Berlin, which were armed uprisings of the two nations situated in the centre, the one, of the continent of Europe, the other, of the Mediterranean; two nations until then enfeebled by division and internal strife, and thus fallen under foreign domination. While Italy was subject to the Emperor of Austria, Germany underwent the yoke, not less effective though more indirect, of the Tsar of all the Russias. The consequences of 18 March 1848 freed both Italy and Germany from this disgrace; if from 1848 to 1871 these two great nations were reconstituted and somehow again put on their own, it was, as Karl Marx used to say, because the men who suppressed the Revolution of 1848 were, nevertheless, its testamentary executors in spite of themselves.

Everywhere that revolution was the work of the working class; it was the latter that built the barricades and paid with its lifeblood. Only the Paris workers, in overthrowing the government, had the very definite intention of overthrowing the bourgeois regime. But conscious though they were of the fatal antagonism existing between their own class and the bourgeoisie, still, neither the economic progress of the country nor the intellectual development of the mass of French workers had as yet reached the stage which would have made a social reconstruction possible. In the final analysis, therefore, the fruits of the revolution were reaped by the capitalist class. In the other countries, in Italy, in Germany, in Austria, the workers, from the very outset, did nothing but raise the bourgeoisie to power. But in any country the rule of the bourgeoisie is impossible without national independence. Therefore, the Revolution of 1848 had to bring in its train the unity and autonomy of the nations that had lacked them up to then: Italy, Germany, Hungary, Poland will follow in turn.

Thus, if the Revolution of 1848 was not a socialist revolution, it paved the way, prepared the ground for the latter. Through the impetus given to large-scale industry in all countries, the bourgeois regime during the last forty-five years has everywhere created a numerous, concentrated and powerful proletariat. It has thus raised, to use the language of the Manifesto, its own gravediggers. Without restoring autonomy and unity to each nation, it will be impossible to achieve the international union of the proletariat, or the peaceful and intelligent cooperation of these nations towards common aims. Just imagine joint inter-national action by the Italian, Hungarian, German, Polish and Russian workers under the political conditions preceding 1848!

The battles fought in 1848 were thus not fought in vain. Nor have the forty-five years separating us from that revolutionary epoch passed to no purpose. The fruits are ripening, and all I wish is that the publication of this Italian translation may augur as well for the victory of the Italian proletariat as the publication of the original did for the international revolution.

The Manifesto does full justice to the revolutionary part played by capitalism in the past. The first capitalist nation was Italy. The close of the feudal Middle Ages, and the opening of the modern capitalist era are marked by a colossal figure: an Italian, Dante, both the last poet of the Middle Ages and the first poet of modern times.

Today, as in 1300, a new historical era is approaching. Will Italy give us the new Dante, who will mark the hour of birth of this new, proletarian era?

London, 1 February 1893   F. ENGELS

The Manifesto of the Communist Party

A spectre is haunting Europe – the spectre of Communism. All the Powers of old Europe have entered into a holy alliance to exorcize this spectre: Pope and Czar, Metternich and Guizot, French Radicals and German police spies.[17]

Where is the party in opposition that has not been decried as Communistic by its opponents in power? Where the Opposition that has not hurled back the branding reproach of Communism, against the more advanced opposition parties, as well as against its reactionary adversaries?

Two things result from this fact:

I. Communism is already acknowledged by all European Powers to be itself a Power.

II. It is high time that Communists should openly, in the face of the whole world, publish their views, their aims, their tendencies, and meet this nursery tale of the Spectre of Communism with a Manifesto of the party itself.

To this end, Communists of various nationalities have assembled in London, and sketched the following Manifesto, to be published in the English, French, German, Italian, Flemish and Danish languages.

1. *Bourgeois and Proletarians**

The history of all hitherto existing society† is the history of class struggles.[18]

Freeman and slave, patrician and plebeian, lord and serf, guild-master‡ and journeyman, in a word, oppressor and oppressed, stood in constant opposition to one another, carried on an uninterrupted, now hidden, now open fight, a fight that each time ended, either in a revolutionary reconstitution of society at large, or in the common ruin of the contending classes.

In the earlier epochs of history, we find almost everywhere a complicated arrangement of society into various orders, a manifold gradation of social rank. In ancient Rome we have patricians, knights, plebeians, slaves; in the Middle Ages, feudal lords, vassals, guild-masters, journeymen, apprentices, serfs; in almost all of these classes, again, subordinate gradations.

---

* By bourgeoisie is meant the class of modern Capitalists, owners of the means of social production and employers of wage labour. By proletariat, the class of modern wage-labourers who, having no means of production of their own, are reduced to selling their labour power in order to live. [*Note by Engels to the English edition of 1888.*]

† That is, all written history. In 1847, the pre-history of society, the social organization existing previous to recorded history, was all but unknown. Since then, Haxthausen discovered common ownership of land in Russia, Maurer proved it to be the social foundation from which all Teutonic races started in history, and by and by village communities were found to be, or to have been the primitive form of society everywhere from India to Ireland. The inner organization of this primitive Communistic society was laid bare, in its typical form, by Morgan's crowning discovery of the true nature of the *gens* and its relation to the *tribe*. With the dissolution of these primeval communities society begins to be differentiated into separate and finally antagonistic classes. I have attempted to retrace this process of dissolution in: *Der Ursprung der Familie, des Privateigenthums und des Staats (The Origin of the Family, Private Property and the State)*, 2nd edition, Stuttgart 1886. [*Note by Engels to the English edition of 1888.*]

‡ Guild-master, that is, a full member of a guild, a master within, not a head of a guild. [*Note by Engels to the English edition of 1888.*]

The modern bourgeois society that has sprouted from the ruins of feudal society has not done away with class antagonisms. It has but established new classes, new conditions of oppression, new forms of struggle in place of the old ones.

Our epoch, the epoch of the bourgeoisie, possesses, however, this distinctive feature: it has simplified the class antagonisms. Society as a whole is more and more splitting up into two great hostile camps, into two great classes directly facing each other: Bourgeoisie and Proletariat.[19]

From the serfs of the Middle Ages sprang the chartered burghers of the earliest towns. From these burgesses the first elements of the bourgeoisie were developed.

The discovery of America, the rounding of the Cape, opened up fresh ground for the rising bourgeoisie. The East-Indian and Chinese markets, the colonization of America, trade with the colonies, the increase in the means of exchange and in commodities generally, gave to commerce, to navigation, to industry, an impulse never before known, and thereby, to the revolutionary element in the tottering feudal society, a rapid development.

The feudal system of industry, under which industrial production was monopolized by closed guilds, now no longer sufficed for the growing wants of the new markets. The manufacturing system took its place. The guild-masters were pushed on one side by the manufacturing middle class;[20] division of labour between the different corporate guilds vanished in the face of division of labour in each single workshop.

Meantime the markets kept ever growing, the demand ever rising. Even manufacture no longer sufficed. Thereupon, steam and machinery revolutionized industrial production. The place of manufacture was taken by the giant, Modern Industry, the place of the industrial middle class, by industrial millionaires, the leaders of whole industrial armies, the modern bourgeois.

Modern industry has established the world market, for which the discovery of America paved the way. This market has given an immense development to commerce, to navigation, to communication by land. This development has, in its turn, reacted on the extension of industry; and in proportion as industry, commerce, navigation, railways extended, in the same proportion the bourgeoisie developed, increased its capital, and pushed into the background every class handed down from the Middle Ages.

We see, therefore, how the modern bourgeoisie is itself the product of a long course of development, of a series of revolutions in the modes of production and of exchange.

Each step in the development of the bourgeoisie was accompanied by a corresponding political advance of that class. An oppressed class under the sway of the feudal nobility, an armed and self-governing association in the medieval commune;* here independent urban republic (as in Italy and Germany), there taxable 'third estate' of the monarchy (as in France), afterwards, in the period of manufacture proper, serving either the semi-feudal or the absolute monarchy as a counterpoise against the nobility, and, in fact, corner-stone of the great monarchies in general, the bourgeoisie has at last, since the establishment of Modern Industry and of the world market, conquered for itself, in the modern representative State, exclusive political sway. The executive of the modern State is but a committee for managing the common affairs of the whole bourgeoisie.[21]

---

* 'Commune' was the name taken, in France, by the nascent towns even before they had conquered from their feudal lords and masters local self-government and political rights as the 'Third Estate'. Generally speaking, for the economical development of the bourgeoisie, England is here taken as the typical country; for its political development, France. [*Note by Engels to the English edition of 1888.*]

This was the name given their urban communities by the townsmen of Italy and France, after they had purchased or wrested their initial rights of self-government from their feudal lords. [*Note by Engels to the German edition of 1890.*]

The bourgeoisie, historically, has played a most revolutionary part.

The bourgeoisie, wherever it has got the upper hand, has put an end to all feudal, patriarchal, idyllic relations. It has pitilessly torn asunder the motley feudal ties that bound man to his 'natural superiors', and has left remaining no other nexus between man and man than naked self-interest, than callous 'cash payment'.[22] It has drowned the most heavenly ecstasies of religious fervour, of chivalrous enthusiasm, of philistine sentimentalism, in the icy water of egotistical calculation. It has resolved personal worth into exchange value, and in place of the numberless indefeasible chartered freedoms, has set up that single, unconscionable freedom – Free Trade. In one word, for exploitation, veiled by religious and political illusions, it has substituted naked, shameless, direct, brutal exploitation.

The bourgeoisie has stripped of its halo every occupation hitherto honoured and looked up to with reverent awe. It has converted the physician, the lawyer, the priest, the poet, the man of science, into its paid wage-labourers.[23]

The bourgeoisie has torn away from the family its sentimental veil, and has reduced the family relation to a mere money relation.

The bourgeoisie has disclosed how it came to pass that the brutal display of vigour in the Middle Ages, which Reactionists so much admire, found its fitting complement in the most slothful indolence. It has been the first to show what man's activity can bring about. It has accomplished wonders far surpassing Egyptian pyramids, Roman aqueducts, and Gothic cathedrals; it has conducted expeditions that put in the shade all former Exoduses of nations and crusades.

The bourgeoisie cannot exist without constantly revolutionizing the instruments of production, and thereby the relations of production, and with them the whole relations of society.

Conservation of the old modes of production in unaltered form, was, on the contrary, the first condition of existence for all earlier industrial classes. Constant revolutionizing of production, uninterrupted disturbance of all social conditions, everlasting uncertainty and agitation distinguish the bourgeois epoch from all earlier ones. All fixed, fast-frozen relations, with their train of ancient and venerable prejudices and opinions are swept away, all new-formed ones become antiquated before they can ossify. All that is solid melts into air, all that is holy is profaned, and man is at last compelled to face with sober senses, his real conditions of life, and his relations with his kind.

The need of a constantly expanding market for its products chases the bourgeoisie over the whole surface of the globe. It must nestle everywhere, settle everywhere, establish connexions everywhere.

The bourgeoisie has through its exploitation of the world market given a cosmopolitan character to production and consumption in every country. To the great chagrin of Reactionists, it has drawn from under the feet of industry the national ground on which it stood. All old-established national industries have been destroyed or are daily being destroyed. They are dislodged by new industries, whose introduction becomes a life and death question for all civilized nations, by industries that no longer work up indigenous raw material, but raw material drawn from the remotest zones; industries whose products are consumed, not only at home, but in every quarter of the globe. In place of the old wants, satisfied by the productions of the country, we find new wants, requiring for their satisfaction the products of distant lands and climes. In place of the old local and national seclusion and self-sufficiency, we have intercourse in every direction, universal inter-dependence of nations. And as in material, so also in intellectual production. The intellectual creations of individual nations become common property.

National one-sidedness and narrow-mindedness become more and more impossible, and from the numerous national and local literatures, there arises a world literature.[24]

The bourgeoisie, by the rapid improvement of all instruments of production, by the immensely facilitated means of communication, draws all, even the most barbarian, nations into civilization. The cheap prices of its commodities are the heavy artillery with which it batters down all Chinese walls, with which it forces 'the barbarians' intensely obstinate hatred of foreigners to capitulate. It compels all nations, on pain of extinction, to adopt the bourgeois mode of production; it compels them to introduce what it calls civilization into their midst, i.e., to become bourgeois themselves. In one word, it creates a world after its own image.

The bourgeoisie has subjected the country to the rule of the towns. It has created enormous cities, has greatly increased the urban population as compared with the rural, and has thus rescued a considerable part of the population from the idiocy of rural life.[25] Just as it has made the country dependent on the towns, so it has made barbarian and semi-barbarian countries dependent on the civilized ones, nations of peasants on nations of bourgeois, the East on the West.

The bourgeoisie keeps more and more doing away with the scattered state of the population, of the means of production, and of property. It has agglomerated population, centralized means of production, and has concentrated property in a few hands. The necessary consequence of this was political centralization. Independent, or but loosely connected, provinces with separate interests, laws, governments and systems of taxation, became lumped together into one nation, with one government, one code of laws, one national class-interest, one frontier and one customs-tariff.

The bourgeoisie, during its rule of scarce one hundred years, has created more massive and more colossal productive forces than have all preceding generations together. Subjection of Nature's forces to man, machinery, application of chemistry to industry and agriculture, steam-navigation, railways, electric telegraphs, clearing of whole continents for cultivation, canalization of rivers, whole populations conjured out of the ground – what earlier century had even a presentiment that such productive forces slumbered in the lap of social labour?

We see then: the means of production and of exchange, on whose foundation the bourgeoisie built itself up, were generated in feudal society. At a certain stage in the development of these means of production and of exchange, the conditions under which feudal society produced and exchanged, the feudal organization of agriculture and manufacturing industry, in one word, the feudal relations of property became no longer compatible with the already developed productive forces; they became so many fetters. They had to be burst asunder; they were burst asunder.[26]

Into their place stepped free competition, accompanied by a social and political constitution adapted to it, and by the economical and political sway of the bourgeois class.

A similar movement is going on before our own eyes. Modern bourgeois society with its relations of production, of exchange and of property, a society that has conjured up such gigantic means of production and of exchange, is like the sorcerer, who is no longer able to control the powers of the nether world whom he has called up by his spells. For many a decade past the history of industry and commerce is but the history of the revolt of modern productive forces against modern conditions of production, against the property relations that are the conditions for the existence of the bourgeoisie and of its rule. It is enough to mention the commercial crises that by their periodical return put on its trial, each time more threateningly, the existence of the entire bourgeois society. In these crises a great part not only of the existing products, but also of the previously created productive forces, are periodically destroyed. In these crises there breaks out an epidemic that, in all earlier epochs, would have seemed an absurdity – the epidemic of overproduction.[27] Society suddenly finds itself put back into a state of momentary barbarism; it appears as if a famine, a universal war of devastation had cut off the supply of every means of subsistence; industry and commerce seem to be destroyed; and why? Because there is too much civilization, too much means of subsistence, too much industry, too much commerce. The productive forces at the disposal of society no longer tend to further the development of the conditions of bourgeois property; on the contrary, they have become too powerful for these conditions, by which they are fettered, and so soon as they overcome these fetters, they bring disorder into the whole of bourgeois society, endanger the existence of bourgeois property. The conditions of bourgeois society are too narrow to comprise the wealth created by them. And how does the bourgeoisie get over these crises? On the one hand by enforced destruction of a mass of productive forces; on the other, by the conquest of new markets, and by the more thorough exploitation of the old ones. That is to say, by paving the way for more extensive and more destructive crises, and by diminishing the means whereby crises are prevented.

The weapons with which the bourgeoisie felled feudalism to the ground are now turned against the bourgeoisie itself.

But not only has the bourgeoisie forged the weapons that bring death to itself; it has also called into existence the men who are to wield those weapons – the modern working class – the proletarians.

In proportion as the bourgeoisie, i.e., capital, is developed, in the same proportion is the proletariat, the modern working class, developed – a class of labourers, who live only so long as they find work, and who find work only so long as their labour increases capital. These labourers, who must sell themselves piecemeal, are a commodity, like every other article of commerce, and are consequently exposed to all the vicissitudes of competition, to all the fluctuations of the market.[28]

Owing to the extensive use of machinery and to division of labour, the work of the proletarians has lost all individual character, and, consequently, all charm for the workman. He becomes an appendage of the machine, and it is only the most simple, most monotonous, and most easily acquired knack, that is required of him. Hence, the cost of production of a workman is restricted, almost entirely, to the means of subsistence that he requires for his maintenance, and for the propagation of his race. But the price of a commodity, and therefore also of labour, is equal to its cost of production.[29] In proportion, therefore, as the repulsiveness of the work increases, the wage decreases. Nay more, in proportion as the use of machinery and division of labour increases, in the same proportion the burden of toil also increases, whether by prolongation of the working hours, by increase of the work exacted in a given time or by increased speed of the machinery, etc.

Modern industry has converted the little workshop of the patriarchal master into the great factory of the industrial capitalist. Masses of labourers, crowded into the factory, are organized like soldiers. As privates of the industrial army they are placed under the command of a perfect hierarchy of officers and sergeants. Not only are they slaves of the bourgeois class, and of the bourgeois State; they are daily and hourly enslaved by the machine, by the overlooker, and, above all, by the individual bourgeois manufacturer himself. The more openly this despotism proclaims gain to be its end and aim, the more petty, the more hateful and the more embittering it is.

The less the skill and exertion of strength implied in manual labour, in other words, the more modern industry becomes developed, the more is the labour of men superseded by that of women. Differences of age and sex have no longer any distinctive social validity for the working class. All are instruments of labour, more or less expensive to use, according to their age and sex.

No sooner is the exploitation of the labourer by the manufacturer, so far, at an end, that he receives his wages in cash, than he is set upon by the other portions of the bourgeoisie, the landlord, the shopkeeper, the pawnbroker, etc.

The lower strata of the middle class – the small tradespeople, shopkeepers, and retired tradesmen generally, the handicraftsmen and peasants – all these sink gradually into the proletariat, partly because their diminutive capital does not suffice for the scale on which Modern Industry is carried on, and is swamped in the competition with the large capitalists, partly because their specialized skill is rendered worthless by new methods of production. Thus the proletariat is recruited from all classes of the population.

The proletariat goes through various stages of development.[30] With its birth begins its struggle with the bourgeoisie. At first the contest is carried on by individual labourers, then by the work-people of a factory, then by the operatives of one trade, in one locality, against the individual bourgeois who directly exploits them. They direct their attacks not against the bourgeois conditions of production, but against the instruments of production themselves; they destroy imported wares that compete with their labour, they smash to pieces machinery, they set factories ablaze, they seek to restore by force the vanished status of the workman of the Middle Ages.

At this stage the labourers still form an incoherent mass scattered over the whole country, and broken up by their mutual competition. If anywhere they unite to form more compact bodies, this is not yet the consequence of their own active union, but of the union of the bourgeoisie, which class, in order to attain its own political ends, is compelled to set the whole proletariat in motion, and is moreover yet, for a time, able to do so. At this stage, therefore, the proletarians do not fight their enemies, but the enemies of their enemies, the remnants of absolute monarchy, the landowners, the non-industrial bourgeois, the petty bourgeoisie. Thus the whole historical movement is concentrated in the hands of the bourgeoisie; every victory so obtained is a victory for the bourgeoisie.

But with the development of industry the proletariat not only increases in number; it becomes concentrated in greater masses, its strength grows, and it feels that strength more. The various interests and conditions of life within the ranks of the proletariat are more and more equalized, in proportion as machinery obliterates all distinctions of labour, and nearly everywhere reduces wages to the same low level. The growing competition among the bourgeois, and the resulting commercial crises, make the wages of the workers ever more fluctuating. The unceasing improvement of machinery, ever more rapidly developing, makes their livelihood more and more precarious; the collisions between individual workmen and individual bourgeois take more and more the character of collisions between two classes. Thereupon the workers begin to form combinations (Trades Unions) against the bourgeois; they club together in order to keep up the rate of wages; they found permanent associations in order to make provision beforehand for these occasional revolts. Here and there the contest breaks out into riots.

Now and then the workers are victorious, but only for a time. The real fruit of their battles lies, not in the immediate result, but in the ever-expanding union of the workers.[31] This union is helped on by the improved means of communication that are created by modern industry and that place the workers of different localities in contact with one another. It was just this contact that was needed to centralize the numerous local struggles, all of the same character, into one national struggle between classes. But every class struggle is a political struggle. And that union, to attain which the burghers of the Middle Ages, with their miserable highways, required centuries, the modern proletarians, thanks to railways, achieve in a few years.

This organization of the proletarians into a class, and consequently into a political party, is continually being upset again by the competition between the workers themselves. But it ever rises up again, stronger, firmer, mightier. It compels legislative recognition of particular interests of the workers, by taking advantage of the divisions among the bourgeoisie itself. Thus the Ten Hours bill in England was carried.[32]

Altogether collisions between the classes of the old society further, in many ways, the course of development of the proletariat. The bourgeoisie finds itself involved in a constant battle. At first with the aristocracy; later on, with those portions of the bourgeoisie itself, whose interests have become antagonistic to the progress of industry; at all times, with the bourgeoisie of foreign countries. In all these battles it sees itself compelled to appeal to the proletariat, to ask for its help, and thus, to drag it into the political arena. The bourgeoisie itself, therefore, supplies the proletariat with its own elements of political and general education, in other words, it furnishes the proletariat with weapons for fighting the bourgeoisie.

Further, as we have already seen, entire sections of the ruling classes are, by the advance of industry, precipitated into the proletariat, or are at least threatened in their conditions of existence. These also supply the proletariat with fresh elements of enlightenment and progress.

Finally, in times when the class struggle nears the decisive hour, the process of dissolution going on within the ruling class, in fact within the whole range of old society, assumes such a violent, glaring character, that a small section of the ruling class cuts itself adrift, and joins the revolutionary class, the class that holds the future in its hands. Just as, therefore, at an earlier period, a section of the nobility went over to the bourgeoisie, so now a portion of the bourgeoisie goes over to the proletariat, and in particular, a portion of the bourgeois ideologists, who have raised themselves to the level of comprehending theoretically the historical movement as a whole.

Of all the classes that stand face to face with the bourgeoisie today, the proletariat alone is a really revolutionary class. The other classes decay and finally disappear in the face of modern industry; the proletariat is its special and essential product.

The lower middle class, the small manufacturer, the shopkeeper, the artisan, the peasant, all these fight against the bourgeoisie, to save from extinction their existence as fractions of the middle class. They are therefore not revolutionary, but conservative. Nay more, they are reactionary, for they try to roll back the wheel of history. If by chance they are revolutionary, they are so only in view of their impending transfer into the proletariat, they thus defend not their present, but their future interests, they desert their own standpoint to place themselves at that of the proletariat.

The 'dangerous class', the social scum, that passively rotting mass thrown off by the lowest layers of old society, may, here and there, be swept into the movement by a proletarian revolution; its conditions of life, however, prepare it far more for the part of a bribed tool of reactionary intrigue.

In the conditions of the proletariat, those of old society at large are already virtually swamped. The proletarian is without property; his relation to his wife and children has no longer anything in common with the bourgeois family relations;

modern industrial labour, modern subjection to capital, the same in England as in France, in America as in Germany, has stripped him of every trace of national character. Law, morality, religion, are to him so many bourgeois prejudices, behind which lurk in ambush just as many bourgeois interests.

All the preceding classes that got the upper hand sought to fortify their already acquired status by subjecting society at large to their conditions of appropriation. The proletarians cannot become masters of the productive forces of society, except by abolishing their own previous mode of appropriation, and thereby also every other previous mode of appropriation. They have nothing of their own to secure and to fortify; their mission is to destroy all previous securities for, and insurances of, individual property.

All previous historical movements were movements of minorities, or in the interest of minorities. The proletarian movement is the self-conscious, independent movement of the immense majority, in the interest of the immense majority. The proletariat, the lowest stratum of our present society, cannot stir, cannot raise itself up, without the whole superincumbent strata of official society being sprung into the air.

Though not in substance, yet in form, the struggle of the proletariat with the bourgeoisie is at first a national struggle. The proletariat of each country must, of course, first of all settle matters with its own bourgeoisie.

In depicting the most general phases of the development of the proletariat, we traced the more or less veiled civil war, raging within existing society, up to the point where that war breaks out into open revolution, and where the violent overthrow of the bourgeoisie lays the foundation for the sway of the proletariat.

Hitherto, every form of society has been based, as we have already seen, on the antagonism of oppressing and oppressed classes. But in order to oppress a class, certain conditions must be assured to it under which it can, at least, continue its slavish existence. The serf, in the period of serfdom, raised himself to membership in the commune, just as the petty bourgeois, under the yoke of feudal absolutism, managed to develop into a bourgeois. The modern labourer, on the contrary, instead of rising with the progress of industry, sinks deeper and deeper below the conditions of existence of his own class. He becomes a pauper, and pauperism develops more rapidly than population and wealth. And here it becomes evident, that the bourgeoisie is unfit any longer to be the ruling class in society, and to impose its conditions of existence upon society as an overriding law. It is unfit to rule because it is incompetent to assure an existence to its slave within his slavery, because it cannot help letting him sink into such a state, that it has to feed him, instead of being fed by him. Society can no longer live under this bourgeoisie, in other words, its existence is no longer compatible with society.[33]

The essential condition for the existence, and for the sway of the bourgeois class, is the formation and augmentation of capital; the condition for capital is wage labour. Wage labour rests exclusively on competition between the labourers. The advance of industry, whose involuntary promoter is the bourgeoisie, replaces the isolation of the labourers, due to competition, by their revolutionary combination, due to association. The development of Modern Industry, therefore, cuts from under its feet the very foundation on which the bourgeoisie produces and appropriates products. What the bourgeoisie, therefore, produces, above all, is its own grave-diggers. Its fall and the victory of the proletariat are equally inevitable.[34]

2. *Proletarians and Communists*

In what relation do the Communists stand to the proletarians as a whole?

The Communists do not form a separate party opposed to other working-class parties.

They have no interests separate and apart from those of the proletariat as a whole.

They do not set up any sectarian principles of their own, by which to shape and mould the proletarian movement.

The Communists are distinguished from the other working-class parties by this only: 1. In the national struggles of the proletarians of the different countries, they point out and bring to the front the common interests of the entire proletariat, independently of all nationality. 2. In the various stages of development which the struggle of the working class against the bourgeoisie has to pass through, they always and everywhere represent the interests of the movement as a whole.

The Communists, therefore, are on the one hand, practically, the most advanced and resolute section of the working-class parties of every country, that section which pushes forward all others; on the other hand, theoretically, they have over the great mass of the proletariat the advantage of clearly understanding the line of march, the conditions, and the ultimate general results of the proletarian movement.

The immediate aim of the Communists is the same as that of all the other proletarian parties: formation of the proletariat into a class, overthrow of the bourgeois supremacy, conquest of political power by the proletariat.

The theoretical conclusions of the Communists are in no way based on ideas or principles that have been invented, or discovered, by this or that would-be universal reformer.

They merely express, in general terms, actual relations springing from an existing class struggle, from a historical movement going on under our very eyes. The abolition of existing property relations is not at all a distinctive feature of Communism.

All property relations in the past have continually been subject to historical change consequent upon the change in historical conditions.

The French Revolution, for example, abolished feudal property in favour of bourgeois property.

The distinguishing feature of Communism is not the abolition of property generally, but the abolition of bourgeois property. But modern bourgeois private property is the final and most complete expression of the system of producing and appropriating products, that is based on class antagonisms, on the exploitation of the many by the few.

In this sense, the theory of the Communists may be summed up in the single sentence: Abolition of private property.

We Communists have been reproached with the desire of abolishing the right of personally acquiring property as the fruit of a man's own labour, which property is alleged to be the ground work of all personal freedom, activity and independence.

Hard-won, self-acquired, self-earned property! Do you mean the property of the petty artisan and of the small peasant, a form of property that preceded the bourgeois form? There is no need to abolish that; the development of industry has to a great extent already destroyed it, and is still destroying it daily.

Or do you mean modern bourgeois private property?

But does wage labour create any property for the labourer? Not a bit. It creates capital, i.e., that kind of property which exploits wage labour, and which cannot increase except upon condition of begetting a new supply of wage labour for fresh exploitation. Property, in its present form, is based on the antagonism of capital and wage labour. Let us examine both sides of this antagonism.

To be a capitalist is to have not only a purely personal but a social *status* in production. Capital is a collective product, and only by the united action of many members, nay, in the last resort, only by the united action of all members of society, can it be set in motion.

Capital is, therefore, not a personal, it is a social power.

When, therefore, capital is converted into common property, into the property of all members of society, personal property is not thereby transformed into social property. It is only the social character of the property that is changed. It loses its class character.[35]

Let us now take wage labour.

The average price of wage labour is the minimum wage, i.e., that quantum of the means of subsistence which is absolutely requisite to keep the labourer in bare existence as a labourer. What, therefore, the wage-labourer appropriates by means of his labour, merely suffices to prolong and reproduce a bare existence. We by no means intend to abolish this personal appropriation of the products of labour, an appropriation that is made for the maintenance and reproduction of human life, and that leaves no surplus wherewith to command the labour of others. All that we want to do away with is the miserable character of this appropriation, under which the labourer lives merely to increase capital, and is allowed to live only in so far as the interest of the ruling class requires it.

In bourgeois society, living labour is but a means to increase accumulated labour. In Communist society, accumulated labour is but a means to widen, to enrich, to promote the existence of the labourer.

In bourgeois society, therefore, the past dominates the present: in Communist society, the present dominates the past. In bourgeois society capital is independent and has individuality, while the living person is dependent and has no individuality.

And the abolition of this state of things is called by the bourgeois, abolition of individuality and freedom! And rightly so. The abolition of bourgeois individuality, bourgeois independence, and bourgeois freedom is undoubtedly aimed at.

By freedom is meant, under the present bourgeois conditions of production, free trade, free selling and buying.

But if selling and buying disappears, free selling and buying disappears also. This talk about free selling and buying, and all the other 'brave words' of our bourgeoisie about freedom in general, have a meaning, if any, only in contrast with restricted selling and buying, with the fettered traders of the Middle Ages, but have no meaning when opposed to the Communistic abolition of buying and selling, of the bourgeois conditions of production, and of the bourgeoisie itself.

You are horrified at our intending to do away with private property. But in your existing society, private property is already done away with for nine-tenths of the population; its existence for the few is solely due to its non-existence in the hands of those nine-tenths. You reproach us, therefore, with intending to do away with a form of property the necessary condition for whose existence is the non-existence of any property for the immense majority of society.

In one word, you reproach us with intending to do away with your property. Precisely so; that is just what we intend.

From the moment when labour can no longer be converted into capital, money, or rent, into a social power capable of being monopolized, i.e., from the moment when individual property can no longer be transformed into bourgeois property, into capital, from that moment, you say, individuality vanishes.

You must, therefore, confess that by 'individual' you mean no other person than the bourgeois, than the middle-class owner of property. This person must, indeed, be swept out of the way, and made impossible.

Communism deprives no man of the power to appropriate the products of society; all that it does is to deprive him of the power to subjugate the labour of others by means of such appropriation.

It has been objected that upon the abolition of private property all work will cease, and universal laziness will overtake us.

According to this, bourgeois society ought long ago to have gone to the dogs through sheer idleness; for those of its members who work, acquire nothing, and those who acquire anything, do not work. The whole of this objection is but another expression of the tautology: that there can no longer be any wage labour when there is no longer any capital.

All objections urged against the Communistic mode of producing and appropriating material products, have, in the same way, been urged against the Communistic modes of producing and appropriating intellectual products. Just as, to the bourgeois, the disappearance of class property is the disappearance of production itself, so the disappearance of class culture is to him identical with the disappearance of all culture.

That culture, the loss of which he laments, is, for the enormous majority, a mere training to act as a machine.

But don't wrangle with us so long as you apply, to our intended abolition of bourgeois property, the standard of your bourgeois notions of freedom, culture, law, &c. Your very ideas are but the outgrowth of the conditions of your bourgeois production and bourgeois property, just as your jurisprudence is but the will of your class made into a law for all, a will, whose essential character and direction are determined by the economical conditions of existence of your class.

The selfish misconception that induces you to transform into eternal laws of nature and of reason, the social forms springing from your present mode of production and form of property – historical relations that rise and disappear in the progress of production – this misconception you share with every ruling class that has preceded you. What you see clearly in the case of ancient property, what you admit in the case of feudal property, you are of course forbidden to admit in the case of your own bourgeois form of property.

Abolition of the family! Even the most radical flare up at this infamous proposal of the Communists.

On what foundation is the present family, the bourgeois family, based? On capital, on private gain. In its completely developed form this family exists only among the bourgeoisie. But this state of things finds its complement in the practical absence of the family among the proletarians, and in public prostitution. The bourgeois family will vanish as a matter of course when its complement vanishes, and both will vanish with the vanishing of capital.

Do you charge us with wanting to stop the exploitation of children by their parents? To this crime we plead guilty.

But, you will say, we destroy the most hallowed of relations, when we replace home education by social.

And your education! Is not that also social, and determined by the social conditions under which you educate, by the intervention, direct or indirect, of society, by means of schools, &c? The Communists have not invented the intervention of society in education; they do but seek to alter the character of that intervention, and to rescue education from the influence of the ruling class.

The bourgeois clap-trap about the family and education,

about the hallowed co-relation of parent and child, becomes all the more disgusting, the more, by the action of Modern Industry, all family ties among the proletarians are torn asunder, and their children transformed into simple articles of commerce and instruments of labour.[36]

But you Communists would introduce community of women, screams the whole bourgeoisie in chorus.[37]

The bourgeois sees in his wife a mere instrument of production. He hears that the instruments of production are to be exploited in common, and, naturally, can come to no other conclusion than that the lot of being common to all will likewise fall to the women.

He has not even a suspicion that the real point aimed at is to do away with the status of women as mere instruments of production.

For the rest, nothing is more ridiculous than the virtuous indignation of our bourgeois at the community of women which, they pretend, is to be openly and officially established by the Communists. The Communists have no need to introduce community of women; it has existed almost from time immemorial.

Our bourgeois, not content with having the wives and daughters of their proletarians at their disposal, not to speak of common prostitutes, take the greatest pleasure in seducing each other's wives.

Bourgeois marriage is in reality a system of wives in common and thus, at the most, what the Communists might possibly be reproached with, is that they desire to introduce, in substitution for a hypocritically concealed, an openly legalized community of women. For the rest, it is self-evident that the abolition of the present system of production must bring with it the abolition of the community of women springing from that system, i.e., of prostitution both public and private.[38]

The Communists are further reproached with desiring to abolish countries and nationality.

The working men have no country.[39] We cannot take from them what they have not got. Since the proletariat must first of all acquire political supremacy, must rise to be the leading class of the nation, must constitute itself *the* nation, it is, so far, itself national, though not in the bourgeois sense of the word.

National differences and antagonisms between peoples are daily more and more vanishing, owing to the development of the bourgeoisie, to freedom of commerce, to the world market, to uniformity in the mode of production and in the conditions of life corresponding thereto.

The supremacy of the proletariat will cause them to vanish still faster. United action, of the leading civilized countries at least, is one of the first conditions for the emancipation of the proletariat.

In proportion as the exploitation of one individual by another is put an end to, the exploitation of one nation by another will also be put an end to. In proportion as the antagonism between classes within the nation vanishes, the hostility of one nation to another will come to an end.

The charges against Communism made from a religious, a philosophical, and, generally, from an ideological standpoint, are not deserving of serious examination.

Does it require deep intuition to comprehend that man's ideas, views and conceptions, in one word, man's consciousness, changes with every change in the conditions of his material existence, in his social relations and in his social life?[40]

What else does the history of ideas prove, than that intellectual production changes in character in proportion as material production is changed? The ruling ideas of each age have ever been the ideas of its ruling class.

When people speak of ideas that revolutionize society, they

do but express the fact, that within the old society, the elements of a new one have been created, and that the dissolution of the old ideas keeps even pace with the dissolution of the old conditions of existence.

When the ancient world was in its last throes, the ancient religions were overcome by Christianity. When Christian ideas succumbed in the 18th century to rationalist ideas, feudal society fought its death battle with the then revolutionary bourgeoisie.[41] The ideas of religious liberty and freedom of conscience, merely gave expression to the sway of free competition within the domain of knowledge.

'Undoubtedly,' it will be said, 'religious, moral, philosophical and juridical ideas have been modified in the course of historical development. But religion, morality, philosophy, political science, and law, constantly survived this change.

'There are, besides, eternal truths, such as Freedom, Justice, etc., that are common to all states of society. But Communism abolishes eternal truths, it abolishes all religion, and all morality, instead of constituting them on a new basis; it therefore acts in contradiction to all past historical experience.'

What does this accusation reduce itself to? The history of all past society has consisted in the development of class antagonisms, antagonisms that assumed different forms at different epochs.

But whatever form they may have taken, one fact is common to all past ages, viz., the exploitation of one part of society by the other.[42] No wonder, then, that the social consciousness of past ages, despite all the multiplicity and variety it displays, moves within certain common forms, or general ideas, which cannot completely vanish except with the total disappearance of class antagonisms.

The Communist revolution is the most radical rupture with traditional property relations; no wonder that its development involves the most radical rupture with traditional ideas.

But let us have done with the bourgeois objections to Communism.

We have seen above, that the first step in the revolution by the working class, is to raise the proletariat to the position of ruling class, to win the battle of democracy.

The proletariat will use its political supremacy to wrest, by degrees, all capital from the bourgeoisie, to centralize all instruments of production in the hands of the State, i.e., of the proletariat organized as the ruling class; and to increase the total of productive forces as rapidly as possible.[43]

Of course, in the beginning, this cannot be effected except by means of despotic inroads on the rights of property, and on the conditions of bourgeois production; by means of measures, therefore, which appear economically insufficient and untenable, but which, in the course of the movement, outstrip themselves, necessitate further inroads upon the old social order, and are unavoidable as a means of entirely revolutionizing the mode of production.

These measures will of course be different in different countries.

Nevertheless, in the most advanced countries, the following will be pretty generally applicable:

1. Abolition of property in land and application of all rents of land to public purposes.
2. A heavy progressive or graduated income tax.
3. Abolition of all right of inheritance.[44]
4. Confiscation of the property of all emigrants and rebels.
5. Centralization of credit in the hands of the State, by means of a national bank with State capital and an exclusive monopoly.
6. Centralization of the means of communication and transport in the hands of the State.

7. Extension of factories and instruments of production owned by the State; the bringing into cultivation of wastelands, and the improvement of the soil generally in accordance with a common plan.

8. Equal liability of all to labour. Establishment of industrial armies, especially for agriculture.

9. Combination of agriculture with manufacturing industries; gradual abolition of the distinction between town and country, by a more equable distribution of the population over the country.[45]

10. Free education for all children in public schools. Abolition of children's factory labour in its present form. Combination of education with industrial production, &c., &c.[46]

When, in the course of development, class distinctions have disappeared, and all production has been concentrated in the hands of a vast association of the whole nation, the public power will lose its political character.[47] Political power, properly so called, is merely the organized power of one class for oppressing another. If the proletariat during its contest with the bourgeoisie is compelled, by the force of circumstances, to organize itself as a class, if, by means of a revolution, it makes itself the ruling class, and, as such, sweeps away by force the old conditions of production, then it will, along with these conditions, have swept away the conditions for the existence of class antagonisms and of classes generally, and will thereby have abolished its own supremacy as a class.

In place of the old bourgeois society, with its classes and class antagonisms, we shall have an association, in which the free development of each is the condition for the free development of all.

3. *Socialist and Communist Literature*

1. Reactionary Socialism

a. Feudal Socialism

Owing to their historical position, it became the vocation of the aristocracies of France and England to write pamphlets against modern bourgeois society. In the French revolution of July 1830, and in the English reform agitation, these aristocracies again succumbed to the hateful upstart. Thenceforth, a serious political contest was altogether out of question. A literary battle alone remained possible. But even in the domain of literature the old cries of the restoration period* had become impossible.

In order to arouse sympathy, the aristocracy were obliged to lose sight, apparently, of their own interests, and to formulate their indictment against the bourgeoisie in the interest of the exploited working class alone. Thus the aristocracy took their revenge by singing lampoons on their new master, and whispering in his ears sinister prophecies of coming catastrophe.

In this way arose feudal Socialism: half lamentation, half lampoon: half echo of the past, half menace of the future; at times, by its bitter, witty and incisive criticism, striking the bourgeoisie to the very heart's core; but always ludicrous in its effect, through total incapacity to comprehend the march of modern history.

The aristocracy, in order to rally the people to them, waved the proletarian alms-bag in front for a banner. But the people, so often as it joined them, saw on their hindquarters the old

---

* Not the English Restoration 1660 to 1689, but the French Restoration 1814 to 1830. [*Note by Engels to the English edition of 1888.*]

feudal coats of arms, and deserted with loud and irreverent laughter.[48]

One section of the French Legitimists and 'Young England' exhibited this spectacle.[49]

In pointing out that their mode of exploitation was different to that of the bourgeoisie, the feudalists forget that they exploited under circumstances and conditions that were quite different, and that are now antiquated. In showing that, under their rule, the modern proletariat never existed, they forget that the modern bourgeoisie is the necessary offspring of their own form of society.

For the rest, so little do they conceal the reactionary character of their criticism that their chief accusation against the bourgeoisie amounts to this, that under the bourgeois *régime* a class is being developed, which is destined to cut up root and branch the old order of society.

What they upbraid the bourgeoisie with is not so much that it creates a proletariat, as that it creates a revolutionary proletariat.

In political practice, therefore, they join in all coercive measures against the working class; and in ordinary life, despite their high-falutin phrases, they stoop to pick up the golden apples dropped from the tree of industry, and to barter truth, love, and honour for traffic in wool, beetroot-sugar, and potato spirits.*

As the parson has ever gone hand in hand with the landlord, so has Clerical Socialism with Feudal Socialism.

Nothing is easier than to give Christian asceticism a Socialist tinge. Has not Christianity declaimed against private property,

---

* This applies chiefly to Germany where the landed aristocracy and squirearchy have large portions of their estates cultivated for their own account by stewards, and are, moreover, extensive beetroot-sugar manufacturers and distillers of potato spirits. The wealthier British aristocracy are, as yet, rather above that; but they, too, know how to make up for declining rents by lending their names to floaters of more or less shady joint-stock companies. [*Note by Engels to the English edition of 1888.*]

against marriage, against the State? Has it not preached in the place of these, charity and poverty, celibacy and mortification of the flesh, monastic life and Mother Church? Christian Socialism is but the holy water with which the priest consecrates the heart-burnings of the aristocrat.[50]

b. Petty-Bourgeois Socialism

The feudal aristocracy was not the only class that was ruined by the bourgeoisie, not the only class whose conditions of existence pined and perished in the atmosphere of modern bourgeois society. The medieval burgesses and the small peasant proprietors were the precursors of the modern bourgeoisie. In those countries which are but little developed, industrially and commercially, these two classes still vegetate side by side with the rising bourgeoisie.

In countries where modern civilization has become fully developed, a new class of petty bourgeois has been formed, fluctuating between proletariat and bourgeoisie and ever renewing itself as a supplementary part of bourgeois society. The individual members of this class, however, are being constantly hurled down into the proletariat by the action of competition, and, as modern industry develops, they even see the moment approaching when they will completely disappear as an independent section of modern society, to be replaced, in manufacture, agriculture and commerce, by overlookers, bailiffs and shopmen.

In countries like France, where the peasants constitute far more than half of the population, it was natural that writers who sided with the proletariat against the bourgeoisie, should use, in their criticism of the bourgeois *régime*, the standard of the peasant and petty bourgeois, and from the standpoint of these intermediate classes should take up the cudgels for the working class. Thus arose petty-bourgeois Socialism. Sismondi was the head of this school, not only in France but also in England.[51]

This school of Socialism dissected with great acuteness the contradictions in the conditions of modern production. It laid bare the hypocritical apologies of economists. It proved, incontrovertibly, the disastrous effects of machinery and division of labour; the concentration of capital and land in a few hands; over-production and crises; it pointed out the inevitable ruin of the petty bourgeois and peasant, the misery of the proletariat, the anarchy in production, the crying inequalities in the distribution of wealth, the industrial war of extermination between nations, the dissolution of old moral bonds, of the old family relations, of the old nationalities.

In its positive aims, however, this form of Socialism aspires either to restoring the old means of production and of exchange, and with them the old property relations, and the old society, or to cramping the modern means of production and of exchange, within the framework of the old property relations that have been, and were bound to be, exploded by those means. In either case, it is both reactionary and Utopian.

Its last words are: corporate guilds for manufacture; patriarchal relations in agriculture.

Ultimately, when stubborn historical facts had dispersed all intoxicating effects of self-deception, this form of Socialism ended in a miserable fit of the blues.[52]

c. German, or 'True', Socialism

The Socialist and Communist literature of France, a literature that originated under the pressure of a bourgeoisie in power, and that was the expression of the struggle against this power, was introduced into Germany at a time when the bourgeoisie, in that country, had just begun its contest with feudal absolutism.

German philosophers, would-be philosophers, and *beaux esprits*, eagerly seized on this literature, only forgetting, that when these writings immigrated from France into Germany,

French social conditions had not immigrated along with them.[53] In contact with German social conditions, this French literature lost all its immediate practical significance, and assumed a purely literary aspect. Thus, to the German philosophers of the Eighteenth Century, the demands of the first French Revolution were nothing more than the demands of 'Practical Reason' in general, and the utterance of the will of the revolutionary French bourgeoisie signified in their eyes the laws of pure Will, of Will as it was bound to be, of true human Will generally.[54]

The work of the German *literati* consisted solely in bringing the new French ideas into harmony with their ancient philosophical conscience, or rather, in annexing the French ideas without deserting their own philosophic point of view.

This annexation took place in the same way in which a foreign language is appropriated, namely, by translation.

It is well known how the monks wrote silly lives of Catholic Saints *over* the manuscripts on which the classical works of ancient heathendom had been written. The German *literati* reversed this process with the profane French literature. They wrote their philosophical nonsense beneath the French original. For instance, beneath the French criticism of the economic functions of money, they wrote 'Alienation of Humanity', and beneath the French criticism of the bourgeois State they wrote, 'Dethronement of the Category of the General', and so forth.

The introduction of these philosophical phrases at the back of the French historical criticisms they dubbed 'Philosophy of Action', 'True Socialism', 'German Science of Socialism', 'Philosophical Foundation of Socialism', and so on.[55]

The French Socialist and Communist literature was thus completely emasculated. And, since it ceased in the hands of the German to express the struggle of one class with the other, he felt conscious of having overcome 'French onesidedness' and of representing, not true requirements, but the requirements of

Truth; not the interests of the proletariat, but the interests of Human Nature, of Man in general, who belongs to no class, has no reality, who exists only in the misty realm of philosophical fantasy.

This German Socialism, which took its schoolboy task so seriously and solemnly, and extolled its poor stock-in-trade in such mountebank fashion, meanwhile gradually lost its pedantic innocence.

The fight of the German, and, especially of the Prussian bourgeoisie, against feudal aristocracy and absolute monarchy, in other words, the liberal movement, became more earnest.

By this, the long wished-for opportunity was offered to 'True' Socialism of confronting the political movement with the Socialist demands, of hurling the traditional anathemas against liberalism, against representative government, against bourgeois competition, bourgeois freedom of the press, bourgeois legislation, bourgeois liberty and equality, and of preaching to the masses that they had nothing to gain, and everything to lose, by this bourgeois movement. German Socialism forgot, in the nick of time, that the French criticism, whose silly echo it was, presupposed the existence of modern bourgeois society, with its corresponding economic conditions of existence, and the political constitution adapted thereto, the very things whose attainment was the object of the pending struggle in Germany.

To the absolute governments, with their following of parsons, professors, country squires and officials, it served as a welcome scarecrow against the threatening bourgeoisie.

It was a sweet finish after the bitter pills of floggings and bullets with which these same governments, just at that time, dosed the German working-class risings.

While this 'True' Socialism thus served the governments as a weapon for fighting the German bourgeoisie, it, at the same time, directly represented a reactionary interest, the interest of the German Philistines. In Germany the *petty-bourgeois* class, a relic of the sixteenth century, and since then constantly cropping up again under various forms, is the real social basis of the existing state of things.

To preserve this class is to preserve the existing state of things in Germany. The industrial and political supremacy of the bourgeoisie threatens it with certain destruction; on the one hand, from the concentration of capital; on the other, from the rise of a revolutionary proletariat. 'True' Socialism appeared to kill these two birds with one stone. It spread like an epidemic.

The robe of speculative cobwebs, embroidered with flowers of rhetoric, steeped in the dew of sickly sentiment, this transcendental robe in which the German Socialists wrapped their sorry 'eternal truths', all skin and bone, served to wonderfully increase the sale of their goods amongst such a public.

And on its part, German Socialism recognized, more and more, its own calling as the bombastic representative of the petty-bourgeois Philistine.

It proclaimed the German nation to be the model nation, and the German petty Philistine to be the typical man. To every villainous meanness of this model man it gave a hidden, higher Socialistic interpretation, the exact contrary of its real character. It went to the extreme length of directly opposing the 'brutally destructive' tendency of Communism, and of proclaiming its supreme and impartial contempt of all class struggles. With very few exceptions, all the so-called Socialist and Communist publications that now (1847) circulate in Germany belong to the domain of this foul and enervating literature.*

* The revolutionary storm of 1848 swept away this whole shabby tendency and cured its protagonists of the desire to dabble further in Socialism. The chief representative and classical type of this tendency is Herr Karl Grün. [*Note by Engels to the German edition of 1890.*]

II. Conservative, or Bourgeois, Socialism

A part of the bourgeoisie is desirous of redressing social grievances, in order to secure the continued existence of bourgeois
society.

To this section belong economists, philanthropists, humani-
tarians, improvers of the condition of the working class, organ-
isers of charity, members of societies for the prevention of cruelty
to animals, temperance fanatics, hole-and-corner reformers of
every imaginable kind. This form of Socialism has, moreover,
been worked out into complete systems.

We may cite Proudhon's *Philosophie de la Misère* as an example
of this form.[56]

The Socialistic bourgeois want all the advantages of modern
social conditions without the struggles and dangers necessarily
resulting therefrom. They desire the existing state of society
minus its revolutionary and disintegrating elements. They wish
for a bourgeoisie without a proletariat. The bourgeoisie naturally conceives the world in which it is supreme to be the best;
and bourgeois Socialism develops this comfortable conception
into various more or less complete systems. In requiring the
proletariat to carry out such a system, and thereby to march
straightway into the social New Jerusalem, it but requires in
reality, that the proletariat should remain within the bounds
of existing society, but should cast away all its hateful ideas
concerning the bourgeoisie.

A second and more practical, but less systematic, form of this
Socialism sought to depreciate every revolutionary movement
in the eyes of the working class, by showing that no mere
political reform, but only a change in the material conditions of
existence, in economical relations, could be of any advantage
to them. By changes in the material conditions of existence, this

form of Socialism, however, by no means understands abolition of the bourgeois relations of production, an abolition that can be effected only by a revolution, but administrative reforms, based on the continued existence of these relations; reforms, therefore, that in no respect affect the relations between capital and labour, but, at the best, lessen the cost, and simplify the administrative work, of bourgeois government.

Bourgeois Socialism attains adequate expression, when and only when, it becomes a mere figure of speech.

Free trade: for the benefit of the working class. Protective duties: for the benefit of the working class. Prison Reform: for the benefit of the working class. This is the last word and the only seriously meant word of bourgeois Socialism.

It is summed up in the phrase: the bourgeois is a bourgeois – for the benefit of the working class.

III. Critical-Utopian Socialism and Communism

We do not here refer to that literature which, in every great modern revolution, has always given voice to the demands of the proletariat, such as the writings of Babeuf and others.[57]

The first direct attempts of the proletariat to attain its own ends, made in times of universal excitement, when feudal society was being overthrown, these attempts necessarily failed, owing to the then undeveloped state of the proletariat, as well as to the absence of the economic conditions for its emancipation, conditions that had yet to be produced, and could be produced by the impending bourgeois epoch alone. The revolutionary literature that accompanied these first movements of the proletariat had necessarily a reactionary character. It inculcated universal asceticism and social levelling in its crudest form.

The Socialist and Communist systems properly so called,

those of Saint-Simon, Fourier, Owen and others, spring into existence in the early undeveloped period, described above, of the struggle between proletariat and bourgoisie (see Section 1. Bourgeois and Proletarians).[58]

The founders of these systems see, indeed, the class antagonisms, as well as the action of the decomposing elements in the prevailing form of society. But the proletariat, as yet in its infancy, offers to them the spectacle of a class without any historical initiative or any independent political movement.

Since the development of class antagonism keeps even pace with the development of industry, the economic situation, as they find it, does not as yet offer to them the material conditions for the emancipation of the proletariat. They therefore search after a new social science, after new social laws, that are to create these conditions.

Historical action is to yield to their personal inventive action, historically created conditions of emancipation to fantastic ones, and the gradual, spontaneous class organization of the proletariat to an organization of society specially contrived by these inventors. Future history resolves itself, in their eyes, into the propaganda and the practical carrying out of their social plans.

In the formation of their plans they are conscious of caring chiefly for the interests of the working class, as being the most suffering class. Only from the point of view of being the most suffering class does the proletariat exist for them.[59]

The undeveloped state of the class struggle, as well as their own surroundings, causes Socialists of this kind to consider themselves far superior to all class antagonisms. They want to improve the condition of every member of society, even that of the most favoured. Hence, they habitually appeal to society at large, without distinction of class; nay, by preference, to the ruling class. For how can people, when once they understand their system, fail to see in it the best possible plan of the best possible state of society?

Hence, they reject all political, and especially all revolutionary, action; they wish to attain their ends by peaceful means, and endeavour, by small experiments, necessarily doomed to failure, and by the force of example, to pave the way for the new social Gospel.

Such fantastic pictures of future society, painted at a time when the proletariat is still in a very undeveloped state and has but a fantastic conception of its own position correspond with the first instinctive yearnings of that class for a general reconstruction of society.

But these Socialist and Communist publications contain also a critical element. They attack every principle of existing society. Hence they are full of the most valuable materials for the enlightenment of the working class. The practical measures proposed in them – such as the abolition of the distinction between town and country, of the family, of the carrying on of industries for the account of private individuals, and of the wage system, the proclamation of social harmony, the conversion of the functions of the State into a mere superintendence of production, all these proposals point solely to the disappearance of class antagonisms which were, at that time, only just cropping up, and which, in these publications, are recognized in their earliest indistinct and undefined forms only. These proposals, therefore, are of a purely Utopian character.

The significance of Critical-Utopian Socialism and Communism bears an inverse relation to historical development. In proportion as the modern class struggle develops and takes definite shape, this fantastic standing apart from the contest, these fantastic attacks on it, lose all practical value and all theoretical justification. Therefore, although the originators of these systems were, in many respects, revolutionary, their disciples have, in every case, formed mere reactionary sects. They hold fast by the original views of their masters, in opposition to the progressive historical development of the proletariat. They, therefore, endeavour, and that consistently, to deaden the class struggle and to reconcile the class antagonisms. They still dream of experimental realization of their social Utopias, of founding isolated '*phalanstères*', of establishing 'Home Colonies', of setting up a 'Little Icaria'* – duodecimo editions of the New Jerusalem – and to realize all these castles in the air, they are compelled to appeal to the feelings and purses of the bourgeois. By degrees they sink into the category of the reactionary conservative Socialists depicted above, differing from these only by more systematic pedantry, and by their fanatical and superstitious belief in the miraculous effects of their social science.

They, therefore, violently oppose all political action on the part of the working class; such action, according to them, can only result from blind unbelief in the new Gospel.

The Owenites in England and the Fourierists in France, respectively oppose the Chartists and the *Réformistes*.[60]

---

* *Phalanstères* were Socialist colonies on the plan of Charles Fourier; *Icaria* was the name given by Cabet to his Utopia and, later on, to his American Communist colony. [*Note by Engels to the English edition of 1888.*]

'Home colonies' were what Owen called his Communist model societies. *Phalanstères* was the name of the public palaces planned by Fourier. *Icaria* was the name given to the Utopian land of fancy, whose Communist institutions Cabet portrayed. [*Note by Engels to the German edition of 1890.*]

4. Position of the Communists in Relation to the Various Existing Opposition Parties

Section 2 has made clear the relations of the Communists to the existing working-class parties, such as the Chartists in England and the Agrarian Reformers in America.[61]

The Communists fight for the attainment of the immediate aims, for the enforcement of the momentary interests of the working class; but in the movement of the present, they also represent and take care of the future of that movement. In France the Communists ally themselves with the Social-Democrats,* against the conservative and radical bourgeoisie, reserving, however, the right to take up a critical position in regard to phrases and illusions traditionally handed down from the great Revolution.

In Switzerland they support the Radicals, without losing sight of the fact that this party consists of antagonistic elements, partly of Democratic Socialists, in the French sense, partly of radical bourgeois.[62]

In Poland they support the party that insists on an agrarian revolution as the prime condition for national emancipation, that party which fomented the insurrection of Cracow in 1846.[63]

In Germany they fight with the bourgeoisie whenever it acts in a revolutionary way, against the absolute monarchy, the feudal squirearchy, and the petty bourgeoisie.

---

* The party then represented in Parliament by Ledru-Rollin, in literature by Louis Blanc, in the daily press by the *Réforme*. The name of Social-Democracy signified, with these its inventors, a section of the Democratic or Republican party more or less tinged with Socialism. [*Note by Engels to the English edition of 1888.*]

The party in France which at that time called itself Socialist-Democratic was represented in political life by Ledru-Rollin and in literature by Louis Blanc; thus it differed immeasurably from present-day German Social-Democracy. [*Note by Engels to the German edition of 1890.*]

THE COMMUNIST MANIFESTO

But they never cease, for a single instant, to instil into the working class the clearest possible recognition of the hostile antagonism between bourgeoisie and proletariat, in order that the German workers may straightway use, as so many weapons against the bourgeoisie, the social and political conditions that the bourgeoisie must necessarily introduce along with its supremacy, and in order that, after the fall of the reactionary classes in Germany, the fight against the bourgeoisie itself may immediately begin.

The Communists turn their attention chiefly to Germany, because that country is on the eve of a bourgeois revolution that is bound to be carried out under more advanced conditions of European civilization, and with a much more developed proletariat, than that of England was in the seventeenth, and of France in the eighteenth century, and because the bourgeois revolution in Germany will be but the prelude to an immediately following proletarian revolution.[64]

In short, the Communists everywhere support every revolutionary movement against the existing social and political order of things.

In all these movements they bring to the front, as the leading question in each, the property question, no matter what its degree of development at the time.

Finally, they labour everywhere for the union and agreement of the democratic parties of all countries.

The Communists disdain to conceal their views and aims. They openly declare that their ends can be attained only by the forcible overthrow of all existing social conditions. Let the ruling classes tremble at a Communistic revolution. The proletarians have nothing to lose but their chains. They have a world to win.

WORKING MEN OF ALL COUNTRIES,

UNITE!

258

prairies by railway and the western migration of American immigrants drastically cut cereal prices. In Britain, this fall in agricultural prices created prolonged agricultural depression, lasting through to 1914. In Germany, it was answered by a programme of tariff protection that formed the basis of a conservative nationalist alliance between Junkers and heavy industry.

8. The tsar in 1848–9 was Nicholas I. His successor, Alexander II, who had emancipated the serfs in 1861, was assassinated by Russian populists in 1881. He was succeeded by Alexander III, who remained at Gatshina, the tsar's country residence, for fear that another assassination attempt might be mounted by the executive committee of the People's Will, the main revolutionary populist organisation.

9. *Obshchina*: the village community.

10. In the first edition of *Capital* in 1867, Marx had stated that 'the country that is more developed industrially only shows, to the less developed, the image of its own future.' He had also derided as romantic panslavism Alexander Herzen's view of the uniqueness of the Russian village commune. In the first edition of *Capital*, therefore, Marx implied that Russia, like Germany, must follow the example of Britain by opening itself to capitalist development and industrialization. By the end of 1869, however, Marx had begun to change his mind. Marx was surprised to find that the country in which *Capital* had its greatest success and was most seriously discussed was Russia; and he himself began to be drawn into the discussion. He taught himself Russian and began to follow the debates on the prospects of capitalist development and the fate of the village commune in the decades following the emancipation of the serfs. In the early 1870s, he was particularly impressed by the essays of N. G. Chernyshevsky on the communal ownership of land. Chernyshevsky argued that 'the development of certain social phenomena in backward nations, thanks to the influences of the advanced nation, skips an intermediary stage and jumps directly from a low to a higher stage'. Concretely, this meant that thanks to the existence of the advanced West, Russia could move from the village commune directly to socialism without undergoing an intermediate bourgeois stage.

Revolutionary populism was an offshoot of this argument. For after peasant emancipation and the apparent progress of Russia along the same path as Western Europe, it was clear that the days of the village commune were numbered. The choice was, therefore, either to push for immediate revolution before the village commune disappeared (hence the resort to terrorism and assassination), or else to wait many decades for capitalist development and the growth of an industrial proletariat to make possible a Western path to socialism. The Black Repartition, a group of exiles in

Geneva, led by Plekhanov and Vera Zasulich, pushed for the latter strategy and based its case on the arguments of the 1867 edition of *Capital*. But editorial changes made by Marx to subsequent editions of *Capital* suggest that his sympathy lay with the revolutionary populist position, that he therefore supported the People's Will rather than the 'Marxist' group around Plekhanov.

This also seems to have led to an implicit divergence between Marx's position and that of Engels. Engels believed that a transition from the village commune to advanced communism in Russia could only occur if there were a successful proletarian revolution in the West. Marx's position seems to have been more equivocal. In one of the (unsent) drafts of a letter to Vera Zasulich replying to her request that he publicly make clear his position, he appeared to suggest that a transition from village commune to advanced communism might be possible without a proletarian revolution in the West. It therefore seems that the supposedly joint position expressed in this preface to the 1882 Russian edition was an expression of Engels' views. See H. Wada, 'Marx and Revolutionary Russia', in Shanin (ed.), *Late Marx*, pp. 40–75.

11. Marx, who had been suffering from chronic bronchitis and recurrent bouts of pleurisy, died of a haemorrhage of the lung on 14 March at his house, 41 Maitland Park Road in London.

12. Ferdinand Lassalle (1825–64) was a Hegelian and an active supporter of Marx's position in the democratic movement in the Rhineland in 1848. In 1863, he founded the *Allgemeine Deutsche Arbeiterverein* (General Association of German Workers), the forerunner (together with the *Sozialdemokratische Arbeiterpartei* (Social Democratic Workers' Party) founded at Eisenach in 1869) of the *Sozialdemokratische Partei Deutschlands* (the German Social Democratic Party). Lassalle was generally regarded as the founder of the German labour movement. He died as a result of a duel in 1864. Lassalle respected Marx's ideas, but (despite Engels' claims) could not be regarded as a follower of Marx. In the early 1860s, Louis Blanc's ideas on state-assisted cooperatives and the Chartist campaign for the suffrage provided more immediate inspiration for his ideas. In the period between 1875 and 1914, the Social Democratic Party became the strongest organized workers' party in Europe. Its programme, laid out in Erfurt in 1891, drew upon Marx, Lassalle and radical democratic ideas.

13. On the First International, see Introduction, pp. 17–18.

14. Engels is referring to the theory expounded in Charles Darwin, *On the Origin of Species by Means of Natural Selection, or the Preservation of Favoured Races in the Struggle for Life*, London, 1859.

15. The International Socialist Workers' Congress – what became the Second International – met in Paris, 14–18 July 1889. It passed a resolution to mark 1 May 1890 as a day of meetings and demonstrations in all countries in support of the 8-hour day.

16. Louis-Napoléon Bonaparte (1808–73) was a nephew of Napoleon I. He was elected President of the Second Republic in France (1848–52) and then through a *coup d'état* declared himself Emperor of the French (1852–70). He abdicated after the French defeat in the Franco-Prussian War.

Otto Prince von Bismarck (1815–98) became Prime Minister of Prussia 1862–71 and then, after defeating both the Austrians and the French, first Chancellor of the newly founded German Empire (the Second Reich) 1871–90

17. The Holy Alliance was an association of European monarchs founded on 26 September 1815 by the Russian tsar, Alexander I, and the Austrian chancellor, Metternich, to suppress revolutionary threats to the European status quo.

François Guizot (1787–1874) was a French liberal historian and, from 1840 until the February Revolution of 1848, premier of France.

18. Notions of class struggle are present in the works of Aristotle (see for instance *The Politics*, Cambridge, 1996, bk 4, pp. 96–110) and Machiavelli (see *The Discourses*, Harmondsworth, 1970, pp. 113–15). But Marx's usage drew mainly upon the work of liberal and socialist theorists and historians in France in the 1815–48 period. See in particular the group around J. B. Say – Augustin Thierry, Charles Comte, Charles Dunoyer. According to Comte, for example, 'the history of the human species is comprised in one word, of struggles which have arisen from the desire to seize the physical enjoyments of the entire species and to impose upon others all the pain of the same kind'. C. Comte, *Traité de Législation*, Paris, 1826, bk 11, p. 91.

The other group, particularly prominent in depicting history as a process of class struggle, were the Saint-Simonians. The sixth session of the *Doctrine of Saint-Simon* was entitled 'The successive Transformation of Man's Exploitation by Man and of the Rights of Property', and its subtitle was: 'Master and Slave; Patrician and Plebeian; Lord and Serf; Idle and Worker'. Iggers (ed. and tr.), *The Doctrine of Saint-Simon*, p. 80.

In a letter to Weydemeyer (5 March 1852), Marx particularly recommended the work of Thierry, Guizot, and the Englishman John Wade, on the 'past history of classes'. *MECW*, vol. 39, p. 61.

19. The idea of 'the epoch of the bourgeoisie' had many sources after the 1830 Revolution. But one particularly energetic exponent of the idea was the republican and socialist historian and journalist Louis Blanc. For Blanc's impact on Marx, see Introduction, p. 103.

20. The German term here is 'Mittelstand', more accurately 'middle estate'.

21. It is not always realized how literally this idea is to be taken. A passage in 'The German Ideology' illuminates its meaning: 'To this modern private property corresponds the modern state, which, purchased gradually by the owners of property by means of taxation, has fallen entirely into their hands through the national debt, and its existence has become wholly dependent on the commercial credit which the owners of property, the bourgeois, extend to it, as reflected in the rise and fall of government securities on the stock exchange.' K. Marx and F. Engels, 'The German Ideology', *MECW*, vol. 5, p. 90. The idea almost certainly came from Engels, drawing upon Chartist and radical sources, which in turn went back to the early eighteenth-century civic humanist critique of the new Whig political order of Hanoverian Britain. See J. G. A. Pocock, *The Machiavellian Moment*, Princeton, 1975; A. Hirschman, *The Passions and the Interests*, Princeton, 1977; Stedman Jones, 'Rethinking Chartism', *Languages of Class*.

22. 'Cash payment' – this refers to the work of Thomas Carlyle. For Carlyle's impact on Engels see Introduction, p. 60, and see also p. 175.

23. See for instance Adam Smith's picture of labour 'unproductive of any value'. 'They are the servants of the public, and are maintained by a part of the annual produce of the industry of other people . . . In the same class must be ranked, some both of the gravest and most important and some of the most frivolous professions: churchmen, lawyers, physicians, men of letters of all kinds, buffoons, musicians, opera singers, opera-dancers etc.' Smith, *Wealth of Nations*, vol. 1, p. 352.

24. The term world literature, 'Weltliteratur', comes from Goethe, who in later years used the term increasingly and had attempted to apply it in some of his own work, for instance the *West-Eastern Divan*. See Prawer, *Karl Marx and World Literature*, p. 144.

25. The identification of progressive movements with the towns and conservative deference with the countryside was particularly marked in Western Europe in the 1830s and 1840s. 1789 had been accompanied by peasant revolts in France and in 1831 there had been an agricultural labourers' revolt in the south of England (the 'Captain Swing' riots). But movements such as Chartism enjoyed little rural support, and the radicalism of the working population of Paris was offset by the hostility of its rural hinterland. In the twentieth century, when revolutionary movements in the Third World often drew their most enduring support from the countryside, this phrase became something of an embarrassment.

26. The causal sequence outlined in this paragraph would seem relatively unambiguous. But in the twentieth century, Marx's followers began to question the precise definition of 'forces' and 'relations' of production and what was meant by ascribing a priority of the one over the other. Behind this doctrinal dispute lay a political battle between the old Socialist and Social Democratic Parties dating back to the period before 1914 and the new Communist Parties constructed on Leninist lines. The question posed by the October 1917 revolution in Russia was whether socialism could be established in a backward and at best semi-industrialized country, a country of peasants.

In the 1840s, given the impact of Chartism upon the industrial regions of Britain and of the 1830 Revolution in Paris, soon followed by the revolt of the silk-workers in Lyons, it seemed self-evident that a revolutionary crisis would proceed from those areas in which the forces of production were most developed, the most industrialized regions of the world. But after 1870, as the relations between classes in Western Europe grew more placid, Marx (but not Engels) seems to have switched his hopes to Russian populists and the possibility of a revolution that would begin in the East. This trend was greatly reinforced by the proclamation of a socialist revolution in Russia in October 1917, unsupported by a proletarian revolution in the West.

Communists thereafter built an alternative theory of revolution based upon Lenin's dictum that 'a chain is as strong as its weakest link'. This meant that capitalism would not necessarily collapse where the forces of production were furthest developed, but where property relations – the relations of production – had become most contradictory and the contrasts sharpest. Although clothed in an emphatic language of orthodoxy, there seems little doubt that this approach fundamentally contradicted the intentions of Marx's original argument. For an incisive discussion of the relationship between 'forces' and 'relations' of production, see G. Cohen, *Karl Marx's Theory of History: A Defence*, Oxford, 1978.

27. These were the 'plethoric' crises discussed by Fourier, Carlyle and Engels. The first sustained discussion of the relationship between commercial crisis, modern industry and overproduction had taken place around 1819 and had involved Malthus, Jean Baptiste Say, Sismondi and others, and it had been recommenced in the industrial depression of 1826–7.

28. Marx's economic analysis in the *Manifesto* is not entirely coherent. Later on (p. 236) Marx appears to espouse a Ricardian subsistence theory of wages. Such a theory implied a (subsistence) limit beneath which wages could not fall without curtailing the long-term supply of labour. Here by contrast, it is implied that wages are defined solely in relation to supply and demand. The worker does not sell a commodity (what he would eventually define as 'labour power') but was himself a commodity, whose value rose and fell like that of any other commodity. Since the division of labour increased the competition between workers, competition grew and wages decreased. In this way, economic progress generated increasingly poverty.

29. At the time of the *Manifesto*, Marx had not yet formulated his later theory of exploitation. From the late 1850s, Marx always specified that what the labourer sold was not his 'labour', but his 'labour power', that is, his capacity to labour. This became the core of his theory of exploitation in the form of the extraction of 'surplus' value. For in purchasing so many hours of 'labour power' the capitalist was left free to extract as much work or effort as he could from the labourer within any given hour.

30. This account of proletarian development largely summarized that presented by Engels in his *Condition of the Working Class in England*, which appeared in 1845.

31. Marx and Engels remained reluctant to accept that workers could make any sustainable *economic* gains from trade union activity. They continued to maintain that trade union activity should simply be seen as part of 'the ever-expanding union of the workers' and of the transformation of the working class into a mass political party.

Around the end of the nineteenth century, Karl Kautsky, the major Marxist theorist of the Second International in Central Europe, drew a far sharper distinction between 'trade unionist consciousness' (a state of mind spontaneously arrived at by workers as a result of their direct experience) and 'political consciousness', a position which presupposed knowledge and education. Lenin in turn used this distinction to reject the idea of a mass party for its low level of engagement and its tendency to opportunism. Together with the profits of empire, which enabled employers and politicians to 'bribe' their workers, Lenin thought that an inability to get beyond trade union consciousness explained the political passivity of the workers of Western Europe and their willingness to follow their parties and governments into the First World War. In place of the mass party, Lenin's Bolshevik model presupposed an elite vanguard party composed of professional revolutionaries.

32. The Ten Hours Bill regulated the working day in textile factories and became law in 1847.

33. The end of bourgeois rule is ascribed in this passage to something akin to absolute immiseration (see footnote 28, p. 227). As more and more persons from intermediate classes fall into the proletariat, competition between proletarians increases and larger and larger numbers become paupers. In *Capital*, vol. 1 (1867), the picture presented is more nuanced. Competition between wage workers and 'the reserve army of labour' (the unemployed) keeps wages fluctuating near subsistence, when evened out over a trade cycle. But immiseration was described in qualitative terms and presented as relative rather than absolute. See *Capital*, vol. 1, parts 6 and 7, especially ch. 25.

34. It is possible that this famous image of the bourgeoisie producing its own grave-diggers might have been provoked by Proudhon. Proudhon's picture referred to the phenomenon of overproduction, but in his account it was the worker who prepared for his self-destruction: 'at the first sign of a shortage . . . everybody returns to work. Then business is good, and both governors and governed are happy. But the more they work today, the more idle they will be afterwards; the more they laugh now, the more they will weep later. Under the regime of property, the flowers of industry serve only as funeral wreaths, and by his labour the worker digs his own grave.' Proudhon, *What is Property?*, p. 146. I am grateful to my student, Edward Castleton, for drawing my attention to this passage.

35. The sources of Marx's view that capital as a form of private property was a 'collective product' and a 'social power' were partly Adam Smith's notion of capital as 'accumulated labour' and more immediately, Proudhon's idea of 'collective force'. 'A force of a thousand men working for twenty days has been paid the same as a force of one working fifty five years; but this force of one thousand has done in twenty days what a single man, working continuously for a million centuries, could not accomplish: is this exchange equitable? . . . No, for when you have paid all the individual forces, you have still not paid the collective force. Consequently, there always remains a right of collective property which you have not acquired and which you enjoy unjustly.' From this, Proudhon inferred that 'all capital is social property' and therefore that 'no one has exclusive property in it'. See Proudhon, *What is Property?*, pp. 93–4.

36. In Britain, the effect of female factory work upon marriage and the family was widely debated by political economists, factory reformers, Chartists, trade unionists, evangelicals and feminists in the 1830s and 1840s. It was also discussed in Engels' *Condition of the Working Class in England*. Engels described the condition of an unemployed operative forced to take on domestic tasks, while his wife went out to work: 'can any one imagine a more insane state of things than that described in this letter? And yet this condition which unsexes the man and takes from the woman all womanliness . . . is the last result of much praised civilization.' But Engels conjoined this argument with a criticism of the original patriarchalism of the family before this transformation. 'If the reign of the wife over the husband, as inevitably brought about by the factory system, is inhuman, the pristine rule of the husband over the wife must have been inhuman too.' F. Engels, 'The Condition of the Working Class in England', *MECW*, vol. 4, p. 439.

37. The association of communism with 'the community of women' derived from ancient Greece. Plato in the name of Socrates argued in *The Republic*, apparently without irony, for a eugenic programme involving control of mating and communal nursing arrangements which would ensure that motherhood would not interfere with women's civic and military functions. Then women could form part of the guardian class and participate in the same education and military training as men. By abolishing the family, the guardians, as 'the city', would themselves form a single great family. Plato reiterated the argument in *The Laws*. A similar case for 'the community of women' was put forward by Diogenes the Cynic and Zeno, the founder of the Stoics.

Early Christians, for example Tertullian, were forced to deny that treating each other as brothers and sisters and having all things in common included the community of women. The accusation surfaced again at the time of the Reformation and was levelled at Anabaptists and other radical Protestant sects for more than a century. In 1525, Thomas Münzer under torture allegedly confessed that Anabaptists believed that everything should be held in common and this accusation was soon extended by Zwingli and others to the charge of practising the community of women (probably a malicious reading of the Anabaptist practice of rejecting faithless partners and establishing new spiritual unions).

Finally, the accusation was made again against the followers of early Socialism in the 1820s and 1830s. The charge was most plausibly levelled at Fourier, whose critique of civilization was directed as much against monogamy as wage labour, and who looked forward to the (eventual) replacement of the isolated household by the amorous corporation. The main arguments put forward by the Owenites in Britain centred upon equality between the sexes and easier divorce laws. In France, the Saint-Simonian position derived from the master's closest disciple, Olinde Rodrigues, who claimed that Saint-Simon on his death-bed had proclaimed, 'man and woman constitutes the social individual'. In October 1830 the 'Fathers' of the Saint-Simonian church, Bazard and Enfantin, declared that the Saint-Simonians 'demand like the Christians, that one man might be united with one woman; but they teach that the wife must become the equal of the husband and that according to the particular grace which God has bestowed on his sex, she must be associated with him in the exercise of the triple function of the temple, the state and the family; in such a way that the social individual, who until now has only been man, shall henceforth be both man and woman.'

Following the schism within the Saint-Simonian movement in November 1831 and the departure of Bazard and his followers, preoccupation with the 'social couple' intensified. Enfantin and forty male 'apostles' went on a celibate retreat at Menilmontant in the spring of 1832, and in 1833 went to Constantinople in search of the female Messiah who would complete 'the supreme couple'. But Enfantin also laid ever greater emphasis upon the sexual connotations of the Saint-Simonian doctrine of the 'rehabilitation of the flesh', including the division between 'the constant' and 'the unconstant' – an apparent endorsement of sexual libertinism. See C. Rowe and M. Schofield (eds.), *The Cambridge History of Greek and Roman Political Thought*, Cambridge, 2000, pp. 219–24, 274–6, 424–6, 443–6, 648; B. Scribner, 'Practical Utopias', *Comparative Study of Society and History*, 1994, pp. 743–72; (on the Owenites) B. Taylor, *Eve and the New Jerusalem: Socialism and Feminism in the Nineteenth Century*, London, 1983; (on the Saint-Simonians) L. Reybaud, *Etudes sur les Réformateurs ou Socialistes Modernes*, Paris, 1864, vol. 1, pp. 106–7.

38. The critique of marriage as 'legalized prostitution' was particularly prominent among the Saint-Simonians. See the declaration of Bazard and Enfantin, 'The religion of Saint-Simon only comes to bring an end to this shameful traffic, to this legal prostitution which in the name of marriage today frequently consecrates the monstrous union of devotion and egoism, of light and ignorance, of youth and decrepitude.' Reybaud, *Les Réformateurs*, p. 107. The treatment of marriage as legalized prostitution was initially found in Fourier. See Fourier, *The Theory of the Four Movements*. But Fourier's criticism of marriage was far more radical than that found among the Saint-Simonians. Fourier condemned marriage for its disregard of the composition of passions within each individual, especially the desire for variety. The Saint-Simonian starting point, on the other hand, was monolithically collectivist. It derived from the imminent advent of the social individual, the couple, whose complementary components embodied and even accentuated conventional distinctions between masculine and feminine. Engels was drawn to Fourier. Marx seems to have been closer to the Saint-Simonian position, especially as expressed by the ex-Saint-Simonian theorist of 'the couple', Pierre Leroux. On these questions, see Bee Wilson, 'Fourier and the Woman Question', Ph.D. dissertation, University of Cambridge, forthcoming 2002.

39. The origins of this idea probably go back to Sismondi, who also reintroduced the Latin term 'proletariat' into nineteenth-century discussion.

In 1819, he argued, 'it is a misfortune to have called into existence a man whom one has at the same time deprived of all pleasures which give savour to life, to the country a citizen who has no affection for it and no attachment to the established order.' Sismondi, *Nouveaux Principes*, vol. 1, p. 368.

40. The word 'material' was added in the English edition of 1888.

41. Instead of 'rationalist ideas', German editions have 'the ideas of enlightenment'.

42. The term, 'exploitation of man by man', was coined by the Saint-Simonians.

43. This was the process which Marx later designated with the term 'dictatorship of the proletariat'. In 1852, Marx considered that his 'own contribution' was 1) to show that the existence of classes was 'bound up *with certain historical phases in the development of production*; 2) that the class struggle necessarily leads to the *dictatorship of the proletariat*; 3) that this dictatorship itself constitutes no more than a transition to the *abolition of all classes* and to a *classless society*'. Marx to Weydemeyer, 5 March 1852, *MECW*, vol. 39, pp. 62–5.

44. This had been the central political demand of the Saint-Simonians.

45. In the 1848 edition, this point was formulated: 'Combination of agriculture with industry, promotion of the gradual elimination of the contradictions between town and countryside'.

46. This was an idea taken from Robert Owen.

47. In the German editions, 'associated individuals' instead of 'a vast association of the whole nation'.

48. 'Saw on their hindquarters the old feudal coats of arms'. The original German reads '*erblickte es auf ihrem Hintern die alten feudalen Wappen*'. The image is taken from Heine's poem: *Germany. A Winter's Tale*.

> Das mahnt an das Mittelalter so schön
> An Edelknechte und Knappen,
> Die in dem Herzen getragen die Treu
> Und auf dem Hintern ein Wappen.

> This is a beautiful reminder of the Middle Ages,
> Of noble servants and squires,
> Who bore loyalty in their heart
> And a coat of arms on their behind.

Cited in Prawer, *Karl Marx and World Literature*, p. 139.

49. Legitimists were those who after the 1830 Revolution continued to support the deposed Bourbon king, Charles X, and his descendants, and

considered Louis Philippe as an usurper. Marx particularly had in mind
J. P. A. Vicomte de Villeneuve-Bargemont, whose *Histoire de l'Economie Poli-
tique* (Brussels, 1839) he cited in his polemic against Proudhon. Villeneuve-
Bargemont's attack upon economic liberalism was made not in the name of
equality, but of Catholicism. See K. Marx, 'The Poverty of Philosophy',
MECW, vol. 6, p. 174.

'Young England' was a conservative literary-political group, which
included Benjamin Disraeli and Lord John Manners. It aimed to promote
paternalism and a regenerated aristocratic leadership. It was formed in
1841, was critical of the liberal conservatism of the government of Sir Robert
Peel, opposed the repeal of the Corn Laws and supported the movement
for the limitation of factory hours. The group broke up in 1848.

50. This is not a reference to the Christian Socialist Movement. In the 1848
German edition, the terms was not 'Christian', but 'holy', except it was
misprinted, not as 'heilige' (holy), but 'heutige' (of today).

51. On Sismondi, see Introduction, pp. 8, 35.

52. In the German editions of *The Manifesto*, this sentence reads, 'in its
further development this trend ended in a cowardly fit of the blues'.

53. In German editions, the beginning of this sentence reads: 'German
philosophers, semi-philosophers and lovers of fine phrases . . .'

54. 'Practical Reason': a reference to the philosophy of Immanuel Kant.
His *Critique of Practical Reason* appeared in 1788.

55. The section on 'True Socialism' was largely a summary of what Marx
and Engels had written in volume two of 'The German Ideology', entitled
'Critique of German Socialism according to its various prophets'. Those
aimed at were a small number of writers and publishers, often past collabor-
ators: among writers particularly, Moses Hess and Karl Grün, among
publishers, Otto Lüning and Hermann Puttmann. Hess was attacked as the
author of 'Philosophy of Action' ('Philosophie der Tat') even though he had
originally participated in the composition of 'The German Ideology' and
had collaborated with Engels in Elberfeld in the publication of *Gesellschaftsspi-
egel* (Mirror of Society). Karl Grün was a close friend and collaborator of
Proudhon and author of *Die soziale Bewegung in Frankreich und Belgien* (The
Social Movement in France and Belgium), which Marx attacked in detail
in chapter 4 of vol. 2 of 'The German Ideology'. On Hess, see Introduction,
pp. 46, 55–9, 122–3; on Grün, pp. 166–7, 170. Hermann Puttmann was the
publisher of *Deutsches Bürgerbuch* (the German Citizen's Book) and *Rheinische
Jahrbücher* (Rhenish Annals), for both of which Engels had written. Otto
Lüning edited *Westphalisches Dampfboot* (The Westphalian Steam-boat) for
which Marx had written his criticism of Karl Grün.

Although these authors and publications had been critical of liberalism, so had Marx and Engels themselves. Politically, this attack in *The Manifesto* was not only sectarian, but lacking in any sense of proportion. First, 'True Socialism' as a distinct literary phenomenon had virtually ceased to exist by 1848; secondly, the supposed anti-liberalism of these authors was greatly exaggerated. According to Franz Mehring, the first major biographer of Marx, writing on the 'True Socialists' in 1918, 'In the revolution which passed sentence of death on all their illusions, they were all without exception on the left wing of the bourgeoisie ... Not one single man amongst the "True Socialists" went over to the enemy, and of all the shades of bourgeois Socialism in their day and since, the "True Socialists" have the best record in this respect.' F. Mehring, *Karl Marx: The Story of his Life*, London, 1936, p. 114. The real offence committed by the 'True Socialists' was to continue with a Socialism built upon a combination of Proudhon and Feuerbach, which Marx and Engels abandoned from the time when they embarked upon 'The German Ideology' in 1845.

56. On Proudhon, see Introduction, pp. 31–2, 103, 109, 162–7, 170, 172–3, 183.

57. On Babeuf, see Introduction, pp. 27–8.

58. On early socialism in France and Britain, see Introduction, p. 8.

59. It is probable that Marx was thinking especially about the Saint-Simonians. Saint-Simon assigned to 'positive philosophy' the task of ameliorating the lot of 'the most numerous and poorest class'. See Iggers (tr.), *The Doctrine of Saint-Simon*, p. 84.

60. Chartism was a British radical movement of unenfranchised wage earners, so called because it was based upon the six points of the Charter – including manhood suffrage, annual parliaments, equal electoral districts and the payment of MPs. Chartism was strongest during the depressed years 1837–42. During this period, it presented two petitions to Parliament, attempted an uprising and provoked a general strike in the textile district. In the following years between 1843 and 1847, a time of renewed expansion of the economy, the movement declined. But activity mounted again with the onset of another commercial crisis and the preparation of a third petition to Parliament in 1847–8. The hostile reception of this petition and the lacklustre character of the accompanying demonstration on Kennington Common on 10 April 1848 was generally seen as a demoralizing defeat. But throughout the rest of 1848, there was continuing agitation combining the demand for the Charter with a campaign for the repeal of the Union with Ireland. Despite this shift in emphasis, the movement never regained its former momentum and finally petered out at the end of the 1850s.

Réformistes referred to the supporters of the Parisian radical newspaper,

La Réforme. Because of the restrictive laws concerning freedom of association in France following radical and revolutionary republican attempts to overthrow the July Monarchy in the 1830–34 period, newspapers took the place of political parties. In provincial France, and in the South in particular, networks of sociability and informal organization, often based on particular cafés, provided the framework of a reform party composed of an alliance of republicans, democrats and socialists. Supporters of *La Réforme* and its more moderate rival, *La Nation*, provided most of the personnel of the provisional government of February 1848.

On Owenites and Fourierists, see Introduction, pp. 8, 31, 43, 46, 62–3, 66, 67–8, 170, 174, 175.

61. This refers to the National Reform Association founded in 1845. The Association agitated for plots of 160 acres for every working man, attacked slavery and a standing army, and called for a ten-hour working day. The Association attracted many German craftsmen including some members of the League of the Just.

62. Until 1848, Switzerland, whose neutrality was guaranteed by five foreign powers, was under the tutelage of the Federal Pact of 1815. The Swiss Diet was made up of 22 Cantons, all republics but Neuchâtel. In the period after the Napoleonic wars, the precocious growth of a textile industry together with the rise of cultural nationalism (despite linguistic diversity) led to the demand for a strong federal state, capable of protecting itself economically against foreigners (by removing internal customs barriers), throwing off the tutelage of the five powers and replacing the inertia of the old Confederation.

In 1829, the Liberal Party was founded, demanding constitutional revision in each Canton, suffrage extension, civic equality, press freedom and separation of church and state. The Conservative Party defended the political monopoly of the privileged, the dominance of the churches and sovereignty of the Cantons. The basic division was between Protestants and Catholics. In 1830–31, threatened by large meetings, most of the Cantons granted constitutional assemblies and suppressed privileges of wealth, birth or residence. After a failure to secure reform in Neuchâtel or to revise the Federal Pact, the left wing of the Liberal Party reconstituted itself as a new 'radical' party. This party strongly resisted demands for the expulsion of German, Polish and Italian refugees and made a frontal attack upon the ultramontane pretensions of the Catholic Church and the Jesuits. In response to radical attacks on the status of the Jesuits, seven Catholic Cantons formed the Sonderbund (December 1845) in violation of the Federal Pact.

By 30 November 1847, General Dufour had subdued the Catholic Cantons. The Swiss civil war gave heart to opposition forces across Europe.

The defeat of the Sonderbund was a defeat for Metternich and a source of discredit for Guizot who had covertly backed the Catholics, while publicly backing compromise. In the Southern German states, the victory of the radicals created euphoria. The famous French historian Elie Halévy argued that the revolution of 1848 did not arise from Parisian barricades, but from the Swiss civil war.

63. The question of Poland was as formative in shaping the left in Europe in the period after 1830 as the question of Spain was to become in the 1930s. Napoleon's creation of the Grand Duchy of Warsaw and memories of the Polish legions in the Grand Army, together with the failed Polish uprising of 1830–31, not only turned Poland into a popular cause among republicans, Bonapartists and socialists, but also provoked the first revolutionary battle in Paris since 1795. The occasion was the funeral in Paris in 1832 of the Bonapartist general Lamarque, who had criticized the government for its inaction over the Russian repression of the Polish uprising. The presence of the aged veteran of the American and French Revolutions, Lafayette, together with the appearance for the first time of the red flag in a workers' procession, further heightened the tensions already inflamed by cholera and economic depression. The funeral ended in a riot and the building of barricades in working-class districts. Similarly in 1848, it was anger over Poland that precipitated the most threatening and radical moment of the revolution, the attack on the National Assembly on 15 May 1848.

Unlike the Italian cause, for which there was also widespread sympathy, the Polish question tended to divide moderates and liberals from radicals, republicans and socialists. Support for Poland was divided between the 'Whites' and the 'Reds'. The largest concentration of Polish refugees was to be found in Paris. The leader of the Whites, Prince Czartoryski, resided there. His aim was to secure through diplomatic pressure on France and Britain the restoration of a Polish monarchy and the recovery of the position of the landed aristocracy. This programme had failed in the past because peasants had remained indifferent to a national movement that paid no attention to the agrarian question. Most Polish refugees and the *Manifesto* supported the Reds, whose platform encompassed both a democratic franchise and land reform.

In Germany after 1830, the cause of the Poles also became central, both among reformers and revolutionaries. According to Heine, writing about Polish refugees in the aftermath of the suppression of the 1831 uprising, 'Yes, that flying visit of the Poles did more to convulse the popular feeling in Germany than any amount of governmental oppression or democratic writing . . . Our hearts beat responsively when, at the fireside they related what they had suffered at the hands of the Russians, what misery, what blows of the knout . . .' H. Heine, *Ludwig Börne – Reflections of a Revolutionist*, tr. T. S. Egan, London, 1881, p. 118.

Anger about Poland surfaced again in November 1846 when Metternich annexed the Republic of Cracow, the last tiny remnant of an independent Poland. In the following year, one of the best-known leaders of the Reds, Mieroslawski, and ten others were arrested and sentenced to death (later commuted) for planning an insurrection in Poznan in the Prussian sector of Poland. Solidarity with Poland, therefore, was not surprisingly the main issue which in London brought together representatives from different nations (including Marx and Engels) in the Fraternal Democrats, the most important predecessor before 1848 of the First International.

64. At the time when the *Manifesto* was composed, Marx and Engels expected that a revolution in Germany would be a repeat of the French Revolution of 1789–95. But what in France had been the result of an unforeseen process of radicalization produced by the resistance of the clergy, the failed flight of the royal family and a desperate war of national defence, was treated as a predictable sequence in relation to which 'the Communists' could position themselves in advance. The resulting strategy – both to insist upon the priority of the battle against 'the absolute monarchy' *and* 'to instil into the working class the clearest possible recognition of the hostile antagonism between bourgeoisie and proletariat' – proved unworkable, once the revolution of March 1848 occurred in Germany.

Marx and Engels returned to Germany in April 1848. They established themselves in Cologne, where they set up the *Neue Rheinische Zeitung* as an 'organ of democracy' opposed to the raising of separate workers' demands of the kind championed by the Cologne Workers' Society led by Andreas Gottschalk. Attempting to reproduce the conditions which had led to the radicalisation of the French Revolution of 1789, the strategy of the *Neue Rheinische Zeitung* was to push for war. As Engels later put it, the political programme consisted of two main points: a single, indivisible, democratic German republic, and war with Russia, which included the restoration of Poland.

But it was not only Marx and Engels who were haunted by 1789. The same was more or less true of every other political grouping. Thus not only were the 'bourgeoisie' quite determined not to proceed down a path leading to terror and the rule of a committee of public safety, but the sequence of events in 1848, far from radicalizing the reform camp, produced confusion, irresolution and a desire for compromise. The June workers' insurrection in Paris made hope of an alliance between communists and liberals unrealistic. In the Rhineland, it produced a climate of repression and renewed press censorship, and led the Marx group to push for a revolutionary government put in place by a popular insurrection. Similarly, the issue of war aided reaction rather than revolution. In the summer of 1848, the war was not against Russia, but against Denmark (over Schleswig-Holstein), and it produced not mass conscription, but a request from the Frankfurt Assembly to the Prussian monarchy to employ its army to aid the German nation. Popular anger was directed at the Malmö armistice, which inconclusively ended this war, and its ratification by the Frankfurt Assembly. An insurrection in Cologne was narrowly averted. Martial law was proclaimed. The *Neue Rheinische Zeitung* was temporarily banned and Engels was forced to flee to France until the following year.

The decisive moment in the German revolutions was reached in October–November 1848. In October, the imminent departure of Hapsburg troops for Hungary provoked an insurrection in Vienna followed by a three-week siege. The city fell on 1 November and 9 November, the Prussian king moved 10,000 troops into Berlin and dissolved the Prussian Assembly. The liberal opposition attempted to organize a campaign of tax refusal in response, but was unwilling to move beyond peaceful protest. By December 1848 in a series of articles, 'The Bourgeoisie and the Counter-Revolution', Marx formally acknowledged the failure of the 'bourgeois revolution' strategy. 'The Prussian bourgeoisie was not, like the French bourgeoisie of 1789, the class which represented the whole of modern society . . . It had sunk to the level of a type of *estate*.' Thereafter, until forced to close down the paper and leave Cologne on 19 May 1849, Marx increasingly distanced himself from the former democratic strategy and backed instead the formation of an independent workers' party. On Marx's political tactics during 1848, see Karl Marx, *The Revolutions of 1848*, ed. D. Fernbach, Harmondsworth, 1973.

Index